D0768912

This book is a gift of

THE MORAGA GARDEN
CLUB

Moraga Branch, Contra Costa County Library

The New Book of
SALVIAS

The New Book of
SALVIAS

SAGES FOR EVERY GARDEN

Betsy Clebsch

Drawings by Carol D. Barner

Timber Press
Portland♦Cambridge

Title page illustration: *Salvia recognita*

First edition, *A Book of Salvias*, published 1997.
Second edition, *The New Book of Salvias*, published 2003.

Published in 2003 by
Timber Press, Inc.
The Haseltine Building
133 S.W. Second Avenue, Suite 450
Portland, Oregon 97204, U.S.A.

Timber Press
2 Station Road
Swavesey
Cambridge CB4 5QJ, U.K.

Reprinted 2003

Designed by Bruce Taylor Hamilton

Printed in Hong Kong

Library of Congress Cataloging-in-Publication Data

Clebsch, Betsy.
    The new book of salvias: sages for every garden / Betsy Clebsch; drawings by Carol D. Barner. — 2nd ed.
        p. cm.
        Rev. ed. of: A book of salvias. c1997
        Includes bibliographical references (p.)
        ISBN 0-88192-560-8 (hb)
        1. Salvia. I. Clebsch, Betsy. Book of salvias. II. Title.

SB413.S22 C58 2003
635.9'3396—dc21   2002020457

To *Salvia*

In these times of fashionable rages
Let us honor enduring sages.
Known to cure, to mend, to ease;
Companions to cooks; splendid teas.
Hundreds of species our world adorn,
Richly diverse in flower and form.
Hail to Salvia, *that scented salvation,*
Worthy of study and our admiration.

Andy Doty

Contents

Acknowledgments 9

A Note from the Author 11

Foreword to the Second Edition 13

Foreword to the First Edition 15

Introduction 17

Description of Plants 25

Where to See Salvias 309

Where to Buy Salvias 311

Flowering Guide by Season 314

Cold Tolerance Guide 317

Shade Tolerance Guide 318

Salvias for a Hot and Humid Climate 319

Water-wise Salvias 320

Salvias with Especially Handsome Foliage 321

Salvias for Containers 322

Color Designations of
Unusual Flower or Foliage Color   323

Geographical Origin of *Salvia* Species   328

Bibliography   331

Index of Plant Names   335

CONTENTS

Acknowledgments

My profound thanks go to all the following, friends old and new, a few no longer with us, who have generously shared their knowledge and resources while enthusiastically encouraging my efforts by word and deed.

My research for the original edition would have foundered long ago but for the generous help of these and many other people:

Frank Almeda, Sherrie Althouse, Christine Andrews, Carol Barner, Dennis Breedlove, Fred Boutin, Ed Carman, Bill Clebsch, James Compton, Jean Coria, Andy Doty, Richard Dufresne, John R. Dunmire, John Fairey, Martin Grantham, Ginny Hunt, Gerda Isenberg, Barbara Keller, Robert Kourik, John MacGregor, David Madison, Don Mahoney, Virginia Mann, William A. McNamara, Pat McNeal, Bart O'Brien, Adam Reyes, Jeff Rosendale, Carl Schoenfeld, M. Nevin Smith, Greg Starr, John Hunter Thomas, Philip Van Soelen, Sarah Veblen, who asked the first questions, and my ever-helpful editor, Neal Maillet.

This second edition has come to fruition because of teamwork, and I am grateful to all those who have been a part of it. Working on this edition would not have been possible—or as much fun—without the help and input from many knowledgeable people. With his wide and deep understanding of the genus, James Compton provided me with the names of a number of different species; his proficient help throughout the project included clarifying sticky problems that came up along the way and assisting me in solving them. John Sutton's *The Gardener's Guide to Growing Salvias* is a pleasurable addition to salvia literature and a useful reference tool. Sonja Wilcomer contributed many fine photographs, and Carol Barner's drawings are particularly instructive. I especially want to thank Ginny Hunt, who grows many hundreds of plants; her practice of always sharing plants with others in the expectation that they will have success in growing them has worked well and produced a great quantity of cultural information. Her talents do not lie just in growing plants but are also evident in how she evaluates and photographs them. Ginny's help with the manuscript, particularly her willingness to proofread it at many different stages, has also been invaluable.

A Note from the Author

When *A Book of Salvias* was first published in 1997, there were a sizeable number of salvias flourishing in my garden that were not included in the book. I omitted them because I and other enthusiasts had not grown them long enough to be able to describe both their habit and performance in the garden. As you might suspect, there were also some salvias that had no names, which provoked intriguing puzzles and problems. These omitted salvias are just waiting to be discovered by gardeners—and I am sure everyone will be delighted by them. Since the book's initial publication there has been a lively interest in the genus *Salvia*, both in the United States and abroad. This revision speaks to that heightened interest by adding descriptions and photographs of more than 50 new species and cultivars.

Africa is now well represented with 11 new entries, which brings the total to 17. All, without exception, do well in my garden. Although this revision contains 19 salvias from Asia, embracing the Near East and extending to China, this figure does not begin to represent all those found in such a large and diverse area. Seed collected on plant exploration trips to China and elsewhere are only just beginning to be identified and distributed. The same is true, though to a lesser extent, of both Mexico and South America.

Our gardens can now flourish with salvias that provide nourishment to wildlife as well as a lively beauty that engenders a sense of joie de vivre in the gardener.

Foreword
to the
Second Edition

The excellent first edition of *A Book of Salvias* clearly shows the deep passion and innate feeling that Betsy Clebsch has for these remarkable plants. Her own interest in sages spans that often unbridgeable gap between botany and horticulture. In the pages of her book it is evident that she is as interested in the botanical histories of her subjects as she is in how they can be cultivated.

I have never met Betsy although we have communicated frequently. In all our correspondence I have been put on my own botanical mettle. I too have been interested in these extraordinarily beautiful plants for many years. My interest in salvias is principally botanical but I have seen them growing in the wild in many parts of the world and have been privileged enough to describe some.

The genus *Salvia* displays a wide variety of features. Some species are tall, others very humble; some have large, exquisitely vibrant blue, red, or purple flowers, others have small flowers. Few species are not garden worthy, however, as those with small flowers usually compensate by producing them in mighty quantities, often with strikingly colored stems or bracts, and sometimes even with superbly felted, silvery textured leaves. I have no doubt that these contrasts are at the heart of Betsy's fascination with them too.

I have thoroughly enjoyed learning about Betsy's experiences of growing salvias in her native California. I remember well the coast road north from San Francisco, how it was scented in late summer with sticky mimulus and tree lupins. I remember too the pizza restaurant near Point Reyes behind which grew a clump of the sweetly aromatic *Salvia clevelandii*. This blue-flowered native species epitomizes to me the heat of California—and the beauty of

Salvia at the core of these pages. Betsy's knowledge of *Salvia* is our good fortune. In this book she shows us not only how we can be ardent admirers of some of nature's great beauties but also how to grow them.

James Compton
Professor of Botany
University of Reading
Reading, Berkshire

Foreword
to the
First Edition

Few groups of plants add as much to a garden as salvias. They are as diverse in fragrance as they are in bloom, habit, and color. I was first drawn to salvias because of the exquisite scents of the leaves of California's native coastal species. Later, I came to appreciate their beauty in flower and their value as a nectar source for hummingbirds. I believe that once you have grown salvias you will always have space for a few in your garden. Strong herbal fragrances are usually an element of native habitats, and salvias are essential garden ingredients if you wish to recapture the complete sensory experience of natural settings.

In recent years, many subtropical salvias have become available, greatly expanding the ranges of color, texture, and leaf fragrance that are now accessible to the gardener. The genus *Salvia* has arguably the truest blues and brightest reds of any group of plants, and some species also have strikingly large flowers. It has been great fun to watch the expanded use of these plants in garden landscapes throughout the San Francisco Bay area where Betsy Clebsch makes her home. The increased availability of superior plant forms in nurseries has been helped by her influence. Now, with this book, we have descriptions as well as cultural information on many species and cultivars that can be widely incorporated into the garden.

One of my favorite personal pursuits is the encouragement of urban wildlife, in particular birds and butterflies. Salvias are a major source of nectar for hummingbirds, and those with red blooms are the ideal lure with their long, tubular flowers. Many species of butterflies feed on salvia nectar and pollen, while birds such as goldfinches relish the nutritious seeds.

For years botanical gardens and arboreta have cultivated many of the salvias described in this book, but their introduction to the gardening public has been slow because of the lack of cultural information. Betsy has observed the successes and failures of these numerous plantings and has cultivated both common and rare salvias in her own wonderful garden in the Santa Cruz Mountains. A wealth of information will finally be available to all of us with the publication of this book.

Don Mahoney
Horticulture Manager
Strybing Arboretum
San Francisco, California

Introduction

Plants of innate beauty and bearing, salvias have been especially popular since the 1970s with those who garden for pleasure. Gardening has become a widespread avocation throughout the English-speaking world and Europe, and those who have chosen to grow salvias have found them handsome and dependable plants that are, by and large, easy to grow. Rapid and reliable transportation now makes it possible for many species and selections of *Salvia* to be introduced to horticulture from the wild. Nursery stock also benefits from modern transportation because of the reduced chance of injury to plants. My hope is that this book will not only help gardeners in selecting from the impressive, sometimes overwhelming, array of salvias, but that it will also stimulate and encourage the study of these plants.

The Roman scientist and historian Pliny the Elder was the first to use the Latin name *Salvia*. The name derives from *salvare*, to heal or save, and *salvus*, meaning uninjured or whole, and refers to the several species of *Salvia* with medicinal properties. Pliny's interest in plants was utilitarian, and his encyclopedic compilation, *Natural History*, included salvias in the vegetable kingdom. In his botanical writing he dealt almost exclusively with the agricultural and medical attributes of plants.

Information on the virtues of sages is also to be found in the old herbals of medieval and renaissance Europe, usually illustrated with woodcuts or engravings. Not only are medicinal recipes given, but charms and spells are also described. The common name *sage* originated in England and is probably a corruption of the old French *sauge*. Sage refers specifically to *Salvia officinalis*, a plant widely used long ago as a "simple" or household remedy. This well-known herb was highly touted, and popular sayings such as the following were widespread in England and on the continent:

Sage helps the nerves and by its powerful might
Palsy is cured and fever put to flight.

The early herbals contain entries for many different species of *Salvia*, coming from far and wide. Their description and cultivation, as well as their medicinal and other uses, received careful attention through word and picture.

Salvias are members of the mint family, Lamiaceae, and comprise the largest genus in that family. The fragrant foliage of many salvias has been used for more than 20 centuries to heal the minds and bodies of people of many different climates and cultures. Salvias may be described by growth habit as perennial, biennial, or annual herbs, or as evergreen or deciduous shrubs. Some species are scandent and appear to climb, but they lack organs such as tendrils for support. The genus is distributed throughout the temperate and sub-tropical regions of the world, occurring from sea level to elevations of 11,000 ft (3400 m) or more. The temperature ranges where they are found is equally great. Some habitats experience 0°F (-18°C) or lower, while others may have readings of more than 100°F (38°C). One can only marvel at the complex and rich diversity of the genus and at humankind's discovery of the healing or soothing qualities of different species occurring in regions spread throughout the world.

How can a gardener be positive that a plant is a salvia? Is there a simple set of easily observed characteristics that will help assure a reliable decision? First, look for opposite leaves and square stems that with age sometimes become round. Next, observe an individual flower closely. The corolla, the colorful tube, can have a variety of shapes (as the botanical drawings, which are not drawn to scale, throughout this book will illustrate), but it must have two lips of unequal length; the upper lip is variable in shape and the lower lip is usually spreading. The calyx must also be two lipped. The upper lip may have two or three teeth or it may be undivided. The lower lip is often two-toothed. There are always two fertile stamens and sometimes two infertile ones called staminodes. Usually four seeds are produced; they are frequently mucilaginous when dampened. Botanists use many technical characteristics in describing salvias or any other plant, but only a few specific characteristics will be referred to in the salvia portraits in this book.

More than 900 species of *Salvia* exist worldwide, with well over half occurring in the Americas, but none occur in Australasia. Add to that number both cultivated hybrids and natural hybrids from the wild as well as gardens, and the total figure increases by several hundred or more. Selected cultivars also raise the total significantly. Because of the large number of species and their diverse native locations, botanists have been unable to treat all of them in a single work. Luckily, monographs and floras for a number of geographical areas do exist, representing many years of work by competent authorities. Regional floras give essential information as to identification, geographical location, and habitat, and quite a number are available, particularly for areas within the United States. Monographs offer a wealth of information that is restricted to a genus within a specific location. An example is *A Revision of* Salvia *in Africa Including Madagascar and the Canary Islands* (1974) by Ian C. Hedge of the Royal Botanic Garden, Edinburgh. This imposing work not only describes 59 species, but the introductory remarks are also rich with information as to *Salvia* characteristics, geography, and groupings. Botanical drawings of many species are also included.

California has a rich history of botanists and botanical exploration. LeRoy Abrams, Carl Epling, Willis Linn Jepson, and Philip A. Munz are a few who have participated in this tradition. Epling's definitive work (1938) on California salvias defines the geographical distribution and speciation of the genus. It is interesting to note that all the 17 *Salvia* species that occur in California, including both annuals and perennials, freely hybridize with one another. Epling clearly states this fact and places all California salvias in a section called *Audibertia*. Nearly 500 *Salvia* species are native to Mexico and Central and South America. This vast group is placed in a section named *Calosphace* and, according to Epling, only two species within this large group suggest any connection with the section *Audibertia*. Gardeners know from first-hand experience the ability of certain species within the section *Calosphace* to freely produce hybrids.

A year after his work on California salvias, Epling (1939) produced his sweeping monograph describing salvias from South America, Central America, Mexico, and those areas in the United States that border Mexico. Many other invaluable monographs, floras, and articles are set out in the bibliography.

Since the 17th century, the British, with their profound interest in natural history and deep desire to learn about the world, have conducted many explorations. From these far-ranging explorations have come field notes and drawings with priceless plant information and specific botanical information in the form of plants, seed, and herbarium specimens. Growing and distributing plants has also been of prime importance. The Royal Botanic Gardens, Kew, and the Royal Horticultural Society's garden at Wisley have been and remain at the center of this activity, and the tradition of plant exploration continues today, as does the conservation and distribution of plants. Great Britain has three national salvia collections (see "Where to See Salvias").

Both private and public gardens along the French and Italian Rivieras have long exhibited an interest in the collection and cultivation of salvias. By 1889, more than 60 species were being grown in that region. Gabriel Alziar, the director of the Jardin Botanique in Nice, France, is carrying on this tradition by continuing his study and work on *Salvia*, and the botanic garden contains an impressive number of salvias representing many geographical regions. Over a period of six years, beginning in 1988, Alziar published a catalog of all recorded salvias indicating habit, flower color, distribution, bibliography, and, perhaps most important of all, synonymy. Through his intensive study, Alziar estimates there are between 600 and 700 *Salvia* species, which is considerably fewer than the more frequently cited 900.

In France quite near the Mediterranean, Marie-Thérèse and Yols Herve supervise the French National Collection at Pépinière de la Foux in Le Pradet. It was a great pleasure for me to be able to visit them in 1995 and to be introduced to many salvias new to my eyes. I also saw old favorites that, because of the gentle climate, were growing luxuriously with companion plants that in my garden require shade. In March 2002 I received word that the nursery has been moved to a location in France that has a colder climate in winter.

Gardening has been a thread pulled tight throughout my life, a steady interest that binds the pages that follow. I have made and tended five gardens, the first in Virginia, the second in Texas, the following three in California. In my second California garden the handsome evergreen foliage and striking flowers of many distinctly different salvias led me to grow them. This garden was a country retreat, and several weeks would frequently pass between my visits. Plants had to be sturdy and able to survive with irregular care and water. Many salvias, the majority from Mexico, flourished, but although they gave me pleasure, they were also perplexing. They often had no name or else the ubiquitous "sp." (species undetermined) designation. Sometimes two dissimilar plants would have the same name—a confusing situation indeed. I sought accurate information from reliable sources, and nursery people and botanists who visited my garden supplied invaluable information as to a plant's source and who had grown it. The next stage of my search involved visiting botanic gardens and arboreta to see salvias that had been collected in their native habitats and to gather data about those collections. This activity put me in touch with many professionals who showed great interest in salvias in general and who have given me enthusiastic support in this project over the years.

In selecting plants to be described in this book, I have chosen those that are, in my experience, both beautiful and interesting garden subjects. Each salvia I describe can be grown well if you have some practical cultural information, and they will thrive for some time if you nurture them. Obviously, some salvias are not appropriate for specific gardens because of temperature range, light patterns, or soil conditions. The descriptions should allow gardeners to make choices based on their own specific garden conditions. I include a few plants that are as difficult to grow as they are to find, such as *Salvia cedrosensis*. I describe these exceptional salvias for the benefit of collectors and to draw attention to the tremendous diversity of the genus.

I wish I were able to say that I have grown all the salvias that have horticultural merit, but that is not the case. Securing seed or cuttings of little-known or rarely grown salvias is exceedingly difficult. Species that are frequently grown abroad may be unknown or unavailable in the United States. I continually seek and incorporate into my garden salvias that are new to me. For example, seed of salvias from China, Japan, and India is being sent to this country and England through botanical exploration, and the adventurous gardener will be able to look forward to new lists from the Far East from which to choose their salvias as nurseries grow and propagate these exciting newcomers.

Writing about the culture of salvias would not have been possible had I not had a large garden in which to grow, observe, and enjoy the plants. My home and garden, Jardin del Viento, are in the Santa Cruz Mountains of California, 30 miles (48 km) south of San Francisco at an elevation of 2000 ft (600 m). The garden is on a slope facing due south with the Pacific Ocean 12 miles (19 km) distant as the crow flies. Nothing protects the garden from the storms that come directly from the ocean, and gusty 50 mph (80 km per hour) winds are common. As the name implies, Jardin del Viento was dedicated to the winds in the hope of appeasing their winter violence. The soil is friable, a medium clay that is easily amended. Two fences, 4 ft (1.3 m) in height and 5 ft (1.5 m) apart, surround the garden to protect plants from deer predation. Jardin del Viento has good drainage, an adequate water supply, and excellent airflow. Temperatures rarely reach the low 20°s F (around -6°C) or high 90°s F (around

33°C). The garden is alive with the activity of numerous pollinators: several species of hummingbirds, butterflies, moths, bees, flies, ants, and bats gather pollen and nectar throughout the year. I have referred to the garden throughout the book and think of it not only as a place in which to find comfort and stimulation but also as a much needed workroom where plants are observed by myself and others.

It has been my good fortune to see many species of *Salvia* in their native habitat. To walk on the desert and watch *Salvia carduacea* standing 2.5 ft (0.8 m) high among tall grasses, all waving in the wind, is to experience a heady delight. Hover moths and insects add to the activity of the scene, and scents that are carried on the breeze bring much enjoyment. A completely different experience is to walk in the evergreen cloud forest habitat, areas of layered vegetation that experience fog, clouds, and seasonal rain. The evergreen cloud forest is the habitat of *S. holwayi* in Chiapas, Mexico. When flowering, this salvia adds a subtle splash of deep rusty red to a sea of green. An understory plant, it covers the ground and shrubs as it weaves its innumerable stems with trusses of flowers over and around the trunks and stems of other plants.

The salvias I have selected are treated alphabetically in this book, and in dealing with each species, I have provided the name of the plant and cited a synonym when a name change has caused confusion. Information about the meaning of the plant's scientific name and the plant's native habitat, including elevation ranges and temperature tolerance, are provided. I describe each salvia and also appraise the cultivars and hybrids, and I offer simple and straightforward cultural practices, including pruning, that have proved successful. Suggestions for companion plantings are given to help readers envision their own combination of well-liked plants that require similar culture. Of prime importance is the initial placement of the salvia in the garden, and the gardener's subsequent observation will help ensure its well being.

Few, if any, cardinal rules can be made as to the culture of all salvias. The need for soil with good drainage applies to the plants discussed in this book even though *Salvia uliginosa*, as its name implies, grows in wet and marshy places. I have found well-draining soil to be especially advantageous during the dark and cold months of winter. Waterlogged clay soil spells disaster and a hasty demise by drowning or disease. Soil that drains rapidly prevents fungal problems and promotes the circulation of air around the root cavities, an essential condition for healthy plants. Friable soil is usually recommended for all species, and I draw attention to those plants needing very sharp drainage or additions of lime or humus.

Although not prone to disease, salvias are occasionally struck by fungal attack and wilt and die. I know of no remedy for this. It occurs so seldom that it has never been a problem in my garden. Good air circulation, however, will help in general with the overall health of the garden. I believe the volatile leaf oils and other chemicals in salvias not only encourage good health but also discourage predation by insects, butterflies, snails, slugs, birds, and even deer. Arthur O. Tucker of Delaware State University has defined and continues to define and quantify the foliar essential oils found in salvias occurring in California. The components of the oils are numerous and differ in number and quantity from species to species. Work of this nature is being carried out on salvias from many floristic provinces throughout the world.

Propagation of annuals and of biennials and perennials that mature as quickly as annuals is by seed that is usually sown outdoors. I sow seed in pots in late spring after both day and night air temperatures have warmed. Seedlings must be protected from birds at all times. I sow herbaceous and woody perennials and shrub species from late spring through early summer, allowing ample time for the plant's root system to become established before frost. Cuttings are sometimes a faster means of establishing a new plant, and woody perennials and shrubs respond well to this method. I have used a greenhouse for propagation, but because of white fly and aphid attacks, I have found a shaded area in the garden where cuttings can be closely watched to be convenient and satisfactory.

Color is close to the heart of the gardener and, at the same time, very ephemeral. Seeing and describing color is as elusive as planting and tending the plant is tangible. The quality or strength of light on a given plant determines our perception of its colors, as does the time of day or time of year. The texture of leaves and bark and the light they absorb and reflect are also elements affecting what we see. Architectural objects such as paths and walls modify color perception, and neighboring plants greatly affect impressions. Because of the numerous factors influencing color perception, I have used adjectives throughout the plant descriptions that are related to commonplace objects, such as butter yellow and grassy green. In addition, I have included an appendix giving colors for most salvias I describe according to the Royal Horticultural Society's Colour Chart (1966). This chart is arranged by color groups with designated numbers and can be readily referred to if needed. A new edition of the chart, available from the United Kingdom, was released in 1995. The color groups and numbers are exactly the same as the 1966 edition. Even these helpful tools are far from perfect in describing color, a subjective concept given concrete terms.

I hope the reader will find the drawings (including the black and white line drawings), photographs, and text of this book stimulating and valuable. I, with my struggle for clarity, am the richer for attempting this project.

Description
of Plants

Salvia aethiopis Linnaeus

Native to a large area of central and southern Europe and western Asia, *Salvia aethiopis* is described botanically as being either biennial or perennial. It has become widely naturalized on several continents and in the United States in California and Colorado. Roadside banks, rocky slopes, and disturbed fields provide good habitat for this salvia, which has been called tumbleweed. The specific epithet, *aethiopis*, is from the Greek and refers to the sage being from Ethiopia, although surprisingly the botanist Ian Hedge (1974) has found no specimens of the plant collected from a native habitat on the African continent. Carolus Linnaeus, the genius who brought order to natural science and botany, described *S. aethiopis* in 1753.

A geometrically constructed plant, *Salvia aethiopis* has large, furry, pearl-gray leaves, sometimes 1 ft (30 cm) in length, arranged in a handsome rosette. The leaves are covered with hairs that give them a soft, blanketlike appearance. They look whitish gray and have scalloped edges, adding another interesting feature. Flowering occurs in early summer. At that time a 1–3 ft (30–90 cm) stem emerges carrying a large, rounded, candelabra-like inflorescence. Widely branched whorls of falcate (scythe-shaped) white flowers with a pale yellow lip open more or less at the same time.

Salvia aethiopis is a hardy sage known to withstand temperatures to 0°F (-18°C). Propagation is by seed. The culture of *S. aethiopis* includes full sun, fast drainage, and additional water throughout dry periods. Flowering usually continues for two to three weeks, at which time pollination normally occurs and

The conspicuously felted leaves of the biennial *Salvia aethiopis* draw attention to the plant through the winter. (Christine Andrews)

seed is produced. It has been my experience that if the seed production occurs, the plant soon dies; fulfilling the designation *biennial*. If the inflorescence is removed before seed production, however, the plant will bloom again the next year. When the plant starts to look old and in need of rejuvenation, allow it to go to seed in order to start the process afresh with seedlings. You will probably find seedlings near the old plant in the spring. To be on the safe side, save some seed to sow the following spring or summer.

In a mild climate, the foliage of *Salvia aethiopis* is handsome throughout the year, recommending it for space in the winter garden. With leaves arranged in symmetrical rosettes, this salvia may be enjoyed to great advantage when elevated to a rocky mound about 2 ft (60 cm) above ground level. If space can be provided, three plants—one at ground level, the second elevated above ground level, and the third wherever it might be tucked in—make an outstanding visual treat throughout the winter and spring. After the blooming period in early summer, the leaves appear tattered and worn and are replaced with new leaves later in the summer. Mat-forming plants such as thymes and veronicas can be grown in combination with these salvias as they cover the bare ground without obstructing the view of the salvias' attractive basal leaves.

SALVIA AETHIOPIS

Salvia africana-caerulea
Linnaeus

The heavily branched *Salvia africana-caerulea* is an aromatic shrub that is found in South Africa, growing predominantly in a limited coastal area. Found at sea level on coastal dunes, it also occurs on rocky hills to 1000–2000 ft (400–600 m) near the sea where it is no stranger to areas of finely textured brush that grows in dry habitats. South Africans have a word—fynbos—adopted from Afrikaans for this particular habitat. Both South Africans and European settlers have used this plant in treating many health problems. Linnaeus described and named this salvia in 1753.

Salvia africana-caerulea sparkles with eye-catching light blue flowers against rich green foliage. (Ginny Hunt)

A good-looking, upright shrub, *Salvia africana-caerulea* will reach about 2–3 ft (60–90 cm) in garden situations. The round grayish stems are covered with hairs that have oil globules, and when they are stroked a savory odor is released. Evergreen leaves that are thick and mostly elliptic in shape are a soft gray-green on the surface and lighter on the underside. They measure approximately 0.25 in (0.6 cm) in length and 0.5 in (13 mm) in width. Inflorescences are in the range of 12 in (30 cm) in length with flowers numbering two to six in each whorl. The calyx is campanulate, and when it expands with seed it becomes purplish. Both floral leaves and bracts subtend the whorls of pale blue flowers. Flowers are reported to be light violet or pale pink but I have seen only the pale blue ones. The lower lip has whitish markings. Never heavy with flowers, *S. africana-caerulea* tends to come into bloom off and on from April through October. I have read in a book on South African wild flowers that it is sometimes confused with *S. chamelaeagnea* but because of its gray-green leaves and calyces that expand with seed its identification has never been problematic in California gardens.

A very utilitarian plant, *Salvia africana-caerulea* also has the virtues of both handsome habit and foliage. It can be used to advantage as a filler in sunny parts of the garden. All its needs are minimal and simple: good drainage, gritty soil, full sun, and a moderate amount of water throughout the summer. It will withstand temperatures into the low 20°s F (around -6°C) for short periods and continue looking good even after long spells in which the days are dark and there is a lot of rain and temperatures that fall below 30°F (-1°C) every night. Although it does produce viable seed, the usual method of propagation is to take cuttings during August and September.

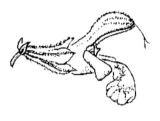

Salvia africana-caerulea

An early spring-blooming border that is cheery with bright yellows and subtle blues would be enhanced with the handsome gray-green foliage of *Salvia africana-caerulea*. The salvia tends to bloom later than the companions I mention as possibilities and will prolong the flowering period in your garden. A bed in full sun that comes into bloom in late February or early March might have a background of *Rosmarinus officinalis* 'Miss Jessop's Upright', which is about 4 ft (1.3 m) tall. If you want a darker blue, the 3 ft (1 m) tall *R. officinalis* 'Collingwood Ingram' is admirable. The midground could be filled with *S. africana-caerulea* and the beautiful South African fleshy rooted perennial herb *Bulbinella robusta* that carries, as my friend puts it, "torches of glowing yellow" on 2 ft (60 cm) stems. The little bare spots in front can be covered with sweet-smelling, gold-flowered *Erysimum* 'Jubilee Gold' that will quickly weave itself between all the plants.

Salvia africana-lutea Linnaeus

The coast of the Cape of Good Hope in South Africa is the native habitat of *Salvia africana-lutea*. It grows within a limited area at close to sea level on coastal sand dunes, arid and rocky banks, and low hills. This plant was known as *Salvia aurea* until the 1990s.

Salvia africana-lutea is a shrubby, evergreen plant, with numerous woody stems growing out of the rootstock that reach 3 ft (1 m) or more in height and

3–4 ft (1–1.3 m) in width. Young plants are amply covered with small, gray-green, elliptical leaves, but by maturity the leaves have become sparse, giving the plant a twiggy appearance. Flowering begins in early spring, with flushes occurring periodically throughout the summer. Flowers appear in whorls and are held erect. The calyx is large, campanulate, and a dark rusty color on the side that faces the light and olive-green on the opposite side. During fruiting the calyx persists and is an added attraction for a long time. The flowers, when first emerging from the calyx, are a bright, glowing yellow, but as they develop in size they turn a rusty orange. The word *africana* in the specific epithet describes the plant's origin, and *lutea* describes the

Salvia africana-lutea flowers in early spring and has a shrublike habit. (Don Mahoney)

yellow color of the emerging flowers. The mature, rusty orange flowers are 1 in (2.5 cm) or more in length and are held within a showy, funnel-like, tan calyx that resembles paper with age. The flowers are both an attraction and a curiosity. Hedge (1974) says the flowers at maturity give the impression of being withered. He describes them as golden brown or khaki colored, often with a trace of purple at their base.

Light, well-draining soil and full sun are desirable for *Salvia africana-lutea*. Plants need deep watering at least once each month, and a mulch at their base is helpful. Some pruning should be done to keep the plant shapely, but over time, usually about five years or more, a build-up of wood is inevitable. At that point, I recommend a fresh start with a young plant. Propagation is accomplished easily by cuttings.

Salvia africana-lutea is generally accepted as hardy to approximately 20°F (-7°C). On one occasion in my garden, a specimen's top growth was completely killed when the temperature fell well below that, but during the following summer, new growth emerged from the rootstock and the plant regained its pleasing shrubby habit within a few years.

Salvia africana-lutea is rarely seen in gardens or nurseries in my home state of California. It is not clear when it was introduced to horticulture, but William Robinson grew the plant and wrote about it. A famous English gardener and horticultural journalist, Robinson is regarded as the instigator of the herbaceous border, the wild garden, and the alpine rock garden. In his book *The English Flower Garden*, Robinson (1933) describes 39 salvias for the border.

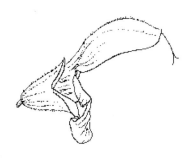

Salvia africana-lutea

Because of its foliage and growth habit, *Salvia africana-lutea* combines nicely with many different manzanitas. For example, *Arctostaphylos stanfordiana* subsp. *bakeri* 'Louis Edmunds' at 6 ft (2 m), *A. pajaroensis* at 4 ft (1.3 m), and *A.* 'Winterglow' at 2 ft (60 cm) make outstanding companions in a shrubbery border. Only *S. africana-lutea* will require summer water. A dry border of flowering shrubs might include the 3 ft (1 m) tall *Cistus palhinhae*, which has gold-centered white flowers, the 4 ft (1.3 m) tall *Eriogonum giganteum*, St. Catherine's lace, which has creamy white clusters of flowers that turn rust-red, and the 4 ft (1.3 m) tall *Phlomis fruticosa*, with its whorls of yellow flowers. All these plants require the same growing conditions. Some blooming will occur from early spring until frost.

Salvia albimaculata Hedge & Huber-Morath

The hardy perennial *Salvia albimaculata* was first described by botanists at the Royal Botanic Garden in Edinburgh in 1957, but the plant was not introduced to gardens until the late 1980s. It was then that Jim and Jenny Archibald of Wales, growers and seed collectors par excellence, made a collecting trip to Turkey and returned with seed of *S. albimaculata* and of many other interesting plants. *Salvia albimaculata* is known to occur naturally in only one area and was found on a steep clay slope over limestone at 4000 ft (1200 m). The location is directly south of Konya in the Taurus Mountains, north of the island of Cyprus. The Archibalds made several trips to this collecting site—first to see the plants in bloom in order to identify them, and subsequently to collect seed.

Under 1 ft (30 cm) in height, *Salvia albimaculata* is about 10–12 in (25–30 cm) wide. Its small, trisected, greenish gray leaves are under 1 in (2.5 cm) in length and impress one as being both unusual and handsome. They are evergreen—a pronounced gray-green during the cold months and grayer in summer. Striking royal purple flowers that measure about 1 in (2.5 cm) long appear in whorls of two to five flowers. Each flower has a prominent white blotch on the lower lip. The epithet *albimaculata* means

Salvia albimaculata is a Turkish endemic that grows on limestone. (Robert Kourik)

"spotted with white." The white blotch has an outline similar to the royal blue lower lip and is neatly banded by that color.

Flowering begins in early summer with many charming inflorescences coming into bloom at the same time. Afterwards, sporadic bloom continues until frost. I would expect *Salvia albimaculata* to be hardy to 10°F (-12°C), perhaps even lower, because of its mountainous origin. A herbaceous plant that is short and shrubby, this salvia builds wood at its base and tends to be short-lived. In my experience, cuttings must be started about every three or four years. The usual method of propagation is by cuttings because seed is rarely found. Flowers and foliage hold well in water and are attractive features in very small bouquets.

Preferring garden loam and good drainage, *Salvia albimaculata* is not a difficult plant to grow. When placed in full sun and given weekly water, its flowers may be enjoyed for an extended period and its foliage year-round. A little lime scattered at the roots each spring is beneficial.

A sunny, exposed rock garden is the ideal setting for *Salvia albimaculata*. Its small size makes it a perfect filler among rocks and other plants such as *Dianthus deltoides*, which is a little over 1 ft (30 cm) tall when in flower, or the old and valued *D. gratianopolitanus*, cheddar pink, which is 8 in (20 cm) tall. The spreading *Diascia barberae* from South Africa is 1–1.5 ft (30–45 cm) tall with flowers the color of strawberry ice cream and is another good mixer. The light pink-flowered hybrid *Saponaria* 'Max Frei', just under 1 ft (30 cm) in height, is also a possible companion. All these plants require the same culture.

Salvia algeriensis Desfontaines

A delightful and charming annual, *Salvia algeriensis* has a limited geographical range in northeast Morocco and northwest Algeria. It is obvious that Réné Louiche Desfontaines, the botanist who described the plant in 1798, thought the specific name *algeriensis* imparted essential information. In its native habitat, the plant grows near sea level at a low altitude, usually just under 2000 ft (600 m), in fields and among shrubs. Not particular as to its cultural conditions, it grows on clay plains as well as on cultivated ground.

Salvia mouretii is another salvia that is indigenous to Morocco. It is an annual, possibly a biennial, that is quite similar to *S. algeriensis*. However, more specimens are needed in order to differentiate between these two species.

In its native habitat, *Salvia algeriensis* is reported to be just under 3 ft (1 m) in height. Plants growing in my garden are much shorter and are usually 1–2 ft (30–60 cm) in both height and width. Bright green leaves are ovate and are typically 3 in (8 cm) in length and width. They either have a short petiole, which is known as a leaf stalk, or are sessile. The uppermost leaves from which the inflorescence emerges are sessile and, being opposite, give the plant an architectural quality. A single plant can produce three or four inflorescences that measure 6 in (15 cm) in length during a productive blooming period. The entire stem is covered with short hairs that have glands on the tips. The tiny reddish brown and green calyx is also hairy and glandular; it is subtended with two small bracts. The stem of the inflorescence and the bracts repeat this warm, reddish brown color. The light violet flowers are strongly falcate, and the lower lip is short and spotted with tiny violet specks. Flowers are in whorls and almost always paired. The space between the whorls is such that the strongly hooded flowers stand out in three dimensions and never look crowded. There is a light scent associated with the plant that is reminiscent of crushed thyme.

A pert and pretty plant, *Salvia algeriensis* gives a fresh touch to the garden. (Ginny Hunt)

This annual will help chase away the blues of winter because it can be sown in autumn and will germinate in late winter or early spring. Where plants have seeded about in my garden, seedlings appear as early as February. The warmth and light of March means the plants are often boldly into bloom by the end of March or the beginning of April. Seedlings do not need to be on such an early schedule, however, and seeds sown later in the spring will come into bloom in summer. It is quite easy to have plants of *Salvia algeriensis* in flower as late as July and August.

The culture of this salvia is simple and straightforward: half to a full day of sunlight, good drainage, porous garden soil enriched with humus, and moderate to light but frequent water. Deadheading will prolong the season of bloom but remember, if you want seeds you will have to let the ovaries in the flowers mature. Propagation is accomplished by saving and then planting seeds or through seeding that occurs naturally in an unpredictable pattern. The spontaneity of random seeding is usually delightful.

Salvia algeriensis is eminently suited for a container because of its perky stance and ability to produce a succession of inflorescences. A raised bed will elevate the plants and allow them to be more clearly seen. Low-growing,

The handsome gray-white leaves of *Salvia apiana*, a California native, embellish the garden throughout the year. (Bart O'Brien)

ground-hugging plants make good companions because the eye can view the splendid detail of the salvias without confusion. The very short, spreading, gray-foliaged *Artemisia caucasica* makes a suitable companion. Erodiums with delicate foliage, such as *Erodium corsicum* 'Album' and *E. corsicum* 'Rubrum', would also be suitable as they are in proportion to the salvia. This combination of plants requires the same culture.

Salvia apiana Jepson
white sage, bee sage

A shrubby and coarsely branched plant, *Salvia apiana* grows 4–5 ft (1.3–1.5 m) tall and about 4 ft (1.3 m) across. Native to California, it occurs from Santa Barbara County through Baja California, growing on dry, rocky hillsides in exposed conditions.

Growing at 5000 ft (1500 m) or lower in its native coastal scrub or chaparral habitat, the white sage typically covers large areas. On a hot day, its fragrance is often evident long before the plant comes into view. Like lavender, a distant relative, the leaves of *Salvia apiana* contain aromatic oils and resins. Although some people find the odor of the leaf offensive when it is rubbed or released by a hot, dry wind moving through a colony, most find the scent both unusual and distinctive. Native Americans and others use the dried or fresh leaves for ceremonial purposes. A tea made from the leaves relieves colds or congestion and may also be used as a soapless shampoo. The specific epithet, *apiana*, pertains to bees and the attraction white sage has for them. Beekeepers have long been aware of this and have kept hives in these chaparral areas.

In spring, several to many flowering stalks 3–4 ft (1–1.3 m) tall rise above the plant's whitish foliage. Leaves are persistent and remain year-round. The stalk is hollow and sometimes a pinkish color, adding interest to the white or pale lavender flowers. The handsome, pink-stalked plant is the one to search for. White sage produces viable seed, and it is not uncommon to see seedlings at the base of the plant. It is hardy to 20°F (-7°C) or less.

White sage hybridizes freely with other *Salvia* species in the wild; plants at the Santa Barbara Botanic Garden and the Rancho Santa Ana Botanic Garden clearly exhibit this tendency. *Salvia apiana* is known to cross with *S. leucophylla* and *S. clevelandii*. Some years ago, a hybrid occurred in the Rancho Santa Ana Botanic Garden that is smaller and more compact than *S. apiana*. The flowering stalk is 3 ft (1 m) high with an inflorescence of lavender-blue flowers in tight whorls similar to those of *S. clevelandii*. It was introduced in 1993 and named *S.* 'Vicki Romo' in honor of a young student at Claremont Graduate School who had been in the Rancho Santa Ana Botanic Garden's doctoral program.

Salvia apiana

Indeed, *Salvia apiana*, with its tall and stiff habit and conspicuous silver foliage has proved to be a fine plant for sunny and dry areas of the garden and will grow in clay or lighter soil when given good drainage. Good air circulation is also important. When established, this drought-tolerant salvia needs no summer water since it is summer dormant with winter growth. After it blooms, prune the tall and coarsely branched flowering stalks in order to encourage compactness.

Good companions are plants that occur naturally in the same habitat, such as the shrubby *Artemisia californica* and *Yucca whipplei*, which has swordlike leaves. This combination features three very different leaf shapes, textures, and shades of gray. A combination that features flowers might include *Rosmarinus officinalis* 'Tuscan Blue' and *Salvia apiana* for the back of the border and drifts of *Penstemon heterophyllus* with its electric-blue flowers and *P. barbatus* with its rich rose flowers at the front. Two perennials that would complement *S. apiana* are the purple-flowered *P. spectabilis* and the low-growing, shell-pink *Sidalcea malviflora* 'Elsie Heugh'. Another drought-tolerant perennial, *Centranthus ruber*, can be mixed in with this pink and purple combination as its fluffy flower heads will add many shades of rich rose, pink, and white to the spring-flowering picture. *Salvia apiana* is particularly beautiful in moonlight so is outstanding in a night garden. The botanist Carl Epling (1938) was referring to this attribute when he called *S. apiana* a snowy shrub.

Salvia argentea Linnaeus

The native habitat of the perennial *Salvia argentea* forms a band across southern Europe from Portugal to Bulgaria. It has no common name at present, but the Latin-based epithet *argentea*, meaning silvery, refers to the color of the leaves and describes the plant admirably.

Here is a plant to be grown and admired for its handsome foliage. A large basal leaf structure measures 3 ft (1 m) across and 1–2 ft (30–60 cm) high, and the leaves persist in all but the coldest climates. At maturity they measure 8–12 in (20–30 cm) in length and 6 in (15 cm) across. The leaves appear to be woolly as they are densely covered with silky hairs on both surfaces. Watch for snails and other pests that feast on foliage because just a little damage would spoil the overall effect of the prominent leaves.

Blooming takes place in spring or summer when a 2–3 ft (60–90 cm) tall candelabra of inconspicuous white flowers, tinged pink or yellow, rises above the foliage. The flowering stalk remains a dramatic feature during the time of its development. After enjoying the stalk at full bloom for a few days, you should remove it, as you lengthen the life of the plant by preventing seed production. Even though it is classified as a perennial, *Salvia argentea* will be short-lived if it produces seed. Eventually, of course, the plant must be allowed to produce a small quantity of seed because this is the quickest and easiest means of propagation. Start new plants every two to three years for continuity in the border. Sow seed in early spring to obtain plants that will bloom the following year.

After the plant flowers, the wonderful woolly leaves lose their silver coloring and remain pale gray-green throughout the summer. Later, with the return of cool weather, the silver-gray color returns and predominates until the next flowering season.

Full sun, sharp drainage, and friable soil are needed for the culture of this plant, as is good air circulation. After it is established, you can work a very small amount of lime around the plant but fertilizer is not recommended. In my garden I have found this salvia to be drought tolerant with little water necessary in summer. It is a hardy species and will take temperatures of 10°F (-12°C) or less.

The dramatic basal leaves of *Salvia argentea*. (Ed Carman)

Plantswoman and garden writer Beth Chatto (1978) enthusiastically praises *Salvia argentea*, while allowing that it is short-lived. Her Essex garden in England is in an area known for its frosts, winds, and dry summers, yet the salvia has survived there for many years in heavy, cold soil, reseeding itself in dry gravel.

Salvia argentea is a bold and strong plant for the front of the border, its leaves providing year-round interest. It fits well into a dry bank of low-growing rosemary combined with the native California *Eriogonum latifolium*, which has short, gray, evergreen foliage. It can also be grouped with the taller *E. fasciculatum*, which has whitish flowering heads that turn an attractive rusty brown in autumn. All require the same cultural conditions.

Salvia arizonica Gray
Arizona sage

A creeping perennial, *Salvia arizonica* can be found growing in large patches in the shade of boulders or in open forests. Categorized as a ground cover, this

Salvia arizonica repeats bloom in summer and autumn. (Ginny Hunt)

salvia has a native habitat that is fairly widespread, covering an area that runs throughout the rich and moist forests of southern Arizona and the Trans-Pecos mountain area of Texas. It is likely that *S. arizonica* also grows in the wild in New Mexico and northern Mexico, but these locations are not included in its established range at the time of publication. Its frequent occurrence at high elevations of 7000–9500 ft (2100–2900 m) suggests that the plant is very cold tolerant.

The trailing stems of Arizona sage have small, triangular or deltoid (in the shape of an arrowhead) leaves that are opposite one another and widely spaced. The numerous stems produced from the plant's running rootstock give the plant an overall appearance of luxuriant foliage. The length of the stem when in bloom is usually less than 1 ft (30 cm). The leaves are mid-green and glabrous with a pleasant minty scent when bruised or crushed. Small indigo-blue flowers with a violet tinge occur in whorls in early summer. If these inflorescences are cut back, the reward is repeated flowerings—as many as three if the growing season is a long one. Water and fertilizer will stimulate reflowering. After you deadhead this salvia, give it several applications of a balanced liquid fertilizer at half strength to encourage new growth. An interval of seven to ten days between applications is sufficient.

Salvia arizonica

Well-drained soil enriched with humus is ideal for *Salvia arizonica.* Humus may be applied as mulch each spring before active growth starts. Water is needed every seven to ten days during hot weather.

Arizona sage is easily grown from seed or by division of the creeping rootstocks. Cutting all stems to the ground before applying humus in early spring will ensure fresh foliage for the coming season. It thrives in the shade of tall herbaceous plants or shrubs such as holly, osmanthus, and viburnum, and its graceful green foliage looks lovely spilling over rocks or walls. *Salvia arizonica* is a graceful and undemanding plant for lightly shaded and woodland gardens. This plant deserves wider attention from gardeners.

Salvia forreri is a similar species, and Epling (1939) reports that more specimens and study are needed to determine if *S. forreri* is a species separable from *S. arizonica*. There is the distinct possibility that *S. forreri* may be only an extension of *S. arizonica* and grow in only five Mexican provinces—Durango, Zacatecas, Sinaloa, Coahuila, and Nuevo-León—between 6500 and 9500 ft (2000 and 2900 m). In my garden, plants of *S. forreri* are similar in flower and leaf to *S. arizonica* but the habit is slightly different in that *S. forreri* is tighter in growth and more mounding. Also, the stems of *S. forreri* are shorter and the leaves are a darker green. These variations do not necessarily suggest a different species, and I hope that botanists will one day solve this problem. Meanwhile, I suggest gardeners turn to *S. forreri* if they need a short plant for full sun that spreads and has herbaceous, dark green leaves.

Salvia austriaca Jacquin
Austrian sage

High and cold altitudes across eastern Europe to Russia are the native habitat of the hardy herbaceous perennial *Salvia austriaca*. It was described in 1776 by Nicholas Joseph de Jacquin, professor of botany at Leiden, Netherlands. It is not known how long the plant has been in cultivation. The specific epithet *austriaca* tells us the origin of the plant and at the same time suggests a convenient common name, Austrian sage.

Salvia austriaca develops a basal rosette of leaves that measures 3 ft (1 m) in width. If brushed the leaves release a somewhat fetid odor. Mid-green in color, the individual leaves measure about 1 ft (30 cm) or more in length. The midrib and veins appear indented and give texture to the surface. In a mild climate it is a late spring-blooming plant with a repeat bloom in late summer. In colder areas, flowering is in summer. Its flowering stalk will eventually rise 2 ft (60 cm) or more above its foliage. Very pale yellow flowers in whorls of six or more comprise an inflorescence that measures 8–10 in (20–25 cm). These erect and slender blooming stems offer a subtle touch to the flowering border. I have read that the calyx is sometimes violet tinged; unfortunately, my plants have

never exhibited this color. The calyx is small, about 0.25 in (0.6 cm) in width, covered with hairs, and light green in color.

Easy to situate in a garden, Austrian sage needs sun for at least half the day and well-draining soil that has been amended with humus. Weekly watering is required and a light application of all-purpose fertilizer in early spring is beneficial. Seed and, consequently, seedlings occur after the plant is well established. Propagation is by seed or division of the basal rootstock. This delicate-looking salvia is long lasting as a cut flower. Austrian sage is hardy to 0°F (-18°C).

Stems of *Salvia austriaca* with soft yellow flowers are prized by flower arrangers. (Christine Andrews)

Many perennials would make outstanding combinations with Austrian sage in either a spring- or early autumn-blooming border. For spring blooming at the front of a border, plant mats of *Achillea* 'King Edward', which has flowers of almost the same color as Austrian sage and fernlike, gray foliage. For autumn bloom, plant patches of trailing California fuchsia, *Epilobium canum* subsp. *canum* (known previously as and persistently referred to as *Zauschneria californica* subsp. *cana*). California fuchsia's green foliage and red-orange flowers will add sparkle and surprise to the composition. Even though drought tolerant, this fuchsia will take the extra water that the other plants require. Another combination includes drifts of the garden hybrid *Aster ×frikartii*, since the aster's clear, violet-blue flowers and yellow-orange discs make fine 2 ft (60 cm) tall companions. 'Monch' and 'Wonder of Staffa' are long-blooming cultivars of the aster.

Salvia axillaris Moçiño & Sessé ex Bentham

Salvia axillaris grows near the central part of Mexico from San Luis Potosí to Oaxaca in a long, ribbonlike line. When Epling described *axillaris* in 1939 he found the plant to be quite variable. In fact, in the 1830s the botanist George Bentham described a species he called *cuneifolia* that Epling later called *axillaris*. Bentham's *cuneifolia* is now synonymous with *axillaris*. A major cause of this identification problem is that *S. axillaris* grows in several different habitats, which results in much variation within the species.

Flowering towards the end of the year, *Salvia axillaris* seldom comes into bloom in my garden until November or early December. Well named, this salvia has short inflorescences that emerge between the axil of the stem and the leaf's petiole. As in all salvias, the leaves are opposite; consequently, the inflorescences are opposite one another as they emerge and mature along the leafy stem. While this arrangement is not unusual for a salvia, what is unusual is that the orderly arrangement of the inflorescences may be easily seen because the lax stems of the plant tend to lie parallel to the ground. This salvia is a herbaceous perennial that creeps across the soil on shoots that root at the nodes making a splendid, low-growing ground cover. It apparently likes warm weather and light but not the hot, full sun of summer. An eastern exposure with good drainage, humusy soil, and regular water are the cultural requirements.

Rarely seen in gardens or nurseries, *Salvia axillaris* makes an excellent filler in gardens where temperatures do not drop below 32°F (0°C) for more than a few hours. On several occasions, however, when temperatures have dropped to the low 20°s F (around -6°C), plants were killed to the ground but came back slowly from their roots the following spring.

About 1 ft (30 cm) in height, this late-blooming salvia produces many stoloniferous shoots. The leaves vary in shape depending on where the plant originated in the wild. My plant has ovate leaves that are dentate on the margins. They are 2–4 in (5–10 cm) in length and hairless on both surfaces. The upper surface is a dull, light green and on the lower surface the veins are prominent. Whorls of six flowers are held on short inflorescences. The flowers themselves are small, a little over 0.5 in (1.3 cm) in length. The white flower tube is almost completely hidden inside the small dark purple calyx. The upper lip of the flower is hooded and dark purple. The lower, dark purple lip is spreading with two very white raindrop lines coming from the throat. Neither the plant nor the flower is conspicuous and both require close observation in order to distinguish their merits.

An east-facing border with good drainage and deep, humusy soil is the perfect setting for *Hydrangea quercifolia* 'Snow Queen', a medium-sized shrub with pure white, conical flowerheads in summer and stunning burgundy foliage in autumn. Several plants of the evergreen *Asarum magnificum*, with its mottled foliage, growing at the base of 'Snow Queen' will give year-round pleasure. Plants of *Salvia axillaris* in the front of the border will weave and work their way in between the other plants. The flowering of the salvia should occur in concert with the purple-red fall foliage of the hydrangea, a native of the southeastern United States.

Salvia azurea var. *grandiflora* Bentham
prairie sage

Described by the botanist George Bentham in 1848, *Salvia azurea* var. *grandiflora* has been popular for 100 years or more and is the kind of plant that has been frequently handed from gardener to gardener because of its beguiling, almost true-blue flowers and ease of propagation. Though there are many old alternatives, I find "prairie sage" an appropriate common name because it describes the plant's native habitat. Found from Nebraska to Colorado and from Texas to Kentucky, it has become naturalized in the southeastern United States. It is able to adapt to many climates and edaphic circumstances and is hardy to 10°F (-12°C).

A herbaceous perennial, *Salvia azurea* var. *grandiflora* is an extremely lax plant that is greatly admired for its cerulean blue flowers. Epling (1939) found that in the wild it has several distinct forms. The form commonly distributed by nurseries has linear to lanceolate leaves that are covered with downy hairs, giving them a dusky green appearance. Many stems are produced from the base of the plant, some reaching 3 ft (1 m) or more in length. September and October are the usual months for prodigious panicles of wonderful blue flowers to appear. On each inflorescence, many flowers bloom simultaneously. It is the large lower lip of each flower, often 0.5 in (1.3 cm) wide, that creates a pool of color. Propagation is by seed, cuttings, or division of the rootstock. Stems of these salvias make good cut flowers if they are first conditioned by being cut under water.

In 1994 an undesignated selection was distributed by Suncrest Nurseries in Watsonville, California. Blooming earlier than the typical prairie sage, this selection has an erect habit that is noteworthy. Its stems are about 2 ft (60 cm) in length and completely upright. Yellow-green leaves are lanceolate in shape and its flowers are pale blue with a whitish splotch on the large lower lip. The plant blooms as early as July and is completely deciduous in winter.

Full sun and friable garden soil are the two necessary cultural requirements for *Salvia azurea* var. *grandiflora*. An inventive gardener I know has made use of the plant's sprawling growth habit by growing it next to a wire fence in order to tie it and force its growth upward. I have placed it next to shrubs that provide support and assure an erect plant. Another friend experimented and found that keeping the plant dryer than normal helped in keeping the subsequently shorter stems more erect. In the wild the roots of this plant descend to great depths seeking moisture during periods of drought, but I am told that flowering depends on regular rainfall.

If you have a fence in a sunny location, the fragrant musk rose 'Buff Beauty' could be trained to a space about 5–6 ft (1.5–2 m) in width and about the same in height. The new foliage of the rose is a rich coppery color that later turns green, complementing its rich, chamois-yellow flowers, which bloom repeatedly. Plant prairie sage on both sides of the rose and weave the sage's long stems among its branches. Throughout the summer the rose will give pleasure, and in the autumn, together with the prairie sage, will provide an intensely colorful display.

Salvia barrelieri Etlinger

A stately herbaceous perennial with sky-blue flowers, *Salvia barrelieri* is found in the wild in northern Africa. Described botanically by Andreas Ernst Etlinger in 1777, it is not known when the plant was first introduced to horticulture. In the 1990s it had a limited appearance in gardens in England and the United States. Occurring in Morocco, Algeria, Tunisia, and the southwestern part of Spain, this salvia's habitat is truly Mediterranean. It is usually found between elevations of 500–4000 ft (150–1200 m) where it grows in many habitats that include the edges of fields, scrub and oak woodlands, and limestone and grassy slopes.

A perpendicular plant with poise, *Salvia barrelieri* will reach 3–6 ft (1–2 m) in height by early summer. Large, wavy, gray-green leaves completely cover the lower portion of the plant and make a mound about 1.5 ft (45 cm) in height. In my garden this salvia usually comes into bloom around the first of June and continues flowering for approximately a month. The inflorescence has many branches, is showy, and 2–3 ft (60–90 cm) tall. Flower color is a lovely light lavender or sky blue, and many whorls come into bloom at the same time. The

Salvia barrelieri makes a column of sky-blue flowers in the border of the Elizabeth F. Gamble Garden in Palo Alto, California. (Sonja Wilcomer)

upper lip is falcate, and across the top there are tiny hairs tipped with glands. The calyx is bright green, small, and also covered with glandular hairs. The gardener must decide whether to deadhead or not; with deadheading the plant is able to rest and the garden looks very tidy, but if the plant is allowed to produce seeds, those seeds can be saved and sown either in the autumn or the following spring. Seeds are the usual means of propagation, though cuttings can be taken from the plant in August or September.

Salvia barrelieri

    Salvia barrelieri is quite easy to place in the garden. All this plant needs is a sunny border, regular light to medium clay soil, some humus, and good drainage. I recommend a weekly watering and additional waterings during hot spells. Good drainage is especially important during winter months because of the prolonged wet and overcast spells.

    The height of this salvia allows it to work very well with plants of different sizes, but remember that it is 3–6 ft (1–2 m) tall for only about one month while in bloom. After you cut it back, pull other plants over or around it. For example, *Lathyrus latifolius*, perennial pea, which grows 9 ft (3 m) in length, has many selections that have been made as to color. Both 'White Pearl' and 'Pink Pearl', which will continue to give bloom to the border, could be pulled around the salvia. Yarrows too would make good companion plants. Those in the range of 2 ft (60 cm) include *Achillea* 'Hoffnung', a pale yellow cultivar, and *Achillea* 'Moonshine', a deep yellow cultivar. Both are early summer bloomers, as are 'Fire King' and 'Paprika', which have yellow centers and red flowers that age to copper. Among my very favorite companions is *Consolida ambigua*, the annual larkspur that comes from the Mediterranean in habitats similar to those of *Salvia barrelieri*. Seed catalogs are enticing with both singles and doubles; flower colors range from shades of blue and lavender to shades of pinks and salmons to whites. This annual will give the garden its first full look of summer growth with the promise of more to come. Another suitable annual that develops and blooms rapidly includes the corn cockle (*Agrostemma githago*), a wildflower of the Mediterranean that can be sown in late winter or early spring for early flowering. It reaches 2–3 ft (60–90 cm), and this Mediterranean plant's primitive form is a hot pink. There are white, lilac-pink, and purple-red forms too. Seed catalogs list *Saponaria vaccaria* 'Pink Beauty' as a rapidly growing annual. At about 2 ft (60 cm) or a little taller it produces flowers in profusion throughout the summer. All these plants share the same cultural requirements.

Salvia blepharophylla Brandegee
eyelash leaved sage

Even though *Salvia blepharophylla* was introduced into cultivation around 1930, it is little known or seen in gardens. In the wild it is found in the Mexican provinces of San Luis Potosí and Tamaulipas, and quite possibly in other locations. The specific epithet, *blepharophylla*, comes from Greek and means "with leaves fringed like eyelashes." Though it is possible to see a row of tiny hairs on the edge of the leaf with the naked eye, if you use a magnifying glass you will much more clearly see why the plant has the common name eyelash leaved sage.

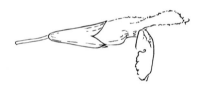

Salvia blepharophylla

Under the right conditions, this stoloniferous plant spreads rapidly. Categorized as a creeping procumbent perennial, *Salvia blepharophylla* is practically evergreen in protected places in areas where temperatures seldom go below 20°F (-7°C). When winter temperatures in my garden have dipped below 20°F (-7°C), this plant has managed to come back from its rootstock. The leaves of the clone that grows in my garden are more or less ovate in shape and a rich and glossy grassy green, making the plant attractive enough to be grown for the foliage alone. In the wild, however, the shape and texture of the leaves and the hairs on its surface can show variation. From early summer until frost, *S. blepharophylla* is very seldom seen without 1 in (2.5 cm) long flowers of vibrant signal-red with an orange undertone. The flowers, in loose whorls, are spaced about 1 in (2.5 cm) apart on an inflorescence that elongates to 1 ft (30 cm) or more. The balance between the glossy foliage and the richly colored flowering spike is strikingly beautiful. The height of the plant in full bloom is about 1.5 ft (45 cm) or more. Eventually it will spread into a patch. Graham Stuart Thomas (1990a)

The shade-loving *Salvia blepharophylla* 'Sweet Numbers' has a wide, intensely colored lower lip. (Christine Andrews)

calls the roots "fleshy and questing." Propagation is by division, cuttings, and seed.

Positioned in part shade and in good garden soil enriched with humus, eyelash leaved sage flourishes. Fast-draining soil is necessary, as is weekly watering. Occasional removal of spent flowering stalks removes excess weight from the plant and encourages upright growth and repeat bloom.

In 1992, Yucca Do Nursery in Texas introduced a form of *Salvia blepharophylla* collected in Tamaulipas, Mexico, at 5000 ft (1500 m). Called 'Sweet Numbers', it resembles the

The richly colored *Salvia blepharophylla* in part shade. (Robert Kourik)

plant described above except the hairs on the edge of the leaf are easily visible without a magnifying glass and the spreading lower lip of each flower is larger. The cultivar name honors the remote village Dulces Nombres in the northern corner of Tamaulipas where this cultivar was found.

Eyelash leaved sage makes a fine companion for plants with apricot-colored flowers. For example, it can be planted as ground cover at the base of roses. The climbing noisette 'Crepuscule', the shrub musk 'Francesca', or the modern upright shrub rose 'Charles Austin' are all enhanced by the salvia's foliage and showy flowers. The roses in turn protect the salvias with their shade.

Salvia brandegei Munz

An evergreen shrub at 3–4 ft (1–1.3 m) or more in height and width in its native habitat, *Salvia brandegei* will rapidly develop into a handsome garden subject. For many years it was thought to occur naturally only on Santa Rosa, one of the islands of the Santa Barbara Channel. During the 1960s and 1970s, however, six large colonies were found in Baja California. On a hillside above Punta Cabras that overlooks the Pacific Ocean where the vegetation is low and appears to be level, *S. brandegei* is a main component of the 3 ft (1 m) high coastal sage scrub community. Other plants include *Aesculus parryi*, *Artemisia californica*, *Encelia californica*, and *Rhus integrifolia*. The soil is a rich brown color, sandy, and full of disintegrating shells. Wind keeps the plants bushy and low, and fog provides moisture as the rainfall there is both sparse and seasonal. On Santa Rosa Island, *S. brandegei* apparently occurs in a typical coastal sage formation with *Artemisia californica*. On the mainland, the typical sage formation is dominated by *S. mellifera* and *S. munzii*.

Salvia brandegei

In the garden, *Salvia brandegei* will reach 4–5 ft (1.3–1.5 m) in height and 5–7 ft (1.5–2.3 m) in width. Its dark green leaves are linear, the longest measuring about 3–4 in (8–10 cm) in length and barely 0.5 in (1.3 cm) in width. The leaves are particularly beautiful because of the rough and varnished texture of the surface and the scalloping along the entire edge. The underside appears feltlike with its white hairs. When flowering takes place in early spring, the leaves cover the plant fully, but during the hot summer the shrub looks more open and sparsely clothed. The flowers are pale lavender, about 0.5 in (1.3 cm) in length, and held in tight, widely spaced whorls. In spite of their small size, the flowers are showy because the two lips are opened wide. The calyces are violet-gray and very ornamental. The flowering stems hold well and make good cut flowers. The foliage also lasts well in arrangements.

This is a shrub for exposed and sunny areas. Evidently deer never browse on it. Good drainage is a necessity, and after the plant is established no additional water is needed. If it is watered, this drought-tolerant shrub will produce excessive branches

Salvia brandegei has linear, evergreen leaves of unusual beauty. (Robert Kourik)

and foliage. A good time to remove a few branches to keep the shrub shapely is when it blooms in the spring. It is hardy to 20°F (-7°C) or lower for short periods. Propagation is by seed or cuttings.

In a dry Mediterranean garden, *Salvia brandegei* complements the gray foliage of lavender, stachys, and artemisia. All require the same bright exposure and other cultural conditions. A combination of *S. apiana*, *S. brandegei*, and *S. spathacea* would show off three California sages with different foliage. The dark green foliage of *S. brandegei* makes a strong contrast interspersed with the gray foliage of *S. apiana*; both reach about the same height. *Salvia spathacea* can be used as a ground cover. All have evergreen leaves, and the magenta to rose flowering spikes of *S. spathacea* are enhanced by the foliage of the other two sages.

Salvia broussonetii Bentham

A plant of maritime cliffs in its native habitat, *Salvia broussonetii* is a shrubby perennial with a limited distribution on the Canary Islands. It is found grow-

Handsome foliage is the hallmark of *Salvia broussonetii*. It performs quite well in a water-wise border. (Ginny Hunt)

ing on both Tenerife and Lanzarote on dark igneous rock from lava flows known as basalt. Described botanically by George Bentham in 1883, it has received little if any attention from horticulturists or those writing garden literature. This species was named to honor Pierre Marie Auguste Broussonet, a professor of botany in France in the 18th century.

A woody rootstock makes *Salvia broussonetii* a very stiff and upright plant. It is about 2 ft (60 cm) tall and just as wide with a sturdy appearance.

Salvia broussonetii

Large yellowish green leaves are distributed over the short stems and are ovate or elliptic in shape. The leaves persist in areas where the winters are mild. The petiole is usually long—4 in (10 cm)—and the margin of the leaf is irregularly lobed. The average leaf is about 4 in (10 cm) in length and 2.5 in (6 cm) wide and is covered with glandular hairs on both surfaces, which make it sticky to touch. Even though it is covered with glands I can detect no particular aroma or scent. Hairs are plentiful and numerous, and any debris that touches or falls on them tends to stick. Consequently, the plant can have a scruffy appearance. However, because of its tidy but large foliage it provides an excellent contrast with the small foliage of so many different drought-tolerant plants. Blooming takes place any time from early summer to autumn. Short inflorescences that are about 8–10 in (20–25 cm) in length rise above the leaves and are branched. The small flowers are white and usually in whorls of two, but it is reported that there can be as many as six per whorl. The upper lip is falcate and the calyx is small and subtended by bracts. Both calyx and bracts are covered with hairs. Plants usually produce seed, which is the customary means of propagation. After seeds are produced, stems bearing leaves can be used to make cuttings.

Collected in the wild at elevations of 300–400 ft (90–120 m) by the seaside, *Salvia broussonetii* is probably hardy to the low 20°s F (around -6°C) for short periods when given excellent drainage. A sunny aspect is needed throughout the year but is a necessity during the winter months. This salvia seldom if ever needs pruning. Loamy garden soil and a full day of sun are its basic requirements along with weekly deep watering.

After closely watching *Salvia broussonetii* develop and flower in the garden I know that this plant will interest gardeners who want to learn about the structure and general appearance or habit of salvias. I can think of no other salvia that has this particular stocky habit. It has no close allies and is considered a relict species, one that now grows within a small range of its once extensive natural habitat. The compact size and habit make *S. broussonetii* easy to combine with other low-growing plants that will not block the sun's rays. An entire bed of salvias would be an interesting project. For example, the spreading but low-growing and evergreen *S.* 'Purple Pastel', a *S. greggii* hybrid found in the wild by Pat McNeal of Austin, Texas, flowers profusely both in spring and autumn and might be used at either end of a short and narrow bed. Two plants of *S. broussonetii* could be placed towards the center with three or four of the small and compact *S. merjamie* from eastern Africa between them. Sow seeds of the delightful annual *S. algeriensis* over the entire grouping to obtain a pretty sprinkling of flowers from spring through autumn. All these salvias have different growing habits and come from different countries but they require the same culture.

The magenta-flowered *Salvia buchananii*, the gray-foliaged *Helichrysum splendidum*, and the day-flowering evening primrose, *Oenothera speciosa*. (Robert Kourik)

Salvia buchananii Hedge
Buchanan's sage

Salvia buchananii is not known in the wild but is probably of Mexican origin. Seed from a garden plant in Mexico City was taken to Britain and grown in a greenhouse by Sir Charles Buchanan sometime around 1960. He also grew it in his Leicestershire garden during the summer. From this source, Ian Hedge of the Royal Botanic Garden in Edinburgh was able to describe the plant in 1963 and name it in Buchanan's honor.

Occasionally called Buchanan's fuchsia sage, this herbaceous perennial grows 1–2 ft (30–60 cm) in height and 1 ft (30 cm) or more across. Glossy, rich green foliage is widely spaced along the stem with young leaves emerging from the leaf axils. The ovate-lanceolate leaves vary in size; the larger ones are about 2 in (5 cm) in length and 0.75 in (2 cm) wide. In a mild climate, plants will produce a few flowers year-round with heavy blooming occurring in summer and autumn. Rather hairy, rich magenta flowers about 2 in (5 cm) long adorn the plant. Although they are arranged in verticils of three to six flowers, only one or two flowers come into bloom at a given time. Many lax stems arise from the base of the salvia. Propagation is by cuttings. Even though I have grown this plant for many years it has never set seed; I suspect a specific pollinator is needed. However, it is reported to set seed occasionally.

Although suited for only the mildest climates, *Salvia buchananii* has on occasion overwintered in my garden. It strikes roots rapidly from cuttings, making it easy to house indoors as a precaution against light frost.

Some protective shade, good sandy loam, and a mulch of compost are needed along with deep watering every week. You will need to provide more water during hot spells. Remove spent inflorescences and pinch back lax growth in order to encourage more flowers and a shapely plant.

This salvia is eminently well suited to container culture. It performs well in the garden too, particularly when given the safeguard of other plants. Stiff and upright-growing perennials such as *Penstemon* 'Hidcote

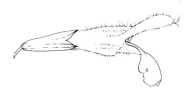

Salvia buchananii

Pink', 'Apple Blossom', or the dark purple-flowered 'Midnight' would encourage upward growth and also give protection from the sun. In a south-facing border, I have three of these salvias planted on the north side of the 8 ft (2.5 m) tall evergreen *Arbutus unedo* 'Compacta'. On either side of the salvias is *Helichrysum splendidum*, the marvelous, gray-foliaged, shrublike perennial from South Africa. It was a pleasant discovery to find that these gray leaves are an excellent contrast to the glossy green ones of *Salvia buchananii*. These two appealing plants make a wonderful feature in any garden.

Salvia cacaliifolia Bentham

In moist or dry mountains in the province of Chiapas, Mexico, and in several similar locations in Guatemala and Honduras, colonies of *Salvia cacaliifolia* frequently occur. Growing at elevations of 5000–8000 ft (1500–2500 m), this perennial herb prefers the high shade and protection of pine or oak forests. The specific epithet, *cacaliifolia*, means "with foliage like *Cacalia*," or "a genus like *Senecio*."

Recognized as a fine garden plant by William Robinson (1933), it has been favored in British gardens for many years. Since the late 1980s, *Salvia cacaliifolia* appears on many nursery lists and catalogs in Britain, France, and the

United States. It is most likely that Strybing Arboretum and Huntington Botanical Gardens are responsible for its introduction in the 1970s to California growers and gardeners.

Coming into bloom in midsummer, *Salvia cacaliifolia* makes racemes of delightful gentian-blue flowers until late autumn. Gardens located in

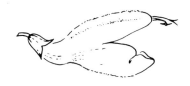

Salvia cacaliifolia

Blooming from summer through autumn, *Salvia cacaliifolia* has flowers that are almost true blue. (Christine Andrews)

mild climates are favored with flowering for eight to ten months. The flowers are short, about 0.5 in (1.3 cm) in length, but plentiful—many reaching full bloom at the same time. The green calyx is tiny and about the same color as the leaves. Deltoid leaves cover this herbaceous perennial amply. Rich grass-green in color, the leaves are covered with gland-tipped hairs. Many stems arise from the creeping, fleshy rootstock, which soon grows into a patch of plants. These roots with stems can be readily divided, assuring easy propagation. Watchful gardeners can find seed in September or October. *Salvia cacaliifolia* has proved to be hardy to 20°F(-7°C) if its crown is protected, and it can be tried in a colder zone using conifer boughs as a safeguard. Robinson apparently grew it outdoors.

A border with some high shade, good drainage, and friable soil will all help this salvia flourish. Weekly water is necessary, along with the removal of spent inflorescences. After danger of a late frost is over, cut the stems almost to the ground to obtain a shapely patch of plants. A dressing of compost in midspring assures an easy root-run. Fertilizer does not seem to be necessary, but occasionally the leaves of my plants turn slightly yellow, indicating an iron deficiency. This deficiency can be treated with applications of chelated iron.

This is a plant that would add summer and autumn color to a collection of spring-blooming viburnums or rhododendrons, whose green foliage would make a fine background for the salvia's gentian-blue flowers. All prefer high shade, soil with humus, and regular water. Quite by chance, I planted a group in front of the deciduous *Viburnum opulus* 'Aureum'. The viburnum's bright yellow leaves make a handsome contrast to the salvia's rich blue flowers. The 3–4 ft (1–1.3 m) tall evergreen *Lonicera nitida* 'Baggesen's Gold', with its yellow summer leaves that turn yellow-green in winter, also makes a highly effective companion.

Salvia caespitosa Montbret & Aucher ex Bentham

A member of the mint family, *Salvia caespitosa* is highly suitable for the rock garden. In the wild it occurs on rocky limestone and volcanic slopes and terraces in central and southern Anatolia, an area that lies between the Black and the Mediterranean Seas. In Asia, the area comprising Anatolia is especially rich in *Salvia*; about half of the 86 species that grow here are endemic to the area, and there are many naturally occurring hybrids. *Salvia caespitosa* is an endemic species that makes its home on a high plateau between 4600 and 7900 ft (1400 and 2400 m), where temperatures can swing from hot to cold in a short period of time. Described botanically in 1836, *S. caespitosa* was grown horticulturally in alpine houses in England in the 1950s. I had a plant in my own garden as early as 1980 but lost it before it set seed. This species is available in both England and the United States. It is enjoying a small popularity among rock garden enthusiasts in the United States.

A herbaceous perennial that develops some wood at its base, *Salvia caespitosa* can be referred to as a dwarf, mat-forming plant. The specific epithet, *caespitosa*, means "growing in dense clumps or tufts" and precisely describes the habit of the plant. Less than 6 in (15 cm) in height, mats can be 2–3 ft (60–90 cm) in width. The

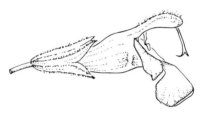

Salvia caespitosa

divided leaves and stems are lightly covered with hairs that grow in bunches rather than spaced evenly along the stem, which gives a tufted appearance. Individual leaves are charming but difficult to see because of the plant's dense growth. The inflorescence is condensed and congested, scarcely exceeding the length of the leaf. Flowers are a very pale pinkish lilac, about 1.6 in (4 cm) in length, and look so inflated they verge on being out of proportion to the plant. The calyx is two lipped and has vague green and white stripes. It is subtended by bracts that have similar markings. Flowering begins in late spring and continues well into the summer.

Here is a salvia that is well suited for dry and hot garden areas. Sunlight and good air movement throughout most of the day are essential, as is rapid drainage. Rocky soil that contains some clay is preferable to a rich or humusy soil. Planting on a mound is another way to achieve fast drainage. After the plant is established, give it a regular amount of water on a weekly basis. Propagate it by taking cuttings in late summer; you can obtain cutting materi-

A perfect bun for the rock garden, *Salvia caespitosa* has large flowers that are a delightful, pale pink surprise. (Sonja Wilcomer)

al by judiciously removing little tufts of leaves on the stems. This salvia takes care of itself—no pruning or deadheading is required—if its habitat requirements are met.

Plants of this species need their special niche to thrive: a large mound of rocks and soil positioned in full sunlight offers such a habitat. A rocky mound, because of its height, also allows viewers to more easily see the raised plants. One mound I envision includes the good-looking *Teucrium pyrenaicum*, its spoon-shaped flowers of creamy white and green foliage making an absolutely flat, reliable mat that creates a handsome background for flashier plants. Two more teucriums can be added to this mound, *T. polium* 'Aureum', which has gray foliage and yellow flowers, and *T. cossonii*, which has grayish white foliage and rosy purple flowers. The stars of this mound are two salvias: *Salvia albimaculata*, which is almost 1 ft (30 cm) tall when its violet flowers with the prominent white beeline (the beeline guides the insect or hummingbird to the nectar and pollen within the flower) are in bloom, and *S. caespitosa*, of course, whose mats will be clearly visible with short-foliaged plants nearby.

A trough that is positioned free of shadows would also be an ideal spot for growing *Salvia caespitosa*. If combined with the silver-gray foliage of *Artemisia caucasica* and the almost dull green leaves and sulfur-yellow flowers of

Eriogonum umbellatum 'Shasta Sulfur', *S. caespitosa* would find itself in a trough filled with handsome, year-round foliage that would burst into bloom in late spring.

Salvia canariensis Linnaeus
Canary Island sage

From the Canary Islands, with their mild and dry climate, comes *Salvia canariensis*. It is an erect and ample shrub with foliage that not only persists but also looks attractive throughout the winter months in benign climates. Brief periods of temperatures falling to 15°F (-9°C) will kill it to the ground, but it will generally come back from its rootstock the following spring. Even though *S. canariensis* seeds itself readily in the garden, it has not become naturalized in temperate California due to its need for summer water.

Salvia canariensis at Strybing Arboretum. (Christine Andrews)

Canary Island sage will reach 6–7 ft (2–2.3 m) in height and 5 ft (1.5 m) across in a growing season. It can be held to a smaller size by infrequent watering. Its stems are densely covered with long white hairs, and the triangular or hastate leaves are a pale green with numerous long white hairs on the underside. The tips of the hairs have aromatic oil glands. Blooming begins in summer and continues until the days are noticeably shorter and cool. Fine panicles of purplish violet flowers with calyces that are tipped purple-red adorn the shrub throughout this lengthy period. In its native habitat, the plant's panicles range from a pale purple to a strong and deep purplish magenta. When conditioned by being cut under water, the stems make long-lasting and good-looking cut flowers that are prized by flower arrangers. Conditioned branches of foliage are also useful to arrangers.

I have been able to grow *Salvia canariensis* var. *candidissima* for only a short period but have seen it in gardens along the French and Italian Rivieras. It is apparently a more tender plant than the type species. Suitable for climates

In the garden at La Mortola, *Salvia canariensis* var. *candidissima* is in glorious summer bloom. (Ginny Hunt)

free of frost, it develops into a 4–5 ft (1.3–1.5 m) shrub in a long growing season. The beautiful foliage is covered with long hairs and is completely silvery-white. Flowers are large and a particularly fine shade of dusky mauve. The wide calyx reflects this color as well. Young plants are especially charming.

Before the new season of growth begins, usually in late February, cut the main stems to 1 ft (30 cm) or less above the ground. This will encourage a more shapely shrub during the long, upcoming growing season. Full sun, good drainage, and water every two to three weeks will promote moderate growth. Humid or damp air can cause fungal problems, so good air circulation is vital. Propagation is by seed or by cuttings taken from spring through autumn. Seedlings are usually found at the base of the mature plant. They are large and easy to remove or pot up for a friend.

A large shrub rose, such as the deep, red-violet *Rosa* 'Mons. Tillier' or the pale pink, almost single-flowered 'Sparrieshoop', would make impressive companions. Because of their size, *Salvia canariensis* and *S. canariensis* var. *candidissima* can be positioned in a hot and dry sunny border to give shade and protection to smaller herbaceous or shrubby plants. Planted outside my fenced garden, it remains untouched by a large deer population and also provides cover to many species of birds and small animals.

Salvia candidissima Vahl

A perennial herb of modest size, *Salvia candidissima* has a widespread distribution throughout western Greece and parts of Turkey, Iraq, and Iran. This salvia is ubiquitous in the general area of Anatolia. Its various habitats are at elevations between 2000 and 6500 ft (600 and 2000 m) and include rocky limestone and shale-covered slopes. It grows in places that are bushy, in fallow fields, and in areas that are dominated by pine, oak, cedar, and fir. It was described in 1804 by the Norwegian-born, Danish botanist Martin Vahl who studied with Linnaeus in Uppsala and later not only taught botany but also collected plants.

Salvia candidissima is an intriguing plant, and the arrangement and texture of the leaves will immediately capture one's attention. Several to many small stems emerge from the rootstock and at first grow almost parallel to the ground. These tight stems or branches eventually will bear upright inflorescences. This salvia has a span of 2 ft (60 cm) in height and width in my garden but is reported to reach 3 ft (1 m) and form a woody base in the wild. Its overall appearance is neat and tidy—it is almost a rock garden plant but is just a little bit too big. Leaves are a light apple green and slightly covered with hairs on both surfaces. They measure 6 in (15 cm) in length and 4 in (10 cm) in width and can be sessile or have a petiole. Most leaves have notches around the margins. As days lengthen and become hot the leaves become both lighter in color and whiter. Inflorescences are branched and about 8–12 in (20–30 cm) in length. Flowers are 1 in (2.5 cm) long and in whorls. They are a creamy white, sometimes tipped with a yellow lip, and are held in a small calyx that is covered with both glands and hairs. The specific name, *candidissima*, probably refers to the color of the flowers but it could also refer to the leaves. Plants are hardy to the low 20°s F (around -6°C) for short periods but are particularly susceptible to wet spells in winter.

An additional word or two needs to be added to the description of *Salvia candidissima*. Its position is at the center of a group of seven salvias that are closely allied and form a natural species group. *Salvia candidissima* is the one found in the habitats of the six others, and there is hybridization and introgression between the species. This is a volatile group of plants and as a result the characteristics of the species are not very constant. To my knowledge no other plant in this group is grown as a horticultural subject.

Full sun and fast drainage are necessities for *Salvia candidissima*, and both a lean soil and a regular weekly watering are desirable. This plant does not require fertilizer but I have noticed that it attracts insects and slugs that feed on its handsome leaves. A regular treatment of snail bait will prevent predation and insure both healthy-looking leaves and a whole, unimpaired plant.

Salvia candidissima

Salvia candidissima can easily become a feature attraction in a sunny border because of its attractive and almost evergreen leaves. Since they are small salvias, place three or four of them in the front of a bed and mix them with a number of purple-leaved plants of *S. officinalis* 'Purpurascens' for contrast. Add several *Lavandula* 'Goodwin Creek Grey', which are 3 ft (1 m) tall and wide, for background. At the back of this border, plant as many *Amaryllis belladonna* as you can afford. These bulbs from South Africa are called naked ladies. They produce straplike leaves in the autumn and winter, and then the

Salvia candidissima is a gem with attractive gray foliage and white flowers. (Sonja Wilcomer)

foliage dies in late spring or early summer. About six to eight weeks later stalks rise about 3 ft (1 m) from the bare ground and great clusters of fragrant, trumpet-shaped, satin-pink flowers come into bloom. All these plants have similar minimal requirements: a sunny aspect, good drainage, a lean soil, and water on a weekly basis.

Salvia canescens var. *daghestanica* Menitsky

A small herbaceous perennial with a shapely, trim appearance, *Salvia canescens* var. *daghestanica* is endemic to the Caucasus Mountains, a region that lies between the Black and Caspian Seas. The specific name *canescens* refers to the leaves of the plant being covered with off-white hairs, and *daghestanica* refers to the name of the province Dagestan, which is located north of Azerbaijan and east of Georgia. The Russian botanist Yo Lo Menitsky (1992) revised the treatment of this salvia but even in 2002 I can find no information about its native habitat. There is unequivocal praise for the plant, however, from Panayoti Kelaidis, curator of plant collections at Denver Botanic Gardens. As he says,

"The queen of rock garden salvias at Denver Botanic Gardens is unquestionably *Salvia canescens* var. *daghestanica*." Even though we have no description of its habitat, I have found the plant easy to grow in a garden situation.

Reaching less than 1 ft (30 cm) in both height and width, *Salvia canescens* var. *daghestanica* makes a rounded mound of snowy white leaves. Individual leaves measure 1–4 in (2.5–10 cm) in length and are fuzzy with white hairs on both surfaces. "They look as though they had been dipped in powdered sugar," comments Kelaidis. Very rich, royal purple flowers are produced in whorls in early summer and again in autumn. They measure a little over 0.5 in (1.3 cm) in length and are held in a small calyx that is covered with hairs and glands. Inflorescences are about 1 ft (30 cm) long and are held above the snowy foliage. As it is reluctant to set seed in my garden, I take material for cuttings from the plant's productive mound of growth or from small rosettes that appear on the flowering stem during summer when the plant is active and growing.

Give *Salvia canescens* var. *daghestanica* a very sunny spot in the garden and be sure it has fast drainage and good air movement. It apparently likes a lean soil and does not require fertilizers. Mulching with small, rough-sided rocks (not the rounded ones) will help to conserve water and at the same time will keep the foliage clean and white. Water is needed on a weekly basis, although the plant will need additional water if the weather is extremely hot. It is reported to take temperatures into the teens (-10°C), which would certainly reflect its native habitat.

A rocky mound of earth that is in full sun and not in the shadow of trees or other plants would be an ideal spot for a raised bed of plants that are proportionate in size to *Salvia canescens* var. *daghestanica*. Plants in the mint family, Lamiaceae, will cover the mound with their leaves, and some will come into and go out of flower, off and on, throughout the summer. Since my idea is to create

Salvia canescens var. *daghestanica*

a tapestry of foliage and flowers, I immediately think of two teucriums. One is the gray-foliaged *Teucrium polium* 'Aureum', which makes a mat of handsome foliage about 2 ft (60 cm) square and becomes covered with a mass of bright yellow flowers in summer. The other teucrium is the green-foliaged *T. pyrenaicum*, which will more sharply contrast with the snowy foliage of *S. canescens* var. *daghestanica* and help push it into the limelight. Although *T. pyrenaicum* grows close to the ground it covers a 2 ft (60 cm) square area and has an architectural quality to it. Charming white flowers are produced abundantly in summer, and bloom is repeated in autumn. Several compact *Lavandula angustifolia* cultivars are 1.5 ft (45 cm) when in bloom: 'Blue Cushion', 'Compacta', 'Melissa', and 'Nana' are all the same size and can be counted on for good summer bloom. If there is room for more, try the skullcap *Scutellaria resinosa* that occurs from Texas to Colorado, which is less than 1 ft (30 cm) tall. If deadheaded, it will produce clusters of deep blue-purple flowers from late spring well into the autumn. All these plants have low water needs once they are established.

Well suited for the rock garden, *Salvia canescens* var. *daghestanica* repeats bloom from spring to autumn. (Sonja Wilcomer)

Salvia carduacea Bentham
thistle sage

The single and best word for *Salvia carduacea* is spectacular, whether you are seeing it for the first or the hundredth time. A California native, this annual has a distribution from Contra Costa County south through the central valley and coast ranges and on through the southern deserts into northern Baja. Growing in sun-swept places that are sandy and gravelly, thistle sage is found at elevations below 4500 ft (1400 m). Native grasses and annual wild flowers are its usual companions.

Salvia carduacea

Thistle sage responds dramatically to its environment. With rain and other moisture, plants can reach 3 ft (1 m) in height. In an arid setting plants are dwarfed and may only be 6 in (15 cm) tall. Spring blooming, the whole plant is

In a spring display on the Carrizo Plains in California, *Salvia carduacea* is seen growing in a mass of poppies and *Coreopsis bigelovii*. (Bart O'Brien)

Salvia carduacea

woolly white with basal leaves that resemble a thistle's, being toothed and long spined. The flowers appear in whorls held in congested calyces that are woolly and spiny. Flower color varies little and is usually a lively lavender electrified by bright orange anthers. Epling (1939) is almost lyrical in his description, calling the flower exquisite in color and form, with pungent foliage similar to *Citronella* (it resembles *Salvia greatae*, another California native, in that regard). He concludes by saying that thistle sage flowers soon after the winter rains and, along with that group of plants known as "winter annuals," soon disappears.

Thistle sage can successfully be brought into the garden. On many occasions I have sown seeds directly into beds but they seldom germinated. Only once have I had good luck, when self-sown seedlings appeared in the garden in the spring of 1982. A surer method is to sow seeds in a container in a greenhouse and then transplant the seedlings into individual containers before eventually moving them into the garden. If you follow these steps, the transplanted seedlings will adjust rapidly.

Full sun and well-drained, gritty soil are practically the only requirements of thistle sage. It is necessary to water plants until they become established; after that, watering increases the size of the plants. In the desert, large hover moths help with pollination. These moths are as large as small hummingbirds and their activity is similar. In a garden setting, hummingbirds probably help with pollination, as do butterflies and moths.

A rocky, dry hillside is well suited for the drought-tolerant thistle sage. It looks natural if grown in front of black sage, *Salvia mellifera*. The dusky green foliage of black sage is a perfect foil for the almost completely white thistle sage. A combination that occurs in the wild is thistle sage, *Stipa cernua*, *S. pulchra*, and *S. speciosa*. These grasses are California natives and they prefer the same dry and sunny culture. *Yucca whipplei* is another native companion whose stiff and pointed leaves would add stature to the composition. The 2 ft (60 cm) tall Mexican native *Beschorneria yuccoides*, with its rosettes of soft and flexible apple-green leaves, is another easy candidate for companion planting.

Salvia castanea Diels

A herbaceous perennial plant of subtle and discrete beauty, *Salvia castanea* in bloom is awesome in its unpretentiousness. Discovered in Yunnan in Western China in 1904 by the persistent and patient plant collector George Forrest, this salvia is also known to occur in Nepal, Bhutan, and Tibet, as well as southern China. Described by Friedrich Ludwig Emil Diels in 1912, it was almost unknown to horticulture until 1966. At that time, Tony Schilling, who was curator of Wakehurst Place Gardens, collected seed of the salvia below Mount Everest in Nepal at an elevation of 14,000 ft (4100 m), where it was growing on rocky slopes in and among dwarf shrubs. It is most likely that the plants we grow today came from this very collection.

Forming a basal clump of oblong leaves, *Salvia castanea* is reported to grow 3 ft (1 m) tall in its native habitat, but in England and the United States its height varies between 1 and 2 ft (30 and 60 cm). Leaves are restricted to the basal clump or the lower

Salvia castanea has rich purple-maroon flowers that appear in early summer. (Ginny Hunt)

part of the flowering stems. The largest leaves measure about 7 in (18 cm) long and 4 in (10 cm) wide, and the petioles are as long as the leaf blades. The inflorescence is about 1 ft (30 cm) in length with spaces between each whorl of flowers. The flowers are few, 1–1.5 in (2.5–4 cm) in length, and a wonderful shade of rich purplish maroon. The specific name, *castanea*, is Latin for chestnut colored, and refers to the flower color. The botanical name for chestnut trees is *Castanea*. Flowers are held in a small purple-tinged calyx that expands with maturing seeds. The tube of the flower is fat and wide, and the lower lip hangs open and is gaping. Flowering is in early summer, and in my garden both hummingbirds and insects are attracted to this salvia. Seed is often produced and is the usual means of propagation. However, it is possible to tease cutting material away from the base of the plant in August and September.

Salvia castanea

The culture of *Salvia castanea* is similar to many other salvias that come from China. Place it where it receives at least a half day of sunlight. Good drainage is essential, particularly in the winter because the plant cannot tolerate wet roots. It is a deciduous plant that gives no indication of life during the winter months, so the gardener cannot tell if anything is amiss with the plant. A good garden soil that is friable and has some humus is recommended. I have found that a half-strength liquid fertilizer in spring will help the plant start its growing cycle. Weekly water is needed during the growing season, and an additional amount should be given during hot spells.

A sunny border or bed where it can be protected by other plants but still be in good sunlight is an ideal location for *Salvia castanea*. For the background, several mounding *S. chamelaeagnea* plants that have excellent dark green foliage would be the mainstay. By midsummer they will have pretty clusters of lightly colored violet-blue flowers. Intermingle plants of *Euphorbia characias* 'Portuguese Velvet' with *S. castanea* throughout the front of the border as the interesting, soft gray foliage of the euphorbia will complement the unusual flower color of the salvia. Geoff Genge, who has a National Salvia Collection at his nursery, Marshwood Gardens, New Zealand, regards *S. castanea* as an excellent companion to old roses. He calls the foliage "magnificent" and says the plant is "as good as any hosta." This is indeed high praise, particularly for a salvia that is still relatively unknown to gardeners.

Salvia cedrosensis Greene

Salvia cedrosensis is an evergreen, fruticose plant. Its native habitat is restricted to the Vizcaino Peninsula, situated midway along the western coast of Baja, and the nearby Cedros Island. It occurs in small canyons and dry riverbeds that have rocky and gravelly soil. *Cercidium microphyllum*, *Encelia californica*, *Hyptis emoryi*, and *Solanum hindsianum* are sometimes present in small numbers and give protection to the salvias. The canyon walls in these washes also shade and protect the salvias. These natural habitats are close to sea level and most years experience summer fog, but winter rains are erratic and variable. Measurable rainfall can be less than 0.5 in (1.3 cm) a year, or there can be deluges that drench the area repeatedly.

A charming, herblike plant, *Salvia cedrosensis* usually reaches 1 ft (30 cm) in height and width in cultivation, but in the wild it can be twice that size. Small felted leaves less than 1 in (2.5 cm) long are almost white in appearance when

Salvia cedrosensis in its native habitat on the Vizcaino Peninsula, Baja California Sur. (Bart O'Brien)

they first emerge. At maturity they are pearly gray and reflect the sun's rays, as do the stems and calyces. All parts of the plant except the spreading lower lip of the corolla are covered with fine hairs. The flowers are a lively violet-blue, but in bright sunlight call little attention to themselves. The calyx is pearl gray with a light dusting of violet around the pointed edges. The two verticils hold three to six flowers each with only one or two flowers on the entire inflorescence coming into bloom simultaneously. In my garden there is a long period of meager but alluring bloom throughout the summer, with a few flowers occurring in autumn. Over time, *S. cedrosensis* builds wood at its base.

Salvia cedrosensis looks as though it is a rather delicate plant, but in reality it is able to withstand flaming sunlight and searing temperatures as well as battering rains and wind. It thrives in full sun when planted in gritty soil on the south side of a rocky mound. The rocks give off reflected heat and supply some small protection from the wind. Water the plant regularly until well established, after which only occasional water is necessary. I have not grown the plant long enough to determine its hardiness, but it has survived temperatures in the low 30°s F (around -1°C). Propagation is by seed or cuttings.

A plant that is rarely seen or grown, *Salvia cedrosensis* is proving to be a reliable rock garden specimen and I am hopeful that it will start to enjoy a reputation that will ensure its distribution among gardeners. Look for specimens at Strybing Arboretum, Rancho Santa Ana Botanic Garden, and the University of California Botanical Garden, Berkeley. It is also being grown by several California native plant nurseries.

Salvia chamaedryoides Cavanilles
germander sage

From high and somewhat dry altitudes comes *Salvia chamaedryoides*, an evergreen perennial from Mexico. It occurs at 7000–9000 ft (2100–2800 m), primarily in desertlike habitats throughout the Sierra Madre Oriental. The specific name, *chamaedryoides*, means "dwarflike" and refers to the plant's habit. In a garden situation, germander sage appears dwarflike only in its winter dormancy. The common name, germander sage, refers to the common name of *Teucrium chamaedrys*, wall germander. The plants share the characteristic of a running rootstock.

With many ascending stems, germander sage reaches 2 ft (60 cm) in height when in bloom and spreads freely from an underground rootstock. The small, gray, evergreen foliage gives year-round pleasure. Small, almost true-blue flowers appear sporadically during warm spells throughout the growing season, with full bloom occurring in early summer and again in autumn when nights are cool. The plant is hardy to approximately 10°F (-12°C). Propagation is by seed, cuttings, and division. Division is easily accomplished, particularly in early autumn, because of the plant's running rootstock.

Full sun and loamy, quick-draining soil are prerequisites for growing *Salvia chamaedryoides*. Prune all spent inflorescences two or three times during the growing season in order for the plant to produce more flowers. No fertilizer is needed. This is a drought-tolerant plant, but after pruning the inflorescences you may help induce further flowering by watering once every week or two.

In the 1980s growers from the United States discovered a whole array of plants in neighboring Mexico that make fascinating additions to our gardens. At about that time, *Salvia chamaedryoides* was introduced to horticulture in the United States, though it had been known and grown in European horticulture since the early 1800s.

Two English gardeners Harold and Joan Bawden (1970) wrote of their enjoyment in growing the radiant blue-flowered germander sage. This would

The sparkling blue-flowered *Salvia chamaedryoides* in the author's garden with *S. microphylla* 'Graham's Sage' in the background. (Robert Kourik)

not seem to be a plant for long damp English winters, but clearly the Bawdens were delighted with it.

A compact selection called *Salvia chamaedryoides* 'Desert Green' was introduced in 1990 by nurseryman Pat McNeal of Austin, Texas. Similar to the species in growth, habit, and cultural requirements, 'Desert Green' has soft-colored, apple-green leaves of a different texture and color than the typical species. Blooming best in spring and autumn when the weather is cool, this selection is noteworthy for its uncommon and attractive silver-green foliage. The form of *S. chamaedryoides* with apple-green leaves is frequently seen in gardens along the French Riviera, whereas in the United States the gray-leaved form is more commonly planted.

Sparkling and versatile, *Salvia chamaedryoides* has no attraction for browsing deer and is extremely attractive planted in groups with gray-green ballotas and deep green rosemary plants. Another combination for a

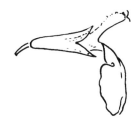

Salvia chamaedryoides

Salvia 'Marine Blue', a likely offspring of *Salvia chamaedryoides*, is a phenomenal flower producer. (Sonja Wilcomer)

sunny site is the gray-foliaged germander sage and the 1 ft (30 cm) tall *Artemisia schmidtiana* 'Silver Mound', which forms a many stemmed, compact mound each year. The light green to gray foliage of the creeping perennial *Silene maritima*, which has large white flowers, ties the gray-foliaged combination together. All three plants require the same culture.

A handsome hybrid from Australia, 'Marine Blue' repeats bloom consistently from early summer through the autumn. It is a little larger in its parts and growth than the type species. Standing erect, a mature plant is about 2 ft (60 cm) tall and wide. It makes an excellent filler for a border that receives limited water. The other parent of this hybrid is unknown.

Salvia chamelaeagnea Bergius

From the coastline of the Cape of Good Hope in South Africa comes *Salvia chamelaeagnea*, a heavily flowering, shrubby sage. Its distribution is apparently limited to the western side of the Cape and the species exhibits little variation. It is commonly found in sandy soil in open fields and streambeds and on roadsides, and appears to be adaptable to many situations.

After several years in the garden, *Salvia chamelaeagnea* will build slowly to about 4 ft (1.3 m). Given time and attention, it will attain 5–6 ft (1.5–2 m) in height and 4 ft (1.3 m) or more in width. Its habit is to send many stems from the rootstock, which may be divided from the plant with care. Propagation is also by seed and cuttings.

Midsummer is the usual time for this freely flowering salvia to start blooming. Clusters of lightly colored violet-blue flowers develop throughout summer into autumn. The inflorescences are crowded because of much branching at the top of each stem. This characteristic gives the

Salvia chamelaeagnea blooms from late summer through autumn. (Christine Andrews)

plant an untidy look when the numerous calyces turn brown while holding the maturing seed. The flowers are falcate and the hood is a light violet-blue. The lower lip is paler and the throat is white. Overall, the flower is about 0.75 in (2 cm) long. The leaves are small, more or less the same length as the flower. Egg-shaped, the leaves are mid-green and give substance to the plant. When brushed they release a light, not unpleasant, medicinal odor.

Cultural conditions include full sun, good drainage, soil prepared with grit and humus, and weekly water in summer. My experience with the plant's hardiness is limited, but it regularly withstands temperatures of 25°F (-4°C) in my garden. I advise taking cuttings for the greenhouse in late August to be on the safe side. Shaping the plant in late winter will help control new growth. In fact, during the entire growing season it is advisable to remove growth when the plant begins to look scruffy.

Described in 1767, *Salvia chamelaeagnea* was given a Latin name that means "dwarf olive," though it is used to mean "shrublike." No reference exists to show that it has ever been introduced to horticulture in South Africa, Britain, or the United States, but it has been introduced and distributed by the nursery that holds the National Collection of Salvias in France, Pépinière de la Foux. In addition, Western Hills Nursery in Occidental, California, a source for many unusual plants, distributed *S. chamelaeagnea* in the spring of 1991, and the salvia may now appear on several seed and nursery lists.

The worthwhile *Salvia chamelaeagnea* is adaptable to many different cultural situations, an outstanding characteristic. In a herbaceous border it provides height, and its handsome, dark green foliage anchors flowering perennials such as penstemons, yarrows, feverfew, asters, veronicas, geraniums, and saponarias. In a bed with annuals it would serve the same function very well indeed. Practicing gardeners are constantly on the lookout for a plant of medium size that has substantial green leaves to be the mainstay of a border of flowering plants, and this is a prime candidate. *Salvia chamelaeagnea* will enhance innumerable spots in the garden because of its size and desirable leaf color.

Salvia chiapensis Fernald
Chiapas sage

To the best of my knowledge, *Salvia chiapensis* has been collected only in the wild near San Cristobal, in the province of Chiapas, Mexico. It grows at elevations of 7000–9500 ft (2100–2900 m) in moist habitats called cloud forests. On a study and collecting trip in 1981, a group from the University of California Botanical Garden, Berkeley, visited this area and returned with seeds and cuttings for the Mesoamerican section of the Garden. Chiapas sage was probably introduced to horticulture from this Botanical Garden sometime after that trip.

A tender, herbaceous perennial, Chiapas sage grows about 1.5–2 ft (45–60 cm) in height and width. Several stems rise out of the plant's rootstock. Ivy-green, glossy, and deeply veined leaves are widely spaced along the stems. The largest measures about 3 in (8 cm) long and 1.5 in (4 cm) wide, giving the plant a lightly clothed look. They are elliptic in shape (broadest at the middle, the ends rather equal) and appear sleek and hairless on both surfaces. The calyx is pea-green and 0.5 in (1.3 cm) long. Three to six flowers in whorls are widely spaced along the inflorescence. They are a bright fuchsia color, about 0.75 in (2 cm) in length, and covered with hairs. This is an attractive, upright, and airy-looking salvia.

Only in frost-free zones can *Salvia chiapensis* survive in the ground year-round. Since it cannot tolerate low temperatures, keep the plant in a contain-

The shiny, deeply veined leaves of *Salvia chiapensis* add to the beauty of the plant. (Ginny Hunt)

er to overwinter indoors or take cuttings to ensure you have plants for the coming spring. Preferring good sandy loam with fast drainage and dressings of rich compost, the plant needs frequent deep watering as well as moisture on its leaves to imitate its cloud-forest habitat. Half-strength solutions of a liquid fertilizer are helpful and may be applied occasionally throughout the growing season.

Blooming commences in the summer, and if the salvia is brought into a light-filled greenhouse in the autumn, flowering will continue throughout the winter. It is a tireless bloomer. Before you move it into the garden in late spring, cut the foliage back hard to encourage a rest period before fresh growth begins. Propagation is easily accomplished by cuttings and seed. Seedlings frequently appear in gardens that have no frost, and it has generously seeded itself in the Mesoamerican section of the Botanical Garden in Berkeley.

Chiapas sage makes an attractive hanging basket, though it requires generous amounts of water. I frequently plant it in a two-gallon, black plastic nursery container and sink it in a bed in the garden. At a moment's notice, it can be retrieved and made safe in the greenhouse. It is very handsome in a large container surrounded by the 6 in (15 cm) tall *Geranium dalmaticum*, which has dainty pink flowers that rise just over its foliage, or by the 2 in (5 cm) tall *Campanula rotundifolia*, which sends up delightful 6 in (15 cm) stems of violet bellflowers in summer and autumn. For the salvia connoisseur, the blue-flowered *Salvia sinaloensis*, with its graceful, plum-purple stems, makes a fine companion.

Salvia chionophylla Fernald

Known to occur in a very limited habitat in northern Mexico, *Salvia chionophylla* may be found near the city of Saltillo in the province of Coahuila. Such a restricted habitat is surprising because the plant has proven to be quite adaptable as a garden subject. It was probably introduced to horticulture in North Carolina, Texas, and California during the summer of 1996, and since then is occasionally seen at arboreta and botanic gardens, nurseries, or in private gardens. It is a treasure that is yet to be discovered. Merritt Lyndon Fernald was the botanist who first described the salvia in 1907, giving it the specific name, *chionophylla*, which emphasizes that it is white leaved.

Salvia chionophylla has small, rounded, dove-gray leaves that measure about 0.5 in (1.3 cm) in length. These evergreen leaves are evenly spaced along the trailing stem, making the salvia appear tidy and uncluttered. The very small, sparkling blue flowers are less than 0.25 in (0.6 cm) long and are held on short inflorescences that have whorls of two to six flowers. Few are open at the same time. Flowering is sporadic, beginning in early summer and continuing through autumn. As seed is sparingly produced, propagation is by removal of a rooted stem or by cuttings. Temperatures in the low 20°s F (around -6°C) do not discolor leaves or damage this salvia if it is given excellent drainage.

A perennial herb that is prostrate and lies close to the ground, *Salvia chionophylla* is a trailing plant that builds very little growth at its center. As it

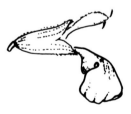

Salvia chionophylla

travels along it tends to root at the nodes, producing more and more trailing stems. It never appears to cover the ground thickly but, given time, will lightly cover a wide border. It is possible to encourage the plant to become more compact and handsome, however, by removing a lot of

A delightfully trailing plant, *Salvia chionophylla* has tiny gray leaves and bright blue flowers.
(Sonja Wilcomer)

the trailing growth. Do not be timid in cutting the plant back when it wants to run rather than clump. This salvia will form attractive clumps if its runners are persistently cut back. If you keep trailing shoots pruned, the plant will have a more pleasing habit. It has been my experience that this salvia produces more vigorous growth if the soil is both well drained and mixed with a lot of humus. Full sun and regular weekly water are also needed. It is interesting to note that plants in pots build up energetically in the center while producing many delightful trailing stems that flower lightly and occasionally.

Indispensable in a dry and sunny rock garden, *Salvia chionophylla* is a charming plant for filling small spaces around rocks and between larger plants such as euphorbias and lavenders. Its small foliage contrasts well with other gray-foliaged plants with large leaves. A hot hillside border featuring four salvias, all with gray leaves but each with a different habit and leaf shape, might include the pleasingly orderly *S. chamaedryoides* and the low-growing sage from Spain and Algeria, *S. lavandulifolia*. *Salvia chamaedryoides* is upright in growth and just over 2 ft (60 cm) tall with sparkling blue flowers. The Spanish sage is noted for its handsome habit rather than its spring flowers of pale lavender. In front of these plants, the less than 1 ft (30 cm) tall *S. thymoides*, with its thyme-like gray foliage and tiny blue flowers, can intermingle with *S. chionophylla*. For contrast, clumps of autumn moor grass, *Sesleria autumnalis*, that reach 20 in (50 cm) in height with beautiful lime-green foliage may be added to the mixture of grays. A cool and composed solution for a difficult hillside, these plants do well with the full sun and quick drainage that it offers.

Salvia clevelandii (Gray) Greene
blue sage

A handsome, rounded shrub, *Salvia clevelandii* is known and enjoyed for its fragrant foliage, which is reminiscent of rose potpourri, and its sparkling, violet-blue flowers. Native to dry chaparral and coastal sage scrub plant communities, it is found below 3000 ft (900 m) in southern California and northern Baja California. Asa Gray named it in 1874 in honor of the plant collector Daniel Cleveland.

Developing a woody base in time, *Salvia clevelandii* is evergreen and grows in a pleasing shape to 3–5 ft (1–1.5 m) in height and width. Its obovate, rugose leaves are less than 1 in (2.5 cm) long, are an ashy green color, and amply cover the plant. After other California native sage species have bloomed and passed their prime, *S. clevelandii* comes into prominence. May or June is the usual time for a three- to four-week flowering period to begin. Luxuriously flowering spikes about 1 ft (30 cm) long, with many whorls of amethyst flowers are held upright. Occasionally, inflorescences are short with only one whorl of flowers.

Flowering stems hold well as cut flowers if conditioned by cutting under water. After the flowers drop, the whorls of tightly packed calyces dry and are quite attractive in the garden or in dried arrangements. A sweet and pleasant odor is released when the calyces are dampened or touched.

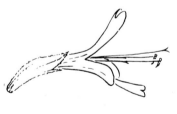

Salvia clevelandii

In cultivation since the 1940s, *Salvia clevelandii* and its cultivars and hybrids are not widely known to gardeners outside California, but of the native California salvias they are the most popular. Preferring a climate with dry summers and winter rains, specimens have proved susceptible to root rot and fungal problems in

In a good year, *Salvia clevelandii* 'Winnifred Gilman' is laden with flowers. (Christine Andrews)

humid areas. Because of the plant's summer dormancy, ideal growing conditions include fast drainage, full sun, good air circulation, and very little additional water after the plant is established. Hardy to 20° F (-7° C), *S. clevelandii* is short-lived and needs replacing every five to ten years. Although its seed is viable, the usual method of propagation is by cuttings taken in spring before flowers and new wood have formed.

Salvia clevelandii 'Winnifred Gilman' is a delightful selection that is both compact and colorful. Unfortunately, records do not reveal the name of the collector or the collection site of this plant. Strybing Arboretum distributed it in 1964 at an annual plant sale under its cultivar name to honor one of their volunteer propagators. In 1989 in the Berkeley, California, garden of Jenny Fleming, a mature plant of *S. clevelandii* 'Winnifred Gilman' came to the attention of Sherrie Althouse and Philip Van Soelen of California Flora Nursery, which is located near Santa Rosa, California. Cuttings were taken, and since 1990, plants of this desirable clone have been distributed from California Flora Nursery and, subsequently, from many nurseries.

A 3 ft (1 m) tall evergreen plant with flower stems and calyces of dark ruby red, *Salvia clevelandii* 'Winnifred Gilman' has intense violet-blue flowers.

Upright in growth, it makes an outstanding filler in a dry border.

In the 1950s at Rancho Santa Ana Botanic Garden, a number of *Salvia clevelandii* plants collected from the wild were placed in the garden. Much later, in 1992, a seedling in the group raised comment because of its unusual random flower color. One flower might be bluish lavender, the next a cool white. Or there might be two or three flowers of one color before another color was repeated—there were even bicolored flowers. The plant is thought to be a true *S. clevelandii*, but one that shows genetic instability through random flower color. After being tested for its ability to adapt to garden conditions, it was introduced in 1994 as *S. clevelandii* 'Betsy Clebsch'. I am honored the plant has been named for me and given cultivar status. It is particularly well suited to the small garden because it reaches less than 3 ft (1 m) in height and width.

Salvia clevelandii 'Pozo Blue' in the author's garden. The green-leaved *Euphorbia* ×*martinii* is in the foreground. (Robert Kourik)

Five hybrids of *Salvia clevelandii* are so similar in overall appearance and performance that it takes a very discerning eye to distinguish one from the other with assurance. 'Allen Chickering' is a hybrid that occurred at Rancho Santa Ana Botanic Garden. The original selection was lost prior to propagation and, consequently, a second generation seedling was selected and named, then introduced in 1949. 'Aromas' occurred in the garden of Ken Taylor, a native plant nurseryman, and was introduced by Saratoga Horticultural Research Foundation in 1981–1982. 'Pozo Blue' occurred as a chance seedling in the Las Pilitas Nursery of Bert Wilson in Santa Margarita, California, and he introduced it in 1989. 'Santa Cruz Dark', a selection made by Ginny Hunt, was introduced by Western Hills Nursery in 1989. 'Whirly Blue' is a selection made by William Nolan; it was named and recommended by the Saratoga Horticultural Research Foundation in 1990.

SALVIA CLEVELANDII

In the spring of 1996 near the Pacific Ocean in northern Baja Calfornia I saw *Salvia clevelandii* in one of its native habitats for the first time. Among the dominant shrubs in a limited area, the plant was 3 ft (1 m) tall and wide, and its graceful stems swept the ground. Several plants exhibited prostrate growth that hugged the ground, making them prime candidates for cultivars. In this location, *S. clevelandii* grew in colonies or with ambrosia, artemisia, and agave as companions.

In a climate with more or less dry summers, *Salvia clevelandii* and its cultivars and hybrids can be the backbone of a difficult garden site. Imagine a hillside where a number of these salvias are interplanted with the 2 ft (60 cm) tall *Yucca whipplei* with rosettes of rigid, gray-green leaves, and with *Y. rostrata*, which has undulating, bluish foliage. Once established, plants of this combination are drought tolerant and can withstand strong winds and predation by deer.

Salvia coahuilensis Fernald

In the wild, *Salvia coahuilensis* is found in Mexico in the Sierra Madre Oriental in the province of Coahuila, west of Saltillo. Apparently, this sage's location is restricted to a mountainous region in the southern part of the province.

Classified as a perennial herb, *Salvia coahuilensis* is a graceful, low-growing, evergreen shrub. Under 2.5 ft (0.8 m) in height and width, the plant builds many slender woody branches from its base. A liberal and relentless bloomer, the small, 1 in (2.5 cm) long, beet-purple flowers grace the garden from early summer though autumn. Linear, olive-green leaves, usually 1 in (2.5 cm) long, are so narrow and widely spaced that the plant looks sparsely clothed. Many different insects and hummingbirds work the flowers for nectar, and pollination is achieved through this activity. *Salvia coahuilensis* produces viable seed, and hybrid seedlings are frequently found near the plant. This salvia is known to hybridize freely with a number of other *Salvia* species, so I advise propagating it by cuttings or division of the rootstock to avoid the risk of cross-pollination.

Fast drainage, friable soil, and full sun are cultural conditions that enable *Salvia coahuilensis* to flower from June until frost. Additional water is needed on a weekly basis. The heavy blooming periods are early summer and autumn when days are hot and nights cool. In my garden the plant has a few flowers

This Strybing Arboretum border of plants native to Mexico includes *Salvia coahuilensis* and *Calylophus hartwegii*, a member of the evening primrose family, Onagraceae. (Christine Andrews)

practically year-round, proclaiming its propensity to stay in bloom. In late winter, you should cut plants back to active growing nodes 6–8 in (15–20 cm) above the ground. Hard pruning will stimulate the growth of new stems that will break into flower in early summer. It is hardy to 20°F (-7°C) or lower, reflecting its native mountainous habitat.

Described by the American botanist Fernald in 1900, *Salvia coahuilensis* remained unknown to gardeners until the late 1980s. I find no mention of the salvia in catalogs or lists until that time. It is rarely seen in nurseries or gardens in spite of its adaptability and long flowering period.

The impact of the small but colorful beet-purple flowers of *Salvia coahuilensis* is intensified when you plant it on a sunny bank beside a drift of the 6–8 in (15–20 cm) tall, blue-silver grass *Festuca cinerea* 'Blausilber'. Add several compact lavenders for their grayish foliage, such as the 1 ft (30 cm) tall *Lavandula angustifolia* 'Loddon Blue' with its 6 in (15 cm) spikes of rich purple flowers. Try arranging these three plants of dissimilar but attractive foliage and flowers in drifts of threes or sixes; each plant's unique and individual characteristics will contribute to the value of the group.

Salvia coccinea Jussieu ex Murray
tropical sage

Widely distributed throughout tropical South America, *Salvia coccinea* is commonly called tropical sage. Due to its adaptability, it has spread far and wide in

The summer-flowering *Salvia coccinea* 'Brenthurst'. (Ginny Hunt)

the subtropical regions of both North and South America. Once thought to have its origins in Brazil, the species's diploid chromosome count suggests that it comes from Mexico. A self-sowing, reliable, and handsome annual (occasionally perennial), it has been carried and commended all over the world.

Salvia coccinea was first described and named in 1778. Carl Epling (1939) found the species had been widely introduced or naturalized in subtropical regions of both hemispheres and was ubiquitous in all warm parts of the Americas. It has been known and grown since the late 18th century.

At Thomas Jefferson's Monticello, *Salvia coccinea* blooms well into October and even November. (Carol Ottesen)

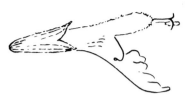

Salvia coccinea

Depending on seed selection and cultural conditions, tropical sage usually grows to 3 ft (1 m). Heights can vary from 2 to 4 ft (60 to 120 cm). Without looking dense, tropical sage has many branches and spreads about 2.5 ft (0.8 m) wide. Leaves are hairy, pea green, and graduated in size along the stems. Widely spaced, the largest leaves measure 3 in (8 cm) in length and 2 in (5 cm) in width and are primarily deltoid. Scalloped at the edge, they clothe the plant lightly. *Coccinea* comes from the Latin for scarlet and refers to the typical flower color for this species. However, flowers come in many shades—orange-red, red, scarlet, pink, salmon, and white—including bicolors, the upper lip a different color from the lower lip. Flower size also varies. 'Lactea' is a particularly attractive white flowering form, and 'Brenthurst' is a fine pink form. These will come true from the seed they produce if cross-pollination with other forms of *Salvia coccinea* does not occur.

Propagation is by seed or cuttings. Seed sown in early spring will produce blooming plants by August. All color forms of tropical sage make fine cut flowers. Be sure to condition each stem by cutting it under water to assure long life in a bouquet.

Cultural requirements include full sun, good garden soil enriched with humus and grit, and weekly watering. It is a good idea to remove inflorescences that have been pollinated and are making seed; this kind of pruning encourages more flower production, as does using stems for cut flowers. Plants will bloom until arrested by cold weather or killed by frost. In very mild climates, *Salvia coccinea* can be perennial. In such circumstances, severe pruning in spring before new growth begins, together with fertilizer applications, will encourage growth and heavy blooming.

Easy to grow, tropical sage is a plant that adds sparkle to a herbaceous border in all climate zones. Three or more plants grouped with late blooming annuals or perennials make a fine combination. In my own garden, tropical sage seeds itself year after year in front of climbing roses and evergreen shrubs. The flowers are in all colors, including the white 'Lactea', which I find to be an exceptionally good mixer.

Salvia columbariae Bentham
chia

Commonly called chia in Mexico and some central American countries, *Salvia columbariae* is an annual that comes into bloom in late spring or early summer. It has a wide distribution in California through coastal and inner coastal ranges from Mendocino County throughout southern California. It is also found in Utah, Arizona, and Baja California. In the wild it is reported to hybridize with *S. mellifera*, a 3 ft (1 m) tall evergreen shrub.

Water and exposure greatly influence the size of chia. Plentiful amounts of moisture will produce a basal clump of wrinkled green leaves with a grayish cast that measures 2 ft (60 cm) across. A clump less than 1 ft

Spring-blooming wildflowers in Antelope Valley, California, including California poppies and *Salvia columbariae*. (Bart O'Brien)

(30 cm) in width is more usual. Individual gray-green leaves are deeply divided and approximately 4–6 in (10–15 cm) long. Their wrinkled texture makes the leaves singularly handsome. Flowering stalks rise about 1 ft (30 cm) over the foliage, and numerous tight whorls of clear amethyst-blue flowers are spaced about 1 in (2.5 cm) apart along the stalk. The purplish calyx and bracts add to the plant's allure. With little or no moisture the flowering stalk and leaves are reduced in size and become tiny miniatures of the full-grown plant. In desert or dry habitats, plants are frequently less than 2 in (5 cm) tall.

The specific epithet, *columbariae*, means "pertaining to a dovecote or niches." I am unsure how to relate this meaning to the plant, unless the structure of the inflorescence reminds one of a dovecote. In his excellent work on California native salvias, Bart O'Brien (1997) states that the epithet refers to *Columbaria*, an old name for the genus *Scabiosa*. He goes on to say that it is anyone's guess as to why this epithet was chosen. Apparently three species of salvia are referred to as chia by Native Americans and rural Mexicans; *columbariae*, *hispanica*, and *polystachya.* All three have seed that is exceptionally high in food value; it was sown as a crop and regularly cultivated along with corn in ancient Mexico. Chia formed part of the diet of Native Americans in the western states before the country was occupied by Europeans. The seeds are very nutritious, are soothing to the stomach, and have thirst-quenching properties. At burial sites on Santa Rosa Island off the coast of California and south of Santa Barbara, *Salvia columbariae* seeds found in pottery jars have been carbon-dated to more than 600 years of age.

Mary Elizabeth Parsons (1921), an early California botanist, wrote of her appreciation of the California flora as it gradually dries and turns warm shades of beige and gold in the late spring and early summer. At that time, she noted, chia covers the hillsides with its dried stems and heads held erect. Later, its abundant small gray seed will cover the hillsides too. For centuries this seed has had economic importance to the aborigines and their descendants.

Once established, this showy annual self-sows and will produce a colony each spring. Try sowing seed in an area that has good drainage and little or no summer irrigation. Protection of seed from foraging birds, mice, and ants is essential. It is reported that seeds of varying color have evolved in order to match the color of the soil and thus avoid predation. Chia and California poppies growing among manzanitas or other drought-tolerant plants will provide a visual springtime treat, and drifts of *Salvia columbariae* would mingle nicely with drought-tolerant Mediterranean plants such as rosemary and lavender.

Salvia confertiflora Pohl

Native to Brazil, *Salvia confertiflora* has been grown in gardens in the United States since the 1960s, and more than likely even earlier in both Britain and France. Only since the late 1980s has it become an ornamental in California gardens. Perhaps its large size is the reason that it is rarely seen in nurseries or listed in catalogs.

Salvia confertiflora

An autumn-blooming plant, *Salvia confertiflora* is a herbaceous perennial that will easily reach 4–6 ft (1.3–2 m) in both height and width in a season. By the time it blooms its stems and branches are heavily weighted with leaves and inflorescences. Consequently, it needs the support of a stake or another shrub. This voluminous growth also necessitates protection from winds. The largest leaves are about 7 in (18 cm) long, 3.5 in (9 cm) wide, and dark green with a yellowish undertone. The surface is quite rugose and the edge of the leaf is serrated. The petiole and stem of the new leaves are covered with velvety, red-brown hairs. The leaves give a strong pattern to the entire plant. As the season progresses, *Salvia confertiflora* grows and develops with age. Inflorescences lengthen to at least 1 ft (30 cm), but an inflorescence that is 2 ft (60 cm) in length is not at all unusual. The inflorescences are spikelike and covered with hairs that give the impression of red-brown velvet. The stems of both the inflorescence and the calyx are velvety red-brown. The flowers are small, less than 0.5 in (1.3 cm) in length, and orange-red. The specific epithet, *confertiflora*, means "crowded with flowers," which is very apt.

The rich, velvety flowers of *Salvia confertiflora*. (Christine Andrews)

Full sun and sharp drainage encourage the complete development of this late-blooming perennial, and a deep weekly watering is needed. The blooming period is from early September until frost. In the mild San Francisco Bay area, *Salvia confertiflora* will winter over in the garden most years, but to be on the safe side cuttings should be made in August or September and kept in the greenhouse. If temperatures fall below 25° F (-4° C) this salvia may succumb to the cold or be severely damaged. Propagation is by cuttings.

Areas of high humidity in Texas and the Gulf of Mexico provide a different habitat for *Salvia confertiflora*. There, the plant is shade loving, blooms in spring and autumn, and is reported to survive temperatures to 10°F (-12°C).

In late winter or early spring, *Salvia confertiflora* should be heavily pruned so that a well-proportioned plant can develop. My mild climate and long growing season allow me to remove woody stems and leave only a few stems show-ing buds that will break near the base of the plant.

Salvia confertiflora needs the support and protection of other plants. In the back of a border next to the dark green foliage of *Osmanthus fragrans* or its cul-tivar 'San José', it will be screened from wind and the color of its cinnabar inflo-rescences will be heightened. It can also be grown with the 6 ft (2 m) tall, butter-yellow *S. madrensis*, which is upright in habit. These two salvias bloom simultaneously, each adding to the other's beauty. Another possibility for a focal point in a large border is to place *S. confertiflora* among clumps of *Panicum virgatum*, a 5 ft (1.5 m) tall grass that reaches maturity in autumn when it blooms. Soon afterward it turns the color of ripe, golden yellow wheat and is a fine companion to the salvia through all stages of development.

Salvia corrugata Vahl

A South American plant of high elevations, *Salvia corrugata* is found in Colombia, Peru, and Ecuador between 8000 and 9800 ft (2500 and 3000 m). Introduced to horticulture in about 2000, the plants we grow in England and the United States probably came from one single source. The chain of events that brought a new and handsome shrub to our gardens is fascinating. It began with Jim and Jenny Archibald who collect seed in the wild and distribute it through their seed business in Wales. On these trips they make many herbari-um specimens of plants in order to study the plants and verify their names. In 1988 they collected in South America, and specimens of the plants they were not able to determine were sent to the Royal Botanic Garden, Edinburgh. The usual procedure is to freeze the material in order not to contaminate any other herbarium specimens; consequently, the Archibald's specimens were held below 0°F (-18°C) for 48 hours. In 1994, some specimens were sent to James A. Compton, a botanist at the University of Reading, who specializes in salvias and

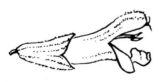

Salvia corrugata

other genera. At Reading, the freezing procedure was repeated once again. Compton, on examining the uniden-tified salvia, found that he was able to put a name on the plant, *S. corrugata*. A few seeds fell from the dried calyces, which Compton then saved and sowed, though as he notes, "without much hope of germination." (pers. comm.). Compton goes on to say that "six seedlings arose from which I believe all living stocks are descended in cultivation today!" (pers. comm.). Dave Fross of Native Sons Nursery in Arroyo Grande, California, introduced *S. corrugata* to California in the summer of 2000 after he returned from visiting English gardens and nurseries.

Wrinkled and furrowed, the leaves of *Salvia corrugata* are deeply textured and present a perfect foil for the rich purple flowers. (Sonja Wilcomer)

An aromatic and substantial shrub that reaches 9 ft (3 m) in its native habitat, *Salvia corrugata*, reaches about 5–6 ft (1.5–2 m) in my California garden. I have noticed that throughout the winter, warm spells trigger the plant into vigorous and active growth. This salvia is well covered with evergreen leaves that are egg shaped and measure about 4.5 in (11 cm) by 1.5 in (4 cm). The upper surface of the leaf is dark green, deeply corrugated (hence the specific name *corrugata*), and hairless. The lower surface has prominent light veining that is delicately covered with a netting of fine hairs that are a pale tan. The small dark purple and green calyx holds dark but brilliant purple-blue flowers that are about 1 in (2.5 cm) long. The lower lip is wider than the hooded, purple-haired upper lip. The flowers are very congested in whorls that are close together. Each whorl numbers between six and twelve flowers. The inflorescences are tight and measure about 3–4 in (8–10 cm) in length. In a sunny climate, flowering can occur throughout the year with summer and autumn being the primary time for bloom.

The cultural requirements for growing *Salvia corrugata* are minimal and straightforward: full sun, garden soil that drains rapidly, and weekly water throughout the growing season. Cuttings from *S. corrugata* root easily at almost any time of the year when there is light and warmth. If you keep cuttings in the greenhouse over winter, however, you will be assured of having a plant to set out in the spring. Rooted cuttings will develop into shrublike plants within several months, and if you remove spent inflorescences, you will encourage continual flowering. From time to time, take out the tip growth of branches to keep the plant's growth in check. Since the usual time for pruning a salvia that grows with great speed is in the early spring after all danger of frost is over, this shrub should be pruned to a small but pleasing size and shape in order to ready it for another season of growth. It has proven to be hardy when temperatures dip to the mid-20°s F (around -4°C) for short periods.

Salvia corrugata has an upright habit and unusual leaves that are quite handsome, so the plant can be used to great advantage with a combination of several plants in a border of shrubs or roses. Use it either as a filler or as a strong element in the background. Dahlias have become featured plants in gardens, and a combination of dark red- and magenta-flowered dahlias, some of which have green foliage and others dark purple-black foliage, would not only be protected with an interplanting of *S. corrugata*, but would also enhance the color of the foliage and the flowers. The cultural requirements for the dahlias include rich soil that has a high humus content and a deep watering twice each week. The salvia needs leaner soil but will respond favorably to additional water.

Salvia coulteri Fernald
Coulter's sage

Even though *Salvia coulteri* has been found in five provinces in Mexico (Nuevo León, Zacatecas, Tamaulipas, Durango, and Hidalgo), it is not a common plant. It grows on dry, hot, rocky mountainsides, sometimes near oak, ash, rhus, and acacia. Collected in Mexico by John Merle Coulter, the plant was described by Fernald in 1900 and named in honor of the collector. In June 1991 it was collected in Nuevo León at 4000 ft (1200 m) by John Fairey and Carl Schoenfeld and was introduced to horticulture through Yucca Do Nursery in Texas.

A many-branched shrub, *Salvia coulteri* is about 2.5 ft (0.8 m) high and 3 ft (1 m) wide and has a graceful appearance. Its woody stems are slender and covered with very short white hairs. Hairs also cover the lanceolate leaves, which are rounded at the tip. The top of the leaf is pale olive-green, and the underside looks whitish. The leaves are widely spaced along the wiry stems, revealing the structure of the plant.

By September, *Salvia coulteri* has produced many inflorescences, and flowering continues until frost. Tight whorls of flowers are jammed together on a flowering stem at the side and top of each branch. These electric lavender-blue flowers are small, measuring less than 0.5 in (1.3 cm), but the vivid color makes this plant seem to bloom as profusely as one with larger flowers. A curious characteristic of *S. coulteri* is the way the calyces are all turned to one side of the flowering stem. Even though they appear in whorls, they sweep to one side. Only about 0.25 in (0.6 cm) long, the calyces persist long after the flowers they hold have bloomed and dropped. If you stroke these dried calyces, they release a pleasant, somewhat mintlike odor.

Salvia coulteri on a shrub-covered hillside in the province of Nuevo León, Mexico. (Carl Schoenfeld)

Full sun and fast drainage are needed for *Salvia coulteri*. In areas with hot summer temperatures, light shade is mandatory. I find deep watering once every week or two is beneficial. In time, the plant will require some pruning in order to keep its shapeliness. Small branches of flowers hold well in arrangements if woody stems are conditioned by cutting them under water. Enjoying the flowers indoors is a way of keeping the plant trimmed and well proportioned.

I have not grown *Salvia coulteri* long enough to test its hardiness, but judging from its collection site, I believe it to be hardy to 20°F (-7°C). It has withstood temperatures in the low 20°s F (around -6°C) on several occasions in my garden. Propagation is by seed or cuttings.

Well suited to a sunny hillside, *Salvia coulteri* would add grace and color to a border of Mediterranean and California native plants. A slope where flowers could be enjoyed from early spring through autumn might include *Rosmarinus* 'Ken Taylor' and *Ceanothus gloriosus* var. *porrectus* for dark green foliage and early flowering, the gray-foliaged herbaceous *Ballota acetabulosa* for early summer blooming and contrasting foliage, and *Eriogonum arborescens*, whose late summer blooming would lead into the flowering period of *S. coulteri*. All these plants require the same cultural conditions and very little attention. Their foliage would look handsome year-round.

Salvia cyanescens Boissier & Balansa

A herbaceous perennial that is endemic to Iran and Turkey, *Salvia cyanescens* was introduced to horticulture in 1959. Even though it readily produces viable seed and is easy to propagate, gardeners and nurseries have been slow to learn about it. In its native habitat it interbreeds freely with *S. candidissima* and seems to be a good candidate for hybridizing.

Developing a small 1 ft (30 cm) clump of gray-green leaves that are ovate in outline, *Salvia cyanescens* is evergreen in a mild climate and tends to look good year-round in the garden. Covered with hairs, the leaves are about 2 in (5 cm) long by 1 in (2.5 cm) wide, and they make a mounding, handsome plant. Although its pale gray-green foliage appears soft and frail, *S. cyanescens* is a hardy and tough plant. During the hot days of summer, as with many gray-foliaged plants, its leaves become whiter and appear silvery. This variation in color may be a mechanism for protecting the leaf surface from excess heat because of the reflection of light; it may also prevent water loss by evaporation.

If warm weather prevails, blooming periods are summer and late autumn. Flowers are small, barely 1 in (2.5 cm) long, and a rather delicate purple-violet color. The inflorescence is candelabra-like and about 1 ft (30 cm) tall. This description sounds spectacular but, in fact, very few flowers are in bloom simultaneously and they are so small that it is easy to walk by the plant and miss the flowering completely. The specific epithet, *cyanescens*, means "bluish" or "becoming blue," a name that is far from precise in this instance.

Good drainage, full sun, and ordinary garden soil with only occasional water are the main requirements of *Salvia cyanescens*. In its native habitat it grows on limestone and igneous rock slopes as well as shale banks and dry, rocky streambeds. Hardy to 0°F (-18°C), it is considered drought tolerant. Propagation is by seed or cuttings.

The handsome foliage of *Salvia cyanescens* is enhanced by the dark green and narrow foliage of the prostrate rosemaries. *Origanum rotundifolium*,

Santolina virens, and *Teucrium chamaedrys* are other suitable companions when arranged on a sunny, rocky bank. All require the same culture. Another grouping for an area set aside for sun-loving annual wildflowers could include *Eschscholzia californica*, the California poppy, and *Salvia columbariae*, chia, planted between drifts of *S. cyanescens*. This grouping results in a delightful spring into summer floriferous display.

Salvia darcyi Compton

The native habitat of *Salvia darcyi* is a very limited area at an altitude of 9000 ft (2800 m) in the eastern range of the Mexican Sierra Madre Oriental. Found in the wild in 1988 by John Fairey and Carl Schoenfeld, *S. darcyi* has been offered by several nurseries under various names. In the autumn of 1991 Fairey and Schoenfeld accompanied a party of plant professionals from Great Britain to northeastern Mexico. The party included botanist James Compton, who was shown this handsome salvia on this trip. He collected and subsequently described it, naming it *S. darcyi* in honor of fellow British botanist William D'Arcy, who had accompanied him on this particular trip.

A perennial herb that reaches 3 ft (1 m) in height in the wild but usually less than that in cultivation, *Salvia darcyi* dies back to its rootstock in winter. The roots are stoloniferous, producing new plants from the shoots with time. I was fortunate enough to see the native habitat of *S. darcyi* in Nuevo León in late spring, when large numbers of the plant were emerging from rich loam among limestone rocks in a wide, dry stream bed. Sycamore trees (*Platanus mexicana*) dotted the valley.

In the garden, *Salvia darcyi* rapidly develops branching top growth, and by early summer its blooming period has begun. Pastel green, deltoid leaves cover the plant amply, making a perfect foil for the 1.5 in (4 cm) long, coral-red flowers. Inflorescences are 6–12 in (15–30 cm) long and they sometimes elongate to 2 ft (60 cm). *Salvia darcyi* generates many widely spaced whorls of flowers until short days and cool nights slow or stop the display. This salvia's high mountain habitat is reflected in its hardiness to 20°F (-7°C), possibly lower.

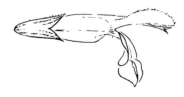

Salvia darcyi

Salvia darcyi has coral-red flowers. *Viguiera* spp. are shrublike sunflowers. (Ginny Hunt)

Easy to care for, *Salvia darcyi* requires three-quarters to a full day of sun, fast drainage, friable soil, and deep watering at least once a week. A light dressing of lime on the root surface in early spring is helpful. Snails and slugs are attracted to new growth. Propagation is by cuttings, but after the plant is well established, rooted shoots can be removed by teasing and then potted for gardening friends.

Gardeners who are interested in working with color will find *Salvia darcyi* an unprecedented plant. When positioned near orange-red or magenta-red flowers or leaves, this plant has the capacity to blend with whichever red group is near. I urge gardeners to experiment with its color in different combinations.

A grouping of plants for a long-blooming, sunny summer border includes in the background the 3 ft (1 m) tall and wide *Phygelius* 'Salmon Leap', with its dark green, glossy, evergreen foliage and pale orange-red flowers. In the midground, incorporate several *Salvia darcyi* plants with the 2–3 ft (60–90 cm) burnt-orange flowered *Agastache* 'Apricot Sunrise'. The front of the border can be cooled with a few clumps of *Festuca amethystina* 'Aprilgrün' or *Briza media*, the perennial quaking grass. Both grasses are about 1 ft (30 cm) in height and width. Chosen primarily for size and color of foliage and flowers, each of these plants requires the same cultural conditions.

SALVIA DARCYI

Salvia dentata is a South African jewel with a flower and calyx of lovely blended colors, such as lavender, blue, pink, and tan. (Ginny Hunt)

Salvia dentata Aiton

A small shrub with short twiggy branches, *Salvia dentata* has a limited habitat in western South Africa, just north of Cape Town. Found between the elevations of 2000 and 5000 ft (600 and 1500 m) it is a plant of dry areas. Usually occurring on low granitic hillsides, dry and rocky slopes, and rock-strewn streambeds, this plant was described by William Aiton in 1789. The salvia's specific name, *dentata*, surprised me because the tiny leaves appear to have an even margin. When I inspect the leaves with a hand lens, however, I can sometimes discern a very, very slight irregular, dentate margin.

This salvia is exceptional in several regards. Described as being a 6 ft (2 m) tall shrub in its native habitat, *Salvia dentata* is 3 ft (1 m) tall in my garden. Another unusual characteristic of this salvia is that its stems are round. Fresh, newly formed stems that are just emerging may be square but they are so small and flat it is difficult to determine their shape. As the round stems age they become light brown, woody, and congested. The gray-green, leathery leaves are clustered and tiny, the average being 0.5 in (1.3 cm) in length. They are also highly aromatic, reminiscent of a closed box in which medicine has been kept for a long time. The inflorescence is short and usually about 2 in (5 cm) long with

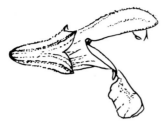

Salvia dentata

crowded whorls of flowers. Measuring less than 1 in (2.5 cm) in length, the flowers can vary in color from light lavender to pale, even sky blue. They are held in a tiny calyx that is subtended by bracts. As the calyces age they expand and turn pink, complementing the color of the flower. Seed is seldom produced, so it is best to take cuttings in midsummer to propagate this salvia. Light frosts apparently do not harm *S. dentata* but temperatures in the 20°s F (around -5°C) for more than several hours will damage or kill the plant.

The merit of this particular salvia lies in its overall appearance. Do not expect it to produce showy, colorful flowers but instead look for the sparkling, medium blue flowers that fairly twinkle against the backdrop of gray-green leaves. Plants come into their main blooming period in spring but also produce a limited number of flowers throughout the summer and well into autumn. The erect habit and the tiny evergreen leaves of suede-like texture and a soft gray-green are very engaging and compelling features. A plant of subtleties, *S. dentata* would be shown to advantage in a container, although a south-facing aspect that receives full sun would also be an appropriate siting. Soil containing humus and grit for good drainage is essential, as is regular watering. A half-strength, balanced liquid fertilizer may be used sparingly, if it is needed at all. An open sunny bed might include two or three plants of *S. dentata* combined with the good green foliage of *Origanum* 'Kent Beauty', *Penstemon heterophyllus* 'Blue Bedder', and *Thymus* ×*citriodorus*. The growth and flowering of these three will spark visual interest throughout the summer without overpowering the salvias. To the front and side of this grouping, add *S. officinalis* 'Purpurascens' for its wonderful purplish velvet leaves. The foliage of all these plants, except *S. dentata*, is less than 1 ft (30 cm) in height. All require good drainage, gritty and lean soil, and only occasional water.

Salvia desoleana Atzei & Picci

A handsome and aromatic plant, *Salvia desoleana* is found on Sardinia, an island in the Mediterranean west of Italy. Sardinia is south of the island of Corsica and was a kingdom that became part of Italy in 1861. An endemic, *S. desoleana* occurs in four or five specific locations on the island, growing in sunny places on limestone, granite, and igneous rock. The plant is named for Luigi Desole who was a botanist and lived from 1904 to 1979. It was botanically described in 1982 by A. D. Atzei and V. Picci.

A herbaceous perennial with rhizomatous roots, *Salvia desoleana* is a low-growing plant with roots that are elongated and grow parallel to the ground. A nicely mounding plant, it has soft green leaves and stems that make a base about 2–3 ft (60–90 cm) high and 3–4 ft (1–1.3 m) wide. The largest leaves are 8 in (20 cm) long, 6 in (15 cm) wide, and ovate in outline. Both the upper and lower surface is lightly covered with hairs and glands. A fresh and strong herbaceous odor is released when the plant is brushed. Flowering begins in late spring and continues for almost a month. The inflorescence rises

The excellent foliage of *Salvia desoleana* warrants it space in the border. A good-looking plant that repeats bloom. (Ginny Hunt)

1 ft (30 cm) or a little more and is branched at the base. The flowering stem is hairy and has an architectural quality, with well-spaced whorls of flowers that are well spaced along the hairy stem. Each individual whorl of six flowers held in calyces is subtended by two, 1 in (2.5 cm) wide, leafy green bracts that look like little nosegays. The bracts dry quickly, then promptly fall away. The calyx is two lipped with three hair-covered veins coming to a hair-tipped point on the upper lip and two on the lower lip. The falcate flowers are about 1 in (2.5 cm) long, and the upper lip is pale lavender while the lower lip is off-white and shaped like a trough. The shape of the lower lip reminds one of the lower lip of *S. indica*. There is just enough space between the whorls for the upper lip to be completely visible.

Often compared botanically with *Salvia sclarea* because they are closely allied, *S. desoleana* appears distinctly different to the gardener's eye. In the wild in Sardinia, *S. desoleana* does well throughout the year, flowering a long time and building a mass of stems, leaves, and flowers that are distillable. The glands produce an intense, long-lasting perfume, which is known to have greater fixative properties than *S. sclarea*. A sugary decoction made from the leaves and branches is used as a remedy for fevers.

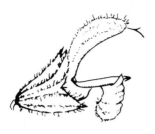

Salvia desoleana

Easy to propagate from seed or cuttings, *Salvia desoleana* requires minimal care from the gardener. Plant the salvia in half to full sunlight in soil that is lean and has good drainage. After the first flowering in late spring, remove spent inflorescences to ensure that *S. desoleana* will repeat bloom quite generously later in summer. A twice-weekly watering schedule is needed to encourage two flowerings. Plants are hardy to temperatures around 25°F (-4°C) for short periods.

This plant is the one to slip into an existing border when an annual is spent or a perennial disappears. It takes up a modest amount of space both horizontally and vertically, and its misty green foliage combines well with other green, gray, or purple foliage of different shades and textures. A combination of Mediterranean plants needing moderate amounts of water include three or more plants of *Salvia desoleana* placed beside or in front of the 3–6 ft (1–2 m) tall *Cistus ladanifer*. The cistus has fragrant, dark green leaves and dark, crimson-spotted white flowers. These plants will usually bloom at the same time as the salvia in late spring. *Erodium corsicum* 'Album' and *E. corsicum* 'Rubrum' are selections from Corsica and Sardinia. The erodiums form a bun about 6 in (15 cm) high and wide and have small, rounded, gray-green leaves that are succulent. The eriodiums bloom in spring and repeat bloom in autumn. *Viola corsica*, also an endemic of Corsica and Sardinia, will repeat bloom too. Given humus it will self sow and spread around the other plants, making a charming addition to the combination.

Salvia digitaloides Diels

A splendid herbaceous perennial, *Salvia digitaloides* occurs in the wild in the Chinese provinces of Guizhou, Sichuan, and Yunnan. Specimens were collected by the highly organized and indefatigable Scotsman George Forrest, who spent most of 28 years in China collecting seeds and plants. It was in 1912 that Ludwig Diels at the university in Marburg, Germany, first described and named this salvia from Forrest's specimens.

In its native habitat *Salvia digitaloides* grows at elevations between 7000 and 11,000 ft (2100 and 3400 m) in dry and shady pine forests, on east-facing mountainsides of scrub oak, as well as on grassy hillsides and valleys. Rarely seen in botanic gardens, it is little known by gardeners, and since 1995 it has appeared sporadically on a few seed lists. In 1990, plant explorers from Quarryhill Botanical Garden in Glen Ellen, California, participated in a joint expedition with those from Howick Arboretum, England, in collecting seed in the province of Yunnan. Plants of *S. digitaloides* are, by 2002, well established in Quarryhill Botanical Garden. In Yunnan, a variety of this salvia is used medicinally.

Known for its purple spotting and subtle beauty, *Salvia digitaloides* blooms in summer. (Ginny Hunt)

When established, *Salvia digitaloides* makes a basal clump of leaves 1–2 ft (30–60 cm) high and wide. The thick, oblong leaf blades that are frequently rounded at the top and base make the plant easily recognizable. The leaf's surface appears to be velvety, and the edges are slightly rolled under. Pronounced white veining occurs on the back of the leaf. Inflorescences are 6 in (15 cm) long and have four to six flowers in whorls that have space between them, which makes the flowers visible and showy. Flowers are a soft shade of yellow and measure more than 1 in (2.5 cm) in length. The upper lip is broadly triangular, and the lower lip is slightly longer and lightly dusted with purple spots. Summer flowers are held in a green calyx that has purple veins. This attractive salvia looks lush because the flower, calyx, and stem of the plant are covered with long, soft, straight hairs. A hardy plant, *S. digitaloides* is deciduous in a cold climate and tolerates temperatures into the teens (-10°C). Plants are usually propagated by seed.

A sunny spot that gets at least a half day of sunlight is desirable for *Salvia digitaloides*. It responds favorably to being planted close to other plants by growing more vigorously. Water on a weekly basis, and good garden soil that is enriched with humus and is well draining are its simple requirements. I have not found it necessary to use fertilizer. Watch for seed, and if there is none, you can remove the spent inflorescence.

A border that features both color and texture of foliage is one way to call attention to the subtle color and shape of *Salvia digitaloides*. It is a very adaptable plant for the summer border and could be planted in threes or fives in front of *S. chamelaeagnea*, which blooms in late summer. The handsome, fresh green foliage of *S. chamelaeagnea* will be a perfect foil for the delicate, pale yellow flowers of *S. digitaloides*. The tightly packed, blue-green, needlelike leaves on the stems of *Euphorbia seguieriana* subsp. *niciciana* appear to creep along the front of the bed. The texture of these tiny leaves is in sharp contrast to the leaves of the two salvias. In a mild climate all these plants have evergreen foliage that is complementary to one another, and they all tend to defy the weather and look good throughout the year.

Salvia discolor Kunth
Andean sage

Salvia discolor is known to occur naturally in only a small geographical location in Peru, and it is equally rare in horticulture. It is unclear exactly when this plant was introduced to horticulture, but William Robinson (1933) wrote of its charm and merits. Its growing habit is scandent, meaning that the plant climbs without the aid of tendrils. With only speculative information about the precise native habitat of *S. discolor*, the following cultural information is inevitably limited.

Salvia discolor is a herbaceous perennial with many wiry white stems arising from the base. It tends to bloom during warm or hot spells throughout the summer and autumn. When situated in a frost-free garden where temperatures do not fall below 32°F (0°C), it builds a strong root system that allows top growth to elongate and extend to about 3 ft (1 m). In areas without the necessary long, warm growing period, pot the plant and move it into the greenhouse or take cuttings in September. Andean sage tends to stay in bloom for a long period if wintered in a greenhouse.

Salvia discolor

Salvia discolor

Along the Rivieras in both France and Italy, *Salvia discolor* is frequently grown as an ornamental specimen plant. In that warm and benign climate, it is not unusual to see a plant reach 3 ft (1 m) in height and width. Its habit is more upright there than in California.

Support is needed for the thin stems of Andean sage if the inflorescences are to be clearly seen. Mistletoe-green leaves of graduated sizes—the largest 4 in (10 cm) long by 1.5 in (4 cm) across—are spaced in pairs about 1–2 in (2.5–5 cm) apart. The back of the leaf is covered with white hairs and veins and is quite noticeable due to the sparse leaf arrangement. The inflorescence usually extends to 1 ft (30 cm) or more. Exceedingly dark purple flowers, saturated with color and less than 1 in (2.5 cm) long, are held in a beautiful, pistachio-green, two-lipped calyx. In certain lights the flowers appear to be black. The stem of the inflorescence looks shiny and is covered with glands that make it sticky to the touch. Often little insects are found stuck to it, prompting a gardening friend to remark, "It's its own flypaper." I do not know the reason for this stickiness, but it may have something to do with detracting predators in the plant's home territory.

The colors of the plant are both subtle and harmonious. The specific epithet, *discolor*, means of two different colors. In the case of this salvia the epithet applies both to the green and white leaf surfaces and to the purple flower in its pale green calyx.

Salvia discolor prefers friable garden soil lightened with humus and deep weekly watering. No more than a half day of sun is needed, and occasional light applications of liquid fertilizer are beneficial. Staking is almost a necessity due to the scandent growth habit, and thin, light bamboo is a suitable material to use. *Salvia discolor* is a collector's plant and does well in a container. Its wiry appearance means that it is most easily seen without the foliage of other plants surrounding it. If kept in a container, *S. discolor* can be easily moved from the greenhouse into the garden for the summer and placed in filtered light. If you grow it in the garden, elevate the plant so the viewer can look directly into it. The long arching stems make it a difficult plant to place in a border.

Salvia disermas Linnaeus

A beautiful and lush plant from South Africa, *Salvia disermas* is a herbaceous perennial with a slightly woody rootstock. In 1762 when Linnaeus described the plant, he gave its habitat erroneously as Syria. In about 1800, the specific name, *rugosa*, became attached to the plant but that was found to be synonymous; the plant is known nowadays in South Africa and elsewhere as *disermas*. Growing with medium conditions of moisture, this salvia is found in stream beds, damp ground among trees, grassland, and river banks, as well as disturbed land. It occurs through western Africa with its chief concentration in South Africa, where it is used medicinally. A tea is made from its leaves, as is a lotion used to treat sores.

An evergreen perennial that reaches about 2 ft (60 cm) in both height and width, *Salvia disermas* has a graceful and pleasing shape. It has numerous stems emerging from its rootstock and each stem carries many

The perfect plant for a cottage garden, *Salvia disermas* has an attractive and relaxed growing habit. It repeats bloom over and over again. (Sonja Wilcomer)

inflorescences that curve upward. The flowers are small, less than 1.5 in (4 cm) long, and can be an icy white color. Some plants have very pale mauvish flowers, while others are white flushed with pale mauve. They are held in a small green calyx that has a rounded upper lip and a divided lower lip with two points. The flowers are far from being spectacular but they compensate by being plentiful, and this plant is seldom out of bloom. By mid-March, plants appear pert and jaunty, signalling the return of warmth and light. Pale apple-green leaves of the plant are long and narrow, as is the petiole. The fragrance is similar to the odor of hay for forage and is released when the glandular hairs covering the stems and petioles are stroked. The plant tolerates temperatures to 25°F (-4°C). It begins active growth in spring and starts flowering with the return of warmth and light. I find its abundant growth in my garden needs to be checked, and it is cut back at least once a month during the summer. Easy to propagate, *S. disermas* produces seed in copious amounts that germinate readily. Cuttings can be rooted quite quickly at almost any time during the growing season.

Salvia disermas

This is a perfect plant for an informal bed in a cottage garden, especially if planted in almost full sun with regular humusy soil that drains freely. The specific epithet, *disermas*, refers to its habit and means "without support," and its pleasing, relaxed shape combines well with the growing habits of many different plants.

Verbascum phoenicium 'Flush of White' is a hardy perennial that sometimes dies after the third year. It will reach 2.5 ft (0.8 m) in height and make a fine background for other plants. Well suited for the middle area, *S. disermas* with its handsome foliage and mounding habit will repeat bloom many times during a long growing season. The fragrant, spring-blooming, orange-flowered *Erysimum pulchellum* makes a lush mat 2 ft (60 cm) high and wide and can be used as a filler in the middle section of the bed. At the front of the border, you could add several clumps of the lax, soft gray *Nepeta* 'Blue Wonder', which is under 2 ft (60 cm) tall. Encourage it to repeat bloom as frequently as the salvia by removing spent flowers. Johnny-jump-ups and other self-sowing annuals that seed randomly on their own would complete the casual border.

Salvia disjuncta Fernald

A late-blooming, shrublike plant, *Salvia disjuncta* is a herbaceous perennial with a woody base. It is native to the Mexican provinces of Oaxaca and Chiapas, and its distribution extends into Guatemala. It is found at high elevations between 7500 and 11,000 ft (2300 and 3400 m) where the warm and moist mountainous habitat receives some summer rain. Collected in the wild by botanists from Strybing Arboretum in the late 1980s, this salvia became available to nurseries and gardeners in 1993 through the Arboretum's plant sales.

Coming into full bloom in late October, *Salvia disjuncta* consistently continues to flower lightly throughout the winter in a mild climate. The species appears in two forms, one with green or pale tan stems and mid-green leaves, the other with raisin-colored stems and mature leaves that are purplish green. Both are shrubby in habit reaching 3–4 ft (1–1.3 m) high and wide with many thin stems emerging from the base of the plant. The stems are lightly covered with short, straight hairs, which are particularly conspicuous when they catch

SALVIA DISJUNCTA

The winter-flowering *Salvia disjuncta* is well suited for a mild climate. (Don Mahoney)

the dew. The few signal-red flowers, 1 in (2.5 cm) or more in length, are held in widely spaced whorls, and their bright color and size blend harmoniously with the deltoid-shaped leaves. Frequently, this salvia has but one pair of flowers in bloom at the end of a branch, making a graceful and delightful display. Stems last well as cut flowers when cut under water.

Salvia disjuncta needs at least a half day of sunlight throughout summer and winter. Regular water and friable garden soil that drains well are also necessary. In a mild climate, the rootstock of a well-established *S. disjuncta* tends to run slightly. Unfortunately, it is not cold tolerant and I have lost plants at 30°F (-1°C). It roots easily from cuttings, however, and using that method you can winter it in a greenhouse. Propagation by cuttings assures selection of the correct form, though seed germinates readily and the seedlings will likely resemble the parent. If plants have wintered over in the garden, cut them above active buds in early spring within a few inches of the ground to obtain a plant of medium size and pleasing proportions by autumn. Occasional light applications of a complete fertilizer will speed growth.

An attractive plant for the border because of its medium size and strong, dark leaf color, *Salvia disjuncta* combines beautifully with the autumn-blooming *Ceratostigma griffithii*. A small shrub, usually 2 ft (60 cm) tall with heavenly blue flowers, *C. griffithii* has leaves that turn red when the days shorten. *Ajuga reptans* 'Jungle Beauty' makes an admirable dark green ground cover. Spikes of indigo-blue flowers 6–8 in (15–20 cm) tall appear in spring above handsome evergreen foliage. All plants require deep weekly watering during the active growth period.

Salvia divinorum Epling & Játiva

A mysterious plant that is both puzzling and perplexing, *Salvia divinorum* was described botanically in 1962 by Carl Epling and Carlos D. Játiva. The specimens used in their description had been given to two Americans, Albert Hofmann, the chemist who discovered LSD, and Gordon Wasson, an ethnomycologist investigating Mazatec rituals, by Mazatec Indians of Oaxaca, Mexico. Hofman and Wasson had traveled extensively in Oaxaca in search of the plant but were never able to find it. They had to prevail on the Mazatec to give them plants so that *S. divinorum* could be described botanically and its chemical properties ascertained. The Mazatec Indians use specific mushrooms, the seeds of certain plants, and the leaves of *Salvia divinorum* for their hallucinogenic properties in divinatory rituals. It was reported for some time that if this salvia was ingested it would produce an illusory experience. Called *hierba de la pastora*, meaning "the herb of the shepherdess," the Mazatec Indians sometimes referred to the salvia as "La Maria, who speaks with a quiet voice."

Botanists working in the area had not been able to locate *Salvia divinorum* because it rarely flowers or sets seed. Known to grow only in the territory lived in by the Mazatec Indians, this salvia is considered by some to be a cultigen, a cultivated plant with an unknown or obscure taxonomic origin. An example of a cultigen is cabbage. By 1985 as many as 15 populations of the salvia had been found, and evidence was mounting that the plant, when it did flower, had no known pollinator and so perpetuated itself by rooting at its nodes.

A perennial herb, *Salvia divinorum* is endemic to the Sierra Mazateca of Oaxaca, Mexico, where it grows between 1000 to 6000 ft (400 to 1800 m) in cloud forests. In the wild, it occurs in fertile soil in hot and humid areas that experience fog. Its habitat is along streambanks where vegetative coverings of low trees and bushes make a congenial environment of low light and high humidity. There is little erect growth on the plant, and the quadrangular stems, which are easily breakable, tend to trail along the ground, rooting copiously at

Easy to root but extremely hard to bring into flower, *Salvia divinorum* is a worthy challenge. (George E. Wilcox)

Salvia divinorum requires low light, warmth, and moisture to flower and flourish. (Don Mahoney)

the nodes and even at the internodes. The green leaves, which have a yellow undertone, taper to a point and are about 4–12 in (10–30 cm) long. They are without hairs on both surfaces, and there is little or no petiole. Inflorescences are about 1 ft (30 cm) long with about six flowers in each whorl. The small violet calyx is covered with both glands and hairs. White flowers are curved in shape, densely covered with hairs, and about 1.25 in (3 cm) in length.

This salvia has been in the literature of ethnobotanists for many years. There is a reference to its being used as a ritualistic herb as early as 1972. Horticulturally, rooted cuttings have been bought, sold, and handed around in California since the 1970s, but the plant has not been advertised or distributed through commercial nurseries. I have found it impossible to find anything written about it in gardening or horticultural magazines or books; my information comes from botanical and ethnobotanical descriptions and from conversations with those who have grown the plant. On several occasions I have grown the plant in a greenhouse but have never succeeded in getting my plants to flower.

Easy to root and establish, *Salvia divinorum* becomes difficult to manage and care for as its stems elongate. Waiting for it to flower may or may not take years, and the time involved makes for many problems in growing the plant. Success in growing the plant outdoors depends on a warm climate where temperatures do not fall below 40°F (5°C) in the winter. If sited in a bed that has lots of humus in the soil, the plant can be grown where trees offer filtered light and shrubs provide support for the clambering stems. You should not only mist this salvia and drench it frequently with water but also give it a monthly feeding of half-strength liquid fertilizer. It is possible to grow *S. divinorum* in a greenhouse throughout the cool months of the year if it receives the protection of low light. Propagation is by cuttings or transplanted rooted nodes. Flower production is always uncertain, but this salvia's flowering season in its native habitat is from September to May.

Salvia dolomitica Codd

A handsome, gray-leaved shrub, *Salvia dolomitica* is found at elevations of 3000–5000 ft (900–1500 m) in the northeast province of Transvaal in South Africa. As its name implies, it grows in dolomite, a rocky soil containing high concentrations of the mineral calcium magnesium carbonate.

Generously covered with leaves, *Salvia dolomitica* usually reaches 3 ft (1 m) in height and width in a garden. In the wild, it can reach twice those dimensions. Elliptic, gray-green leaves held in an upright position are prominently veined on the underside. Blooming in early summer, the inflorescence is short, and the verticils are two flowered. The calyx is pea green and covered with oil globules that smell lemony. The two-lipped calyx has distinct lobes, three on the top lip and two on the bottom. The flowers are pale lilac with a wide cream streak extending into the throat. Though not showy, the inflorescence has many interesting features when observed closely. *Salvia dolomitica* has never produced seed in my garden, though seeds germinate readily. Cuttings are a reliable means of propagation.

If sited in a gravelly soil that drains rapidly and where it receives at the very least a half day of sunlight, *Salvia dolomitica* will thrive. Occasionally, some summer irrigation is needed in order for the root-run not to become dry. I have found that less than a handful of crushed oyster shells sprinkled around the base of the plant in early spring is beneficial. The plant has proved hardy to around 25°F (-4°C), and because of the high elevation of its natural habitat, it may well withstand colder temperatures.

Salvia dolomitica, with its slick, clean, gray-white foliage that is evergreen, deserves a special place in a sunny, hot garden. (Sonja Wilcomer)

A foliage border featuring plants from areas of dry summers and wet winters can be built around salvias native to the Mediterranean, South Africa, and California. I call this a "geography bed" because it demonstrates the similar growing conditions of plants separated in their native habitats by thousands of miles. For a dark green background, *Salvia brandegei* and *S. mellifera* from the California chaparral make a screen 5 ft (1.5 m) high. In the midground, group several plants of *S. dolomitica*, a gray-green leaved salvia, and *S. chamelaeagnea*, a mid-green leaved specimen from South Africa. In a foreground of low-growing Mediterranean natives, feature drifts of the spreading *S. officinalis* 'Berggarten', which has mid-green leaves, and the biennial *S. aethiopis*, which has ornamental leaves and large inflorescences. All plants require more or less the same culture and little time or trouble.

Salvia dombeyi Epling

The native habitat of the spectacularly flowered *Salvia dombeyi* is Peru and Bolivia. An extremely tender plant, this sage is found at altitudes of 9800 ft (3000 m) in the wild. Robert Ornduff, while director of the University of California Botanical Garden, Berkeley, for 18 years, observed *S. dombeyi* grow-

ing as a vine to a height of two stories in the courtyard of the Museum of Archeology at the University of Cusco, Peru. Named in honor of the French botanist Joseph Dombey, this salvia is popular with gardeners in both Peru and Bolivia.

With a woody base and several to many stems, *Salvia dombeyi* is scandent and needs support in order to elongate and flower successfully. In cultivation with ideal conditions it might climb 9–20 ft (3–6 m). Exceedingly sensitive to cold temperatures, I have lost this salvia on several occasions when temperatures dipped to the low 30°s F (around -1°C) for short periods. However, Strybing Arboretum has mature plants growing outdoors in a benign climate on and above a 12 ft (4 m) fence. Tall conifers provide excellent protection from cold air and wind.

Salvia dombeyi has probably the longest flower of any salvia, usually measuring at least 3 in (8 cm) in length. (Christine Andrews)

Heart-shaped leaves that are graduated in size lightly cover the actively growing portion of *Salvia dombeyi*. The dark green leaves have a long petiole covered with short, distinct hairs that sparkle in dew or fog. Late summer and autumn is the usual time for the uncommonly long and beautiful flowers to appear. The 1.5 in (4 cm) currant-red calyx holds a 3.5 in (9 cm) long scarlet corolla, providing a dazzling display. Only a few flowers mature at the same time, so the inflorescence is in bloom for a long period.

Place *Salvia dombeyi* where it will receive support from other plants and a half day of sun. Good garden loam with fast drainage is desirable along with applications of half-strength liquid fertilizer twice each month throughout the active growing season. A mulch over the root area will conserve moisture and condition the soil. If temperatures drop below freezing, pot the salvia and place it in the greenhouse for the winter or take cuttings in early autumn. Growing and caring for *Salvia dombeyi* in a greenhouse is worth this extra effort by gardeners who live in all but the warmest areas. Propagation is by cuttings.

SALVIA DOMBEYI

An excellent plant for a water-conserving border, *Salvia dominica* has a lovely fragrance because of the numerous glands on its leaves. (Ginny Hunt)

Salvia dominica Linnaeus

A strong smelling and much-branched shrub that tends to be evergreen in a mild climate, *Salvia dominica* is found throughout the eastern Mediterranean region. It is particularly abundant in Israel, Lebanon, and Syria, and in its native habitat is a dominant species commonly found in association with *Ballota undulata*. Horticulturally, it has never been a well-known or popular sage. However, in Israel, where Nogah Hareuveni (1980) has interpreted Jewish tradition as reflected in plants, the branched inflorescence of the fragrant *S. dominica* is one of several salvias thought to have inspired the design of the menorah, or seven-branched candelabra.

Linnaeus, in describing *Salvia dominica*, believed it to be from the West Indies and gave it the specific epithet *dominica* to commemorate the island of Dominica, which means "belonging to the Lord." A student of Linnaeus, Martin Hendriksen Vahl, also described this salvia and gave it the specific name *graveolens*. According to the botanical rules of nomenclature, the earlier name stands. Incidentally, *graveolens* means "heavily scented" and refers to the fragrant glands on the hairs covering the leaf, making it a more relevant epithet than the misleading *dominica.*

Reaching about 3 ft (1 m) in both height and width, *Salvia dominica* adapts well to garden situations. It tolerates overhead watering if quick drainage follows. The chalky hills of the plant's native surroundings receive only infrequent water. In my garden it has proved hardy when temperatures have fallen to the low teens (around -11°C). The hastate leaves are gray-green and fuzzy, being covered with the previously mentioned aromatic hairs. The plant blooms in spring or early summer and produces pale, yellowish white flowers in delicate and airy whorls. The inflorescences hold well as cut flowers. In a short time this salvia will build wood at its base and should be replaced every three to four years. This replacement can be smoothly managed because propagation is easily accomplished by layering, cuttings, or seed.

Salvia dominica is considered drought tolerant and can be planted with a rosemary such as 'Collingwood Ingram' on a bank that receives full sun, where the differences in the plants' shape and foliage color will make a pleasant display. This sage also looks handsome planted among herbaceous perennials such as penstemons, agastaches, and the gray-leaved, sterile *Nepeta* ×*faassenii.* The woolly leaves of this salvia are an attractive contrast with the perennials' foliage and also emphasize their colorful flowers.

Salvia dorisiana Standley
fruit-scented sage, peach sage

From Honduras comes *Salvia dorisiana,* a tender perennial that is sometimes called fruit-scented or peach sage. This sage apparently commemorates Doris, daughter of Oceanus, wife of Nereus, and mother of 50 sea nymphs. In its warm native habitat it reaches 3–4 ft (1–1.3 m) in height and is heavily branched. Widely known and grown for the lovely fruity scent that is released when its leaves are brushed, fruit-scented sage is also admired for the large hot-pink flowers it produces in winter.

First named and described in 1950, *Salvia dorisiana* has become a popular greenhouse plant. It requires a warm climate year-round, but I have found it to withstand temperatures as low as the high 20°s F (around -2°C) in my garden for short periods. Cold air will cut the top of the plant down, but with the return of reliably warm weather, new growth will break through from the

plant's base. Frosty and cold spells
coincide with this sage's December to
March blooming period and, consequently, it must be kept indoors in all
but the warmest areas to encourage
flowering. To enjoy its flowers, I keep
pots of the sage in the greenhouse in
winter, then move them into the garden to a spot with filtered light for the
long summer.

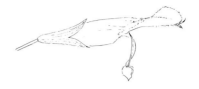

Salvia dorisiana

Large magenta-pink flowers sometimes reach 2 in (5 cm) in length and are
held in a lime-green calyx that can reach 0.75 in (2 cm) in length. The color of
the calyx is repeated in the hairy, ovate leaves. Almost the entire plant is covered with hairs that have glands that release a delightful pineapple-grapefruit
scent when stroked.

A half day of sunlight, friable soil enriched with humus, frequent water,
and light applications of a balanced fertilizer are needed to keep fruit-scented
sage in good condition. Because of its frequent spurts of growth and its branching habit, periodic pruning is required. The flowering shoots are most attractive to hummingbirds and make good, long-lasting cut flowers. Propagation is
by seed or cuttings.

Salvia dorisiana is an excellent choice for a container garden. Its attractive
and heavy foliage furnishes a quiet background for plants that flower for long
periods. Ivy geraniums and impatiens come quickly to mind for companions.
The trailing foliage of variegated ivy, such as *Hedera helix* 'Helena' or one of the
many other ivy cultivars, might be used to soften the edge of the container. All
require similar growing conditions.

Salvia eigii Zohary

Blooming in late winter and early spring, seed of the herbaceous perennial
Salvia eigii came to me from the Jerusalem Botanical Garden in 1982. It has
never been formally introduced, but since the early 1980s its seed has been
passed from one gardener to another in the San Francisco Bay area. In its native
habitat in the Eastern Mediterranean, where it grows in fallow fields on alluvial
soils, it is rarely found in the wild. Botanists believe it endemic to that particular region.

Fresh growth begins in winter as *Salvia eigii* builds a large clump of basal leaves that measures over 1 ft (30 cm) high and 2 ft (60 cm) wide. The dark green leaves are ovate in outline, and the largest measures 1 ft (30 cm) long and 8 in (20 cm) wide. The flowering stalk is 3 ft (1 m) in height and supports many 8–12 in (20–30 cm) inflorescences. The 1 in (2.5 cm) flowers appear in whorls and generously fill the inflorescence. The upper lip of the flower is cyclamen-purple, and the lower lip is a pale pink with ruby beelines into the throat. A prominent ruby calyx, which is distinctly veined and hairy, adds to the beauty of the flower. Many flowers open simultaneously, making this salvia a good candidate for a bouquet, especially since the cut flowers last well.

Large crisp leaves and pink flowers adorn *Salvia eigii* for three or even four months. (Christine Andrews)

Full sun, good garden soil enriched with humus, and sharp drainage are needed for *Salvia eigii* to flourish. Regular, deep watering every week or two is necessary throughout the summer, depending on temperatures. Propagation is by seed. One plant will produce an abundant supply of seed and it is not unusual to find seedlings around the base. Hardy to 10°F (-12°C), *S. eigii*, with the protection of conifer boughs, would probably survive even lower temperatures. In a mild climate it tends to have evergreen leaves, and its blooming period is three to four months long beginning in late winter and continuing through spring. In my garden, plants tend to throw inflorescences throughout the warm months.

Salvia eigii

Named for the botanist Alexander Eig, *Salvia eigii* is a fine addition for an informal cottage garden. Its shape provides a good contrast to hollyhocks, foxgloves, larkspurs, and delphiniums, and its lengthy blooming period would probably overlap with that of these plants, particularly in a cold climate. On a large scale, a combination of early spring-blooming plants might include a drift of pink and ruby *S. eigii* growing under the flowering cherry *Prunus* 'Shirotae' ('Mt. Fuji'), which has semidouble flowers that are pink in bud and white when fully open and that age to purplish pink. *Lychnis flos-jovis*, an airy-looking, well-branched perennial that is 2 ft (60 cm) tall with pink or white flowers, would complete the picture very nicely.

Salvia elegans Vahl
pineapple sage

Among the last sages to come into bloom before the end of autumn is the herbaceous perennial *Salvia elegans*, also known as *Salvia rutilans* Carrière. Seeing it bloom is a treat because the plant is cut down in most winters by cold weather before it can flower. Its native habitat across central Mexico and into the Sierra Madre del Sur provides a long and mild season in which to mature, and a bloom period can last for two to four months. Usually found at elevations of 6000–9000 ft (1800–2800 m), this species colonizes on the edge of woodlands.

In the wild there are two distinct clones, as well as intergradations, of *Salvia elegans*. The clone with larger flowers, called pineapple sage, was known for over a hundred years as *S. rutilans* and was in cultivation before 1873. The British botanist James Compton (1994a) has proposed changing the name of pineapple sage to *S. elegans* in order to show its relationship within the species. He has also proposed that this cultivar be called 'Scarlet Pineapple'.

When able to reach maturity in the garden, *Salvia elegans* is a somewhat shrubby plant about 4–5 ft (1.3–1.5 m) tall. Its roots extend on underground runners and in a moderate climate make a large clump. Deltoid, bright yellow-green leaves with a pale green, white-veined underside are covered with fine hairs and glands. They cover the branches fully and have a downy appearance. Deeply veined and graduated in size, the largest leaves measure 3 in (8 cm) long and 2 in (5 cm) wide. Six to twelve scarlet-red flowers appear in widely spaced, loose whorls. Two stamens and a feathery red pistil protrude and are easily visible. The 8–10 in (20–25 cm) long inflorescence comes into bloom gradually, making the plant a valuable and prolonged source of nectar for hummingbirds.

Salvia elegans was introduced to horticulture in about 1870, but few records and no lore exist to suggest where it came from or by what means. Its

The repeat-blooming *Salvia elegans* 'Honey Melon' with the variegated *Salvia officinalis* 'Icterina'. (Robert Kourik)

fragrance and form have given pleasure to scores of people for years, however. Prized for its pineapple scent, it is one of those beloved plants that is passed from gardener to gardener and wintered over indoors on many windowsills.

If *Salvia elegans* is to flower it needs an area with mild winters, good drainage, and garden soil enriched with humus. Wind protection and weekly watering are also required. As to hardiness, pineapple sage prefers temperatures no lower than the low 30°s F (around -1°C). It will usually withstand winters in the San Fransisco Bay area but on occasion will die down to the ground before returning from established rootstock in late spring. Cuttings and division of the rootstock are easy means of propagation. Seed sown in a warm greenhouse in early winter will produce a large plant by the following September or October. This sage grows rapidly and abundantly.

Easily placed in the garden with shrubs or tall perennials such as hollyhocks (which will also provide shade), pineapple sage attracts hummingbirds and, because of its late flowering, gives great enjoyment. In a mild climate, *Salvia elegans* does well in a protected nook in the garden. Its crisp foliage and showy blossoms will give the garden relief from the sparse look of winter. It also makes a splendid greenhouse plant.

Salvia elegans

Salvia elegans 'Honey Melon' was introduced by the Huntington Botanical Gardens in California in the 1970s. This selection is from a seedling of *S. elegans* collected in 1968 in Jalisco, Mexico, by botanist Fred Boutin. A winsome plant, 'Honey Melon' resembles a miniature *S. elegans*. It is 1.5–2 ft (45–60 cm) tall, spreads on an underground rootstock, and in a short time will make a thick ground cover. Its leaves are smaller than those of *S. elegans*, but when crushed they release the same fruity, pineapple fragrance.

'Honey Melon' begins flowering in early summer, and erect stems carry many inflorescences of scarlet-red flowers that measure about 1 in (2.5 cm) in length. Many come into bloom at the same time and make a fine combination with the fresh-looking, mid-green leaves. The leaves are deltoid in shape, about 1 in (2.5 cm) wide and equally as long. Hardy to 20°F (-7°C) or less, 'Honey Melon' renews itself from its rootstock. During the growing season, cut all inflorescences back as soon as they look spent. The plant will come into bloom again very quickly. The growing season of my specimens are long and I cut this salvia back three times for repeat bloom.

Flourishing in light shade, 'Honey Melon' will also take full sun. Give it good drainage, garden soil enriched with humus, and regular watering every 10–14 days. It may be divided almost any time of the year, and cuttings are also an easy form of propagation. Try it as a ground cover at the base of tall salvias or of shrubs such as *Osmanthus* or *Ilex*. The butter-yellow *Salvia madrensis* or the purple-blue *S. mexicana* would be enhanced with a liberal splash of the red of 'Honey Melon' at their feet.

Salvia farinacea Bentham
mealy sage

The herbaceous perennial *Salvia farinacea* occurs in a wide variety of habitats in central and eastern Texas, New Mexico, and the neighboring Mexican province of Coahuila. Found at elevations from 165 to 6000 ft (50 to 1800 m), *S. farinacea* usually grows on rocky soil that contains limestone. Described and named botanically in 1833, the specific epithet, *farinacea*, is derived from the Latin for flour and refers to the mealy-looking dusting that covers the inflorescence. Mealy sage, as it is commonly called, was soon recognized as a fine plant and was being grown as a garden subject by 1850.

Growing 3–4 ft (1–1.3 m) tall and 2 ft (60 cm) wide, mealy sage is heavily clothed with glossy mid-green, ovate, lancelike leaves. They are 3–4 in (8–10 cm) long and 1 in (2.5 cm) or more wide. The inflorescence is terminal, 6 in (15 cm) long, and tightly packed with whorls of flowers. The calyx that holds each flower is less than 0.5 in (1.3 cm) long and appears farinose but is actually densely covered with matlike woolly hairs that are tinged with white, blue, or purple. It is for the farinose, mealy granular characteristic that the plant is named. Flowers are less than 1 in (2.5 cm) long and usually a dark violet color. *Salvia farinacea* has a long blooming period beginning in April or May and continuing until cold weather and frost stop the display. Hardy to 25°F (-4°C), mealy sage will not come back from its rootstock after a cold winter.

A number of cultivars are offered by nurseries and seed catalogs. Some of the old-time favorites are 'Alba' and 'White Porcelain', which have white inflorescences, 'Blue Bedder', which has darker blue flowers than the typical species, and 'Victoria', which has violet-blue flowers, calyces, and stems. A smaller form of 'Victoria' called 'Mina', has been introduced. It grows about 1 ft (30 cm) high and less in width, and some gardeners regard it as a weak perennial. With the exception of 'Mina', all make good bedding plants.

Undisturbed by pests or insects, mealy sage is a trouble-free plant either in the garden or in pots or tubs. Its attributes include plain and simple culture with little pruning or pinching and a long blooming period. Full sun and fast-draining soil enriched with humus are required, along with ample water. Light applications of a balanced liquid fertilizer are helpful because of its heavy blooming. If winters are mild, the root crown can be protected with lightweight straw or evergreen boughs. When all danger of frost has passed, prune for a shapely plant. Propagation is by cuttings or seed. Many *Salvia farinacea* cultivars will usually come true from seed, but plants are generally treated as annuals.

Mealy sage is often used as a filler in borders of all sizes because of its dependable flowering and very neat and trim appearance. It also excels as a pot plant or in a large container. Pamela J. Harper (1991) praises its ability to be grown either as an annual or perennial and its capacity for mixing well with both yellows and pinks.

A traditional plant combination includes *Salvia farinacea* 'Blue Bedder' and trailing ivy geraniums (*Pelargonium peltatum*) for an ongoing floriferous display. An unconventional combination for a large tub includes the cultivar *S. farinacea* 'Victoria' with red lettuce, purple basil, and the large gray-leaved *S. argentea* spilling over the side of the tub.

Salvia flava Forrest ex Diels

Native to the province of Yunnan in China, *Salvia flava* is found there in large numbers on hillsides at altitudes of 7500–13,000 ft (2300–4000 m). It grows abundantly along streambanks in gravelly soil with maples, willows, viburnums, berberis, and clematis.

Sturdy and upright, *Salvia flava* is a perennial herb with a clump of basal-like leaves. It is sometimes under 1 ft (30 cm) tall but more usually over 2 ft tall (60 cm). The attractive leaves are a rich grassy green color with a puckered surface and about 3 in (8 cm) long with a pointed tip. In mid- to late summer, the salvia's flowering stalk elongates and blooms, reaching approximately 2 ft (60 cm) tall. The widely spaced flowers appear in whorls of four to eight. Individual flowers are covered with long, soft hairs and are tubular in shape, with the upper lip slightly curved at the apex. The flower color is yellow (*flava* means "yellow") or yellow-brown, with a conspicuous purple spot on the lower lip.

Beguilingly beautiful, *Salvia flava* has yellow flowers with a conspicuous purple beauty spot. (Ginny Hunt)

The Flora of China (1994) warns that *Salvia bulleyana*, also found in Yunnan, is very closely related to *S. flava*, and is repeatedly regarded as a synonym. In horticulture both in Great Britain and the United States, *S. flava* is frequently called *S. bulleyana*. The flowers of *S. bulleyana* are purple-blue, with no spotting on the middle lobe of the lower lip. There is no information about the two species hybridizing in the wild but it would be interesting to find out about that possibility. If they do not hybridize in the wild, then both species should be properly recognized.

The specific epithet, *bulleyana*, has its origins in a trip made by the famous plant collector Reginald John Farrer. The industrious and energetic Farrer needed subscriptions in order to finance his journeys to Japan, China, and other places in the East. Arthur K. Bulley, a wealthy cotton broker who in 1904 founded his own nursery, Bees, was approached and was the principal contributor for two of Farrer's plant-hunting expeditions. The salvia that bears his name was collected on one of these trips.

Easy to situate and care for in the garden, *Salvia flava* needs friable soil that drains well, partial sunlight, and water on a weekly basis. Although described by some gardeners as drought tolerant, I have not tested the plant for this attribute, and I keep the soil around it from drying out. In my garden, *S. flava* is completely dormant in winter, returning from its rootstock in early spring after the soil has begun to warm. Plants are hardy to 0°F (-18°C) or lower. Stems hold well in flower arrangements if first conditioned by being cut under water. Propagation is by division of an established clump or by seed.

Salvia flava is well suited for a subdued but important role in a partly sunny herbaceous border. When planning for midsummer bloom, the yellow- to cream-flowered *Phlomis fruticosa*, which reaches 4 ft (1.3 m), and the 2 ft (60 cm) tall *Echinops ritro*, with its bristly, globular heads of light blue flowers, make fine companions for clumps of the subtly colored and long-blooming *S. flava*. If you have space, I recommend *Verbascum chaixii* 'Album', which has off-white flowers and a pronounced mauve eye and grows to 2–3 ft (60–90 cm), as it gives a strong vertical lift to the composition.

Salvia forsskaolii Linnaeus

An endemic of the southeastern part of the Balkan Peninsula, *Salvia forsskaolii* is found from Bulgaria and Greece to the Black Sea coastline of Turkey. A hardy and handsome herbaceous perennial, in its native habitat it occurs at elevations of 6000 ft (1800 m) or less, growing in broad-leaved and coniferous forests, in meadows, and on steep banks. Introduced to horticulture in 1880, it was named in honor of Peter Forsskål of Finland, who collected plants in southwest Arabia in the mid-1700s. There is and has been some confusion in the spelling of his name due to his own and his family's several different spellings.

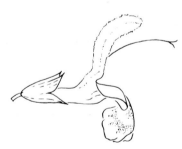

Salvia forsskaolii

Being deciduous in cold climates, *Salvia forsskaolii* starts building its thick and plentiful basal leaves in early spring. Hairy on both surfaces, the leaves are parsley-green in spring, turning dark green by summer. They gradually develop into a large basal clump 2 ft (60 cm) in height and as

The distinctive beelines that guide insects to nectar are prominent on *Salvia forsskaolii*. This clone has particularly richly colored flowers. (Christine Andrews)

much across. In midsummer, flowering stalks rise just above the ample foliage, with a blooming period of six weeks or so. The whorls of flowers are few in number and widely spaced but they make quite a show because the violet-blue, two-lipped flower has white streaks with yellow markings on the lower lip. This beeline tracks the most direct path to the nectar and pollen for insects. Fertile seed is plentifully produced and germinates readily. If you sow seed, try to find a strain that has flowers of deep violet-blue as they show up well in light shade. Inflorescences last well in bouquets.

Loamy soil and two-thirds to a half day of sun will promote a healthy plant and provide good flowering conditions. Weekly watering and sharp drainage are necessary, and a yearly dressing of humus will keep the soil in good tilth. A light application of fertilizer may be helpful in early summer. During a long, warm autumn, flowering will be repeated. *Salvia forsskaolii* plants are reported to be hardy to 0°F (-18°C) and can be protected with pine boughs in gardens that experience low temperatures.

For a border with some light shade, consider the evergreen western chain fern, *Woodwardia fimbriata*, which grows in clumps 6 ft (2 m) tall, in the middle of the border along with *Salvia forsskaolii*. In front, *Geranium macrorrhizum* 'Album', with its creamy petals and pink stamens, becomes a large mat. All have more or less evergreen foliage and will thrive with the same growing conditions in a mild climate. Gardens that have 0°F (-18°C) weather will find this salvia a valuable addition to a sunny herbaceous border. Worthy autumn companions include the 3 ft (1 m) or taller *Helianthus ×laetiflorus* 'Morning Sun', with its clear yellow flowers, and the delightful, similar-sized *Rudbeckia hirta*, black-eyed Susan, with its pale yellow rays and purple-brown discs.

Salvia 'Frieda Dixon'

The herbaceous perennial *Salvia* 'Frieda Dixon' will reach 4–5 ft (1.3–1.5 m) in height in a growing season. Given a favorable situation in light shade, its rootstock increases rapidly and forms a large clump similar to *S. elegans*, the pineapple sage.

Salvia 'Frieda Dixon' is a chance seedling of *S. elegans* that was found by Jon Dixon in his greenhouse in Woodside, California, in the late 1970s or early 1980s. Only one parent is known since many different salvias were growing in the greenhouse and garden at that time. Dixon planted the seedling in a garden situation in order to evaluate its performance, and when it proved to have an upright habit and an attractive appearance, he propagated it from cuttings and distributed it among gardeners. Since 1983 it has been grown in gardens in the San Francisco Bay area and, as well as being beautiful, it also attracts hummingbirds and butterflies. This salvia has demonstrated a pleasing vertical growth habit and hardiness during short periods of 20°F (-7°C). After one extended period of cold weather, when temperatures were about 11°F (-12°C) for several days, this salvia came back from its rootstock the following spring, and by autumn it was blooming as usual.

Salvia 'Frieda Dixon' can frequently be found in California nurseries and on mail order lists. It certainly merits its good reputation for reliable autumn flowering and unusual flower color.

Fast-draining soil enriched with humus and a site that offers protection from the western sun are needed to bring the plant into flower by late summer or early autumn. Deep weekly watering is also necessary. *Salvia* 'Frieda Dixon' has the upright-growing habit of pineapple sage, and the lanceolate leaves have the same fruity fragrance. The largest leaves are about 2 in (5 cm)

The peach-red flowers of *Salvia* 'Frieda Dixon' are stunning in autumn sunlight.
(Christine Andrews)

long and 1 in (2.5 cm) wide and mid-green in color. The flowers are a peachy-red when fully open; when back lit, the peach color is prominent on the two lips of the flower. The color reminds me of tomato soup thinned with heavy cream. Pleasing as cut flowers, flowering stems have a long life in a bouquet. When all danger of a late frost has past, cut stems to the ground to ensure uniform spring and summer growth. Propagation is by cuttings or division of the rootstock.

A number of perennials and grasses require the same cultural conditions as *Salvia* 'Frieda Dixon'. A grouping that features beautiful foliage would include *Panicum virgatum*, the good-looking switch grass, which blooms in autumn and then turns a lovely shade of pale honey. The grass is 2 ft (60 cm) tall and its airy flowering stems, which rise an additional 2 ft (60 cm), could be interspersed with clumps of this salvia. The 1 ft (30 cm) tall *Epimedium* ×*rubrum* placed at the base of these plants would tie the grouping together. Its handsome wine-red leaves with distinctive pea-green veining retain their color from the beginning to the end of the growing season. The shape and color of the three foliages, as well as the height of the plants, would be complementary.

Salvia frigida is both petite and charming, characteristics that make it an excellent rock garden plant. (Ginny Hunt)

Salvia frigida Boissier

Salvia frigida is a candidate for the rock garden not only because of its slight and slender size, but also because of its restrained growing habit. It is a perennial herb that occurs in the wild in northwestern Iran, northern Iraq, and eastern Turkey where it is found at altitudes of 3000–8000 ft (900–2500 m). These high elevations call attention to the specific epithet, *frigida*, meaning growing in cold regions. In Anatolia it grows on the edge of pine, juniper, and fir woodlands as well as in meadows and on limestone slopes and crevices. Apparently an adaptable plant, it grows in many diverse habitats.

Handsome and tidy, almost to the point of being like a small statue, *Salvia frigida* usually bears one flowering stem that is 1 ft (30 cm) tall. In Anatolia it reportedly sometimes grows to 2 ft (60 cm) tall with multiple flowering stems, but this has not been my experience. With a thick, woody rootstock, it has basal leaves that can vary in shape from ovate to oblong. Covered with long and tangled woolly hairs, the slender leaves are more or less 6 in (15 cm) in length and have a smooth and soft texture. In a mild climate the leaves tend to persist through winter but they appear worn and tattered. With the coming of warm weather, however, the plant produces new and fresh hairy leaves. When the inflorescence first emerges, it is both distinctive and ornamental, though small. Buds and bracts are held tightly together, making a decorative braided pattern. Blooming takes place in early summer. The small white or pale lilac flowers, scarcely 1 in (2.5 cm) long, are usually in whorls of two but there can be as many as six. They are held in a tiny calyx that gradually widens and expands with fruit. The inflorescence is not prominent and does not call attention to itself; on one occasion I completely missed its flowering and was surprised to find three or four seedlings near the mother plant the following spring. The usual means of propagation is by seeds.

Give *Salvia frigida* full sun, good garden soil, and an aspect that has excellent drainage throughout the year. Winter sunlight is important, as is weekly water during the growing season. With these cultural requirements in mind, I consider a trough the perfect place for this salvia. It could be combined with the purple form of the hardy *Sedum spathulifolium*, which will, with time, make a mat. Another salvia with a more prostrate habit that would also make a handsome and interesting trough companion is *Salvia caespitosa*. It makes a frothy mound of divided leaves and will bloom with *S. frigida* in late spring and early summer. If there is enough space, the bright and cheerful *Allium oreophilum*, 4–6 in (10–15 cm) tall with deep purplish pink flowers and darker midveins, would add color and sparkle in early summer.

Salvia fruticosa Miller
Greek sage

Among the earliest spring-blooming salvias, *Salvia fruticosa* is evergreen and described as a shrub. Native to the eastern Mediterranean, including southern Italy, it is particularly abundant in Israel. It also occurs on the Canary Islands and in North Africa. Although *S. fruticosa* plants are commonly found in several plant communities, populations comprised only of *S. fruticosa* are not unusual. Valued for centuries for its bountiful beauty, Greek sage has medicinal and culinary properties as well as sweet nectar and pollen. On the Greek island of Crete at the site of the reconstructed Knossos, Greek sage was depicted circa 1400 B.C. in the House of Frescoes.

In a garden setting the bushy *Salvia fruticosa* generally grows 2 ft (60 cm) in height and width and its flowering stalk rises 1 ft (30 cm) or more above the foliage. The entire plant is hairy and has a delightful frosty appearance. Its leaves are numerous, of different sizes, and in clusters, which accounts for the

Salvia fruticosa has a prolonged flowering period in early spring and handsome gray-green foliage year-round.
(Christine Andrews)

bushy look. A long hairy petiole supports a three-part, artichoke-green leaf. The middle portion is obovate or lanceolate with two little segments at its base.

The blooming period usually begins in early March and continues for well over a month. Pinkish lavender flowers about 0.5 in (1.3 cm) in length are held in a small oxblood-red, five-pointed, hairy calyx, making a very pretty combination of colors. The flowers occur in whorls along the inflorescence.

When the plant was described by Linnaeus in 1781, he named it *triloba* to emphasize the unusual leaf. In actuality, the plant had already been described in 1768 by Philip Miller, who, among many other accomplishments, was curator of the Chelsea Physic Garden for 22 years. According to the rules of botanical nomenclature, the earliest name stands. The specific epithet, *fruticosa*, means "shrubby" or "bushy."

A full day of sun, well-draining soil, and good air circulation are all necessities for *Salvia fruticosa*. It is hardy to 20°F (-7°C) and is a drought-tolerant plant that needs little additional water when established. After it blooms, it can be pruned to a desirable size. If flowers are needed for bouquets, pruning can also help with the shaping of the plant. Branches last well in arrangements. Propagation is by seed or cuttings. In June or July, cuttings strike roots rapidly.

Greek sage is highly variable in its form and structure. Its oils are variable too. It has a high oil content, and so its historical uses are similar to those of *Salvia officinalis*. The leaves contain chemicals similar to some lavenders, and druggists in some parts of the world sell the leaves as *Folia salviae*. Dried leaves are used to make tea, and fresh leaves steeped with honey make a refreshing drink.

In its native habitat, *Salvia fruticosa* frequently develops woolly galls that range in size from a cherry to a walnut. The gall-producing insect is more than likely found only in the Middle East. Most galls are about 1 in (2.5 cm) in diameter and are called "apples." Often mistaken for fruit because of the resemblance to little apples, they are very fragrant, juicy, and tasty when young and still green. Considered delicious and healthful, Greeks and Arabs, among others, peel and eat them when they are soft.

On a dry hillside with other evergreen Mediterranean plants such as *Artemisia arborescens, Euphorbia myrsinites, E. rigida,* and *Rosmarinus officinalis* 'Collingwood Ingram', a group of *Salvia fruticosa* will add variety of leaf form to a combination of plants with interesting foliage. All require the same culture, including good drainage and only occasional summer water.

Salvia fulgens Cavanilles
cardinal sage

Botanically classified as a perennial herb, *Salvia fulgens* resembles, in stature, a shrub. Native to Mexico, its range is limited to the central mountains in the province adjoining Puebla. It grows on the edge of oak and coniferous woodlands, particularly in clearings of *Picea religiosa,* at elevations of 8700–11,000 ft (2700–3400 m). These mountains receive moisture in the form of fog practically year-round and in the form of rain during the late spring, the end of summer, and the beginning of autumn. Its common name, cardinal sage, is appropriate, for the flowers stand out as brightly in its native green woodland as the eastern cardinal stands out in its home territory. This salvia is also known by the synonym *S. cardinalis* Kunth.

Growing 4–5 ft (1.3–1.5 m) tall and 3–4 ft (1–1.3 m) wide in a season, cardinal sage needs a long warm autumn in order to produce heavy flowering. The rather pale, yellow-green, heart-shaped leaves are about 1.5 in (4 cm) long and 1 in (2.5 cm) wide and cover the plant amply. Inflorescences are short, usually 4 in (10 cm) in length, and are terminal. Very rarely, a 12 in (30 cm) long inflorescence may be found. The flowers are fire-engine red, 2 in (5 cm) in length, and in loose whorls. The upper lip of each flower is covered with red hairs. The specific epithet, *fulgens,* means "glitter," "glisten," or "shine," which is appropriate because the hairs catch moisture from dew and glisten in the morning light. After the flowers have bloomed, they drop, leaving a reddish brown, 0.5 in (1.3 cm) calyx. Frequently, the calyx drops too, precluding seed production.

Site cardinal sage in full sun, being careful that the slanted October and November sun still reaches the plant. Well-draining soil enriched with humus

The hairy upper lip of each flower of *Salvia fulgens* glistens with the morning dew. (Don Mahoney)

and regular summer watering are needed. Fertilizer in early summer may help this salvia get off to a fast start. Some staking is necessary, and I usually tie twine around the middle of all the plant's stems to hold them up and make the flowers easily visible. Other plants will camouflage the twine. *Salvia fulgens* is hardy to 20°F (-7°C). After all danger of frost has passed, cut cardinal sage within 1 ft (30 cm) of its crown. Propagation is by seed, cuttings, and division of the rootstock.

During the autumn and winter of 1993 and 1994, temperatures were mild, the soil in my garden remained warm, and there was no killing frost. These unusual weather conditions allowed me to have a bouquet of cardinal sage for my desk on 23 January, which was a particular pleasure during the short days of winter.

Introduced to horticulture in the 1800s, cardinal sage has been grown in Britain for many years. Harold and Joan Bawden (1970) call its flowers startling and write that it is at its very best in their Sussex garden in September. They regard it as well worth the extra trouble of keeping it in a greenhouse over winter and finding a warm wall for it in the garden in spring.

A composition of autumn-blooming salvias is outstanding and a joy to behold. For height, the yellow-flowered *Salvia madrensis* and vermilion-flowered *S. confertiflora* will make a 5–7 ft (1.5–2.3 m) tall background. In the midground, clumps of cardinal sage can be interplanted with white and scarlet *S. coccinea*. For the front of the border, a wide ribbon of *S. elegans* 'Honey Melon' will hold the mass of foliage and colorful flowers together. All plants require the same culture and care. In my own garden, *S. fulgens* is allowed very little space and must compete for sun with the rich violet-flowered *S. mexicana* and violet-blue flowered *Aster ×versicolor*. These plants are in the range of 4–5 ft (1.3–1.5 m) tall, and when crowded together they help hold each other up. For well over a month their variously colored flowers are a treat.

Salvia gesneriiflora Lindley & Paxton

A robust, winter- into spring-flowering perennial or subshrub, *Salvia gesneriiflora* occurs in many mountainous provinces of the Sierra Madre Occidental in Mexico. Growing at elevations ranging from 7500 to 10,000 ft (2300 to 3100 m), it is apparently tolerant of cold temperatures into the low 20°s F (around -6°C). Named to honor Conrad von Gesner of Zurich, a celebrated 15th-century naturalist and botanist, the long tubular flowers of this salvia resemble the flowers in the genus *Gesneria*. Both the genus and the family, Gesneriaceae, are named for Conrad von Gesner.

Reputed to grow to 25 ft (7.6 m) tall in its native habitat, *Salvia gesneriiflora* usually attains approximately 5–6 ft (1.5–2 m) in height and 4 ft (1.3 m) in width as a garden plant. Pruning is a contributing factor to the smaller plant size, whether brought about by the gardener or by windy weather. This salvia is a ready candidate for rain and wind damage because it builds multiple woody stems that are heavy with foliage. The heart-shaped leaves are graduated in size, mid-green, and strongly aromatic. Large, vivid, orange-red flowers are 1–1.5 in (2.5–4 cm) long and held in a 1 in (2.5 cm) yellow-green calyx that is tinged with purple glands. Whorls of showy flowers are closely spaced on inflorescences that are 8–12 in (20–30 cm) long. This plant tends to stay in bloom for an extended period during the late winter and early spring. In late May when the weather is very warm, it is advisable to cut the whole plant back to leaf nodes near its base even

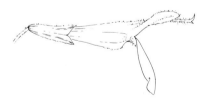

Salvia gesneriiflora

Throughout the winter and well into the spring, *Salvia gesneriiflora* 'Tequila' will repeat bloom. (Ed Carman)

though it may still be in bloom. Hard annual pruning will ensure new growth that will build approximately 6 ft (2 m) in height during the growing season. This pruning will also encourage flowering in the coming year.

Botanists at the Huntington Botanical Gardens made a collecting trip to Mexico in 1970. At this time, Fred Boutin collected seed of *Salvia gesneriiflora* from two distinctly different populations: a form with a green calyx, which is the more common, and a form with a purple calyx and stem, which was given the cultivar name 'Tequila'. The collection site was at 8500 ft (2600 m) on the Volcan de Tequila in the province of Jalisco. Sometime around 1979, John MacGregor, who was on the horticultural staff at the Huntington, selected a seedling from 'Tequila' and called it 'Mole Poblano'. It is reputed to be more floriferous than 'Tequila' with a longer bloom season, but I have been unable to verify this. It is entirely possible that these two selections have become confused, since they are similar.

A sunny spot with good drainage and protection from wind is ideal for *Salvia gesneriiflora* and its two cultivars. Some regular water is needed throughout the summer and autumn. Propagation is by seed or cuttings. It is not unusual to find seedlings near the mother plant from time to time. Remember, late May is the time to cut the plant back even though it may still be blooming. If branching occurs at awkward angles—and it probably will—remove shoots at the main stem in order to keep a shapely plant. Proven to be cold tolerant into the low 20°s F (around -6°C), I would not advise planting this salvia unless your winter climate is both sunny and mild, as those are the conditions that are necessary to generate good flowering. These salvias are striking companions in gardens with mild climates and are also a generous nectar source for over-wintering hummingbirds.

SALVIA GESNERIIFLORA

Salvia gesneriiflora and *S. gesneriiflora* 'Tequila', because of their large stature, combine beautifully with large clumping grasses such as *Miscanthus sinensis*, Japanese silver grass, which reaches 6–8 ft (2–2.5 m) at maturity. Flowering in August, the dried inflorescence of the grass holds through the winter months, complementing the winter-blooming salvia. Late in the season the foliage of Japanese silver grass turns purple-red and then dries to a warm beige, giving form and motion to the garden during the shortest days of the year.

Salvia gilliesii Bentham

A pleasing plant with good vertical qualities, *Salvia gilliesii* comes from a habitat in the Andes Mountains that includes Bolivia, Argentina, and Chile. In this mountainous chain it is reported to occur at elevations as high as 10,000 ft (3100 m). First described by George Bentham in 1873, this attractive plant has taken many years to be discovered by gardeners. On the French Riviera in Hyeres, which is not far from Nice, Pépinière de La Foux grew and distributed *S. gilliesii* in 1994. In 2002 it is still a newcomer to horticulture in the United States.

A very tall and erect plant, *Salvia gilliesii* is said to reach 9 ft (3 m) in its native habitat. In my garden it reaches a full 6 ft (2 m) by the time it starts to bloom in late summer. Although rarely expressing his personal opinion, Epling (1939) described *S. gilliesii* as a "beautiful shrub." Stems of its new growth in early spring are square and light green in color. They mature rapidly, becoming rounded, woody, and soft gray. The plant produces many slender, upright stems within a small space giving the shrub a tall, light, and airy quality. Leaves lightly cover the plant and are lanceolate in shape and graduated in size. The largest are on the lower part of the plant and measure approximately 4 in (10 cm) long and 1.5 in (4 cm) wide. The edge of the leaves is serrated, and the underside is white with pronounced veining. When the surface is rubbed, a faint but pleasing scent is released. Flowering begins in late summer and continues until the short, cool days of autumn. Inflorescences are branched

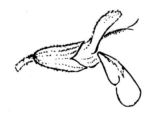

Salvia gilliesii

From late summer until frost, *Salvia gilliesii* will enhance the autumn border. (Ginny Hunt)

with well-spaced whorls of flowers that number three to six in each whorl. Deep sky-blue flowers with a purple undertone are small but easily seen because of their position. They measure 0.75 in (2 cm) in length and are held in a tiny calyx that is purple on the side that is turned to the sun and green on the underside. The top of the narrow upper lip has a farinaceous dusting, which is whitish and mealy. The lower lip is wider and has two white lines that aid insects in finding the nectary.

A sunny spot in the garden that has good air circulation will allow *Salvia gilliesii* to reach its full and graceful height. It needs ordinary friable garden soil that drains fast and regular watering. This salvia produces seed, and after you gather it in late autumn, prune the plant so that all stems are about 3 ft (1 m) from the ground. The portion that remains will help protect the roots from cold weather. These shorter stems should in turn be cut to the ground in spring after the plant shows active growth. Propagation is usually from cuttings taken in early summer that can be held over in the greenhouse until warm spring weather returns. I have not grown this plant long enough to determine its hardiness, but because of its high elevation habitat I would expect it to be hardy to the low 20°s F (around -6°C) for short periods. Cuttings that are planted in the garden in spring have several months to grow and mature before flowering begins in late summer. Seed can be sown in late winter in a warm greenhouse. These plants will probably have a late and short flowering period.

This salvia is a joy to place in the border because it always looks attractive and does not need to be staked. In the background of a sunny border, several of the handsome evergreen *Berberis hookeri* will make beautiful mounding plants about 4 ft (1.3 m) tall and wide. These plants are the perfect foil for many autumn-blooming annuals such as the 4 ft (1.3 m) tall *Tithonia rotundifolia* 'Aztec Sun' with apricot-gold flowers and the less spectacularly flowered *Nicotiana langsdorffii*. The nicotiana is about the same height and has large, beautiful, smooth leaves and small, fresh-looking, lime-green flowers. Many plants of *Salvia gilliesii* can be worked in between these perennials to create a border that will have interesting flowers and foliage from late August until frost. All need the same culture, which includes moderate, regular water.

Salvia glechomifolia Kunth

Native to at least three provinces in central Mexico, *Salvia glechomifolia* is found at altitudes ranging from 7500 to 10,500 ft (2300 to 3200 m). Not a well-known plant in horticultural circles, it became available to gardeners through California nurseries in 1992. The specific name, *glechomifolia*, is derived from the Greek and means "with foliage like *Glechoma*." Linnaeus gave the name *Glechoma* to a small genus in the mint family that comprises creeping and stoloniferous plants.

A creeping perennial herb, *Salvia glechomifolia*, when established, will make an airy colony of yellow-green foliage that is upright and almost sparse. The leaves reflect light and appear to be in widely spaced whorls. Stems are short and reach about 1–1.5 ft (30–45 cm). Flowering lightly throughout the summer, the long, blue-violet flowers have two prominent white lines leading to the nectary and seem to bloom without interruption. The small flowers are less than 1 in (2.5 cm) long and occur in unevenly spaced whorls, usually with fewer than 12 flowers in each whorl. The overall effect is of daintiness.

A half day of sun along with loamy soil enriched with humus are needed for *Salvia glechomifolia*. Friable soil enriched with a large handful of bloodmeal will encourage the plant to colonize. In fact, a small amount of bloodmeal every spring will give plants strength and good foliage color. I also recommend soil that drains well and deep watering at least once a week. Colonies of the salvia profit from the humidity created by the leaves of nearby plants. The

Covering the ground with good green foliage, *Salvia glechomifolia* thrives in the companionship of other plants. (Christine Andrews)

removal of spent inflorescences will help keep the plants flowering over a three-month period during summer. Known to be hardy to 32°F (0°C), *S. glechomifolia* survived in my garden without damage when temperatures fell to the high 20°s F (around -2°C) for short periods. Propagation is by division of the rootstock, seed, or cuttings. Cuttings for overwintering in the greenhouse can be taken in late summer or early autumn.

Another native of Mexico, *Echeveria elegans*, which is sometimes called white Mexican rose, would make an admirable partner for *Salvia glechomifolia*. The leaves of *E. elegans* are a year-round garden feature and grow in bold rosettes. Flat and silver-gray, they are covered with a fine, white powdery meal. Short flowering stalks appear in spring with pinkish, bell-like flowers that are orange and yellow inside. Another possible companion for *S. glechomifolia* is *Anthemis cretica*, a gray-foliaged plant that will bloom at the same time as the salvia. It is an uncommon, cushion-forming perennial that is well worth looking for. About 1 ft (30 cm) in height and width with deeply divided grayish foliage, its small daisylike flowers make a floriferous display. In addition, *A. cretica* is easy to grow from seed. If you are looking for a long blooming companion, the California native *Erigeron glaucus*, with basal leaves in clumps, is a good companion with lots of color. Adaptable to most growing conditions, it has lavender, daisylike flowers and is under 1 ft (30 cm) when in bloom. Suitable for a large container, *S. glechomifolia* combines well with the old-fashioned favorite *Glechoma hederacea* 'Variegata'. These plants will thrive with similar culture.

Salvia glutinosa Linnaeus
Jupiter's distaff

Growing across Europe and western Asia, *Salvia glutinosa* has a native habitat that ranges from central France through central Russia and includes Spain, Italy, and Greece. Usually occurring in mountainous areas, it is found in woodlands and protected, shaded environments. Described by Linnaeus in 1753, *S. glutinosa* was known long ago in central Europe for its pleasant smelling flowers and leaves that were used to give flavor to homemade wines.

A deciduous perennial, *Salvia glutinosa* is a rangy plant that frequently reaches 3 ft (1 m) in height. Hairy, hastate leaves about 5 in (13 cm) in length are widely spaced on the plant's ascending stems. Parsley-green in color, the leaves have petioles that are practically as long as the leaf itself. The flowers, in whorls of two to six, are pale yellow, and the upper lip is heavily flecked with maroon dots. Both the flowers and the small lime-green calyces are sticky, hence the specific name, *glutinosa*. Flowering begins in early summer and continues for about a two-month period. Be sure to look for the flowers because even though the inflorescences can be 1 ft (30 cm) long, flower color is subtle enough that flowering can be easily overlooked. *Salvia glutinosa* bears a remarkable resemblance to *S. nubicola*, a species from China. In a mild climate, flowers still bloom in late autumn. Propagation is by seed or cuttings.

A shady area, friable garden soil containing humus, and water on a weekly basis are the specific cultural requirements for *Salvia glutinosa*. This deciduous plant is cold tolerant and withstands temperatures below 0°F (-18°C). Remove the season's top growth when tidying the garden in late autumn or early winter as it will prevent decomposing stalks from getting into the crown of the plant.

Gardeners in England have made use of this salvia's tendency to reproduce itself freely by seedlings. Harold and Joan Bawden (1970) credit it as a tall ground cover with an outward sprawl. Their plants flowered over a period of three months. Graham Stuart Thomas (1990a) calls it coarse but recommends it for rough places. The experience of these writers will help other gardeners place *Salvia glutinosa* in shady areas that require only occasional water and care.

Salvia greggii Gray
autumn sage

Occurring in rocky soil at elevations of 5000–9000 ft (1500–2800 m), *Salvia greggii* has a lengthy and narrow distribution from southwest Texas throughout the Chihuahuan deserts into the province of San Luis Potosí, Mexico. An evergreen shrub that is common throughout this region, autumn sage is usually found in sunny and dry locations. Described and named by Asa Gray in 1870, the name commemorates J. Gregg, a Mexican trader, who found and collected the salvia in Texas.

Closely related to *Salvia microphylla*, *S. greggii* can be identified, according to Epling (1939), by the lack of a pair of papillae inside the corolla near its base. Both these species hybridize freely, and James Compton (1994a) has given the name *Salvia ×jamensis* to a hybrid swarm of *S. microphylla* and *S. greggii* found in the wild (see the entry for *Salvia ×jamensis*). In my experience, *S. greggii* and its hybrids are fecund, and every summer both the species and their hybrids produce numerous seedlings.

Defying its common name, autumn sage flowers throughout the summer and autumn until short days and cool weather slow then stop their production. A highly variable plant reaching 1–4 ft (0.3–1.3 m) in height and less in width, this salvia's growth habit ranges from upright to mounding. Leaves vary in shape and tend to be less than 1 in (2.5 cm) long. Mid-green and glabrous, the leaves can lightly or profusely cover the plant. Flower size is highly variable, from 0.25 to 1 in (0.6 to 2.5 cm), as is flower color. Tints and shades of scarlet and red are the most common colors in the wild, but rose, white, and occasionally pink, lavender, and violet may also occur. From time to time, plants that exhibit unusual attributes are found. For example, *Salvia greggii* 'Big Pink' was introduced by garden writer Scott Ogden in Austin, Texas, because of the plant's larger than usual lower lip, which clearly flaunts the flower's deep pink color and lavender tint. The cultivar 'Furman's Red' is a selection made in Texas, probably in the 1970s, and named for W. A. Furman, a distinguished plantsman from Kerrville, Texas. It is known for its profuse production of dark red flowers in autumn. Nurseryman Pat McNeal of

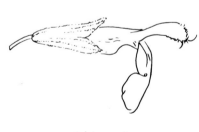

Salvia greggii

Well suited for a shady area, *Salvia greggii* 'Cherry Chief' is an excellent cultivar. (Robert Kourik)

A ripe peach-colored clone of *Salvia greggii* 'Desert Pastel'. (Christine Andrews)

Austin, Texas, has introduced the small and charming 'Purple Pastel', which repeats bloom heavily in autumn. Another of his introductions is 'Purple Haze', with small but intensely colored violet-purple flowers. 'Cherry Chief' was introduced by nurseryman Richard Dufresne of Greensboro, North Carolina, because it blooms reliably in the humid south. These plants have proved to be hardy and suitable for shady spots such as an eastern or northeastern exposure, making them valuable additions to horticulture. Their glossy green foliage intensifies the bright colors of the flowers.

A trim, tidy, and good-looking cultivar, 'Desert Pastel' has proven to be a reliable perennial that comes into heavy bloom in the autumn. Lightly blooming throughout spring and summer, plants are about 2 ft (60 cm) tall and wide. Small and shiny evergreen foliage that is sweet smelling forms little clusters along the woody stems. Flowers are a delightful, pale apricot color that is difficult to describe because the lower lip has a streak of pale yellow that subdues the intensity of the flower color. In a mild climate, 'Desert Pastel' is an attractive plant year-round and is hardy to the low 20°s F (around -6°C).

Easy to grow in areas with low humidity, *Salvia greggii* needs excellent drainage, a half to full day of sun, and loamy soil. Reported to be drought tolerant, these plants will tolerate regular water on a weekly basis. Some pinching

Salvia greggii 'Desert Pastel'

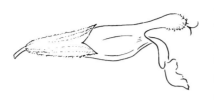

Salvia greggii 'Desert Pastel'

and pruning will be necessary throughout the long growing season to induce continued flowering. Cut back spent inflorescences periodically, and before active growth begins in spring, prune all dead wood and shape the plant for the season ahead. In my mild climate, *S. greggii* blooms from May until November and is tolerant of temperatures into the low 20°s F (around -6°C). Wood builds in the center of the plant so be sure to start afresh. with cuttings every four to five years. Propagation is usually by cuttings because of the great variability of seedlings.

Salvia greggii was introduced to cultivation in 1885 and became popular in the United States on the West Coast a hundred years later. Nurseries propagate reams of cultivars with attractive flowers—'Alba', white; 'Cherry Queen', red; 'Big Pink' and 'Dwarf Pink', pink; 'Keter's Red', orange-red; 'Rosea', pale red; and 'La Encantada', reddish pink. Several undesignated forms have peach or salmon flowers. Sizes and growing habits of all these cultivars differ. Two hybrids that are fine ornamental plants with graceful growing habits are 'Plum Wine' and 'Raspberry Royale'. These hybrids measure 3 ft (1 m) in both height and width.

Known and valued for its long flowering period, *Salvia greggii* can be smoothly slipped into many different kinds of sunny borders. Planted in an area designed to be attractive from late summer through autumn, the purple-leaved *Cercis canadensis* 'Forest Pansy' will anchor a number of pink-flowering *S. greggii* cultivars, drifts of *Aster ×frikartii* 'Monch', with its deep, clear, violet-blue flowers, and *Aster lateriflorus*, which has purple foliage and pink ray flowers. The self-seeding *Viola tricolor* 'Johnny Jump Up', which is purple and gold with a white eye, can fill the bare spots between the other plants. All require the same culture.

Salvia guaranitica Saint-Hilaire ex Bentham
anise-scented sage

From a wide geographical region in South America, including Brazil, Paraguay, Uruguay, and Argentina, comes the exceedingly long-blooming herbaceous perennial *Salvia guaranitica*. Described and named in 1833, it has long been favored by gardeners in the United States and elsewhere because of its adapt-

'Argentina Skies' is a pale blue selection of
Salvia guaranitica, shown here with *Daucus
carota*, Queen Anne's lace, and *Rosa* 'La Marne'
on the right. (Robert Kourik)

ability and brilliant, almost true-blue
flowers.

Sometimes called anise-scented
sage, referring to the scent released
from bruised leaves, this salvia begins
blooming in early summer and continues until frost, flowering being
heaviest throughout the hot summer
months. *Salvia guaranitica* will reach
4–5 ft (1.3–1.5 m) in height in a season
and become a large patch in a few
years because of its running rootstock. Its roots sport little nodules
that look like miniature cigars. The
rootstock is quite easy to divide,
though propagation can be by seed
and cuttings.

Salvia guaranitica is unparalleled in its ability
to repeat bloom over a long period throughout summer and autumn.
(Robert Kourik)

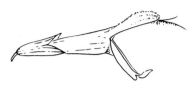

Salvia guaranitica

Inflorescences, which fairly sparkle with rich blue-violet flowers, are 8–10 in (20–25 cm) long. Ovate leaves are 1.5 in (4 cm) long and almost the same in width. They are a fresh mint-green in color and remain so throughout the prolonged flowering period. The calyx is small, usually a dark purple-green on the side facing the sun, and green on the underside. Good for cut flowers, this salvia lasts well in arrangements if stems are conditioned by first cutting them under water.

The culture of *Salvia guaranitica* is similar to that of many of the salvias that come from Mexico. Situate plants in full sunlight or at least in areas that receive sunlight for three-quarters of the day. Fast-draining soil that is enriched with humus is required, and plants should be watered every 7 to 10 days in hot weather. Prune plants to the ground in late winter and divide clumps every three years or so. Anise-scented sage has proved hardy to 10°F (-12°C) when given the protection of pine boughs, but it will be completely dormant in a cold climate. Although Penelope Hobhouse (1985) admires this sage, she warns that cuttings should be taken in autumn and a protective mulch used since it is not reliably hardy in Great Britain.

A number of cultivars are being grown in Britain, France, and the United States. 'Argentina Skies', which was introduced by Charles Cresson in 1990, has pale blue flowers, 'Blue Enigma' has a green calyx, 'Blue Ensign' has large Cambridge-blue flowers, 'Black and Blue' is a subshrub with a very dark violet-blue calyx, and 'Purple Splendour' has rich purple flowers. In my experience, none of the cultivars develop in the same substantial clumps as the species nor flower as profusely. A cultivar that blooms for a long period in autumn and reaches 6 ft (2 m) is 'Costa Rica Blue'. I have found it to be more tender than the other cultivars. A sport with dark violet flowers was growing in my garden in 1993, its thick stems and sturdy, upright habit proving the plant's propensity to be variable.

Easy to situate in the garden because of its dependable upright habit, *Salvia guaranitica* can be the mainstay at the back of a herbaceous border. For a pleasing color scheme, plant a clump with the polyantha rose 'Nathalie Nypels', a repeat-blooming, rosy pink, 3–4 ft (1–1.3 m) shrub. A start of *Geranium dalmaticum*, with its rich green, lush foliage and pink flowers will, in time, make an admirable carpet. Another color scheme combines *S. guaranitica* with the yellow-gold, 1.5 ft (45 cm) tall perennial *Coreopsis* 'Early Sunrise'. Known for flowering early from seed, 'Early Sunrise' can be treated as an annual. The reliable, trailing *Lobelia* 'Crystal Palace' planted at the base of *S. guaranitica* and *C.* 'Early Sunrise' would complement both. The green foliage of these plants is restful and brings the cold blues and warm yellow-gold colors together harmoniously.

Salvia hians Royle ex Bentham

A herbaceous perennial, *Salvia hians* is found in many locations in mountainous regions from Pakistan to Bhutan. Commonly occurring in the Kashmir alpine region at elevations of 7800–13,000 ft (2400–4000 m), its habitats are open slopes and forests. It was first described in 1830 by the naturalist John Forbes Royle, who was superintendent of the East India Company's two hospitals at Saharunpur and curator of the botanical garden there. The gardens were redesigned by Royle and contained both medicinal and economically useful plants that had been collected in the high mountain areas of Kashmir.

Withstanding temperatures below 0°F (-18°C) in a normal growing season, *Salvia hians* makes a mound that measures 2–3 ft (60–90 cm) tall by 2 ft (60 cm) wide. The slightly hairy leaves vary in size and shape, the largest being about 10 in (25 cm) long. Usually lanceolate in shape, with a petiole as long as the blade itself, the leaves appear linear because they are slightly folded in half along the midrib. Deep pea-green in color, the leaves are deciduous in winter, even in a mild climate. Flowering stems are branched and rise well above the foliage. Whorls of only a few dusky violet flowers are airily spaced towards the top of the stem. The calyx is frequently less than 0.5 in (1.3 cm) in length, and though it is small, it is an important adjunct to the flower. It is covered with sticky, glandular hairs and is an unusually dark brown-red color. This rather strange color somehow intensifies the inflated violet flower. The specific epithet, *hians*, means "gaping," referring to the gap between the two lips of the flower.

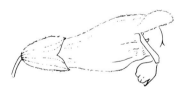

Salvia hians

The dusky violet flowers of *Salvia hians.*
(Robert Kourik)

Salvia hians adapts well to many garden situations. A friable, loamy soil with good drainage is recommended, as is a half to full day of sun and deep watering once each week. Flowering occurs during the summer with repeat bloom where the autumn is long and mild. Propagation is by seed and division. Plantlets (leaves with roots) frequently appear in late summer that can be teased away from the base of the plant.

Salvia hians is known to gardeners on the West Coast of the United States and may be seen at Quarryhill Botanical Garden near Glen Ellen, California, and at the University of California Botanical Garden, Berkeley. It appears with regularity on seed lists. Gardeners in Britain have appreciated this salvia for many years. William Robinson (1933) wrote that it was free in growth and flower. Graham Stuart Thomas (1990a) found its plentiful spikes of purplish blue flowers and purplish brown, hairy calyces an unusual and attractive color scheme.

Well suited for a sunny border, *Salvia hians* combines nicely with many other sun-loving perennials. Planted with groups of the 2 ft (60 cm) tall *Achillea* 'Taygetea', which has pale yellow flowers, it will flower during the same period, and its somewhat long and slender leaf blade will contrast with the achillea's ferny foliage. Included for its eye-catching, pale gray, heart-shaped foliage, *Helichrysum petiolare* will complement the other two plants. Another combination includes the 9 in (22 cm) annual marigold *Tagetes patula* 'Legion of Honour' massed in front of the salvia. The marigold has single, golden yellow flowers with dark brown markings. In the background, the gray-leaved, shrublike *Brachyglottis* 'Sunshine' supplies substance and light. Space permitting, the vertical *Salvia farinacea* 'Victoria' adds another shade of purple and another shape to the picture.

Salvia hierosolymitana
Boissier

Flowering early in spring, *Salvia hierosolymitana* is a perennial herb that is both a handsome addition to the garden and a long-lived plant. Found in the eastern Mediterranean, it has limited habitats in Israel, Palestine, Lebanon, and Syria. Sometimes called Jerusalem sage, it grows in open fields, in rocky soils, and among low-growing native shrubs that would correspond to California's chaparral. This salvia was described in 1853 by the botanist E. Boissier, and the specific epithet, *hierosolymitana*, refers to royal, sacred Jerusalem.

Making a pleasing mound of basal leaves that measure about 2 ft (60 cm) in width but less in height, *Salvia hierosolymitana* tends to be

Blooming in early spring, *Salvia hierosolymitana* has alluring and unusual burgundy flowers. (Ginny Hunt)

evergreen in a mild climate. The ovate leaves are a dull mid-green, lightly covered with hairs, and unevenly scalloped on the margin. The largest measure 8–10 in (20–25 cm) long and have long petioles that are flat on the upper surface and rounded on the underside. There is prominent veining on the underside. Inflorescences are 1 ft (30 cm) in length and usually branched. Alluring and uncommon in color, the wine-red flowers number two to six in whorls that are widely spaced and tend to bloom at the same time. They measure less than 1 in (2.5 cm) long and have a falcate upper lip. The lower lip is splashed white with wine-red spotting, and there are two little appendages attached at the top of the lower lip. Flowers are held in small pea-green calyces that are ribbed with red veins and subtended with pointed, leafy bracts edged in red. Even the square stem of the inflorescence is edged with red. Propagation is generally by seed but even in midsummer there is some cutting material at the base of the plant. Although salvias are generally known for releasing fragrances and odors when the glands are brushed, this salvia is an exception. I can find no reference to it being used medicinally or culinarily where it naturally occurs.

As this is a long-lived plant, you should site this salvia in full sun to partial shade in regular garden soil that is not rich in nutrients and that drains readily. Water it regularly throughout the year. Pruning is not necessary but removal of spent inflorescences will keep the plant looking healthy and tidy. Established plants will bloom in early spring, usually for a period of three to four weeks. In late summer it is not unusual for plants to repeat bloom for a short period, rewarding the gardener who has supplied a minimal amount of watering on a steady basis. It is hardy to the low 20°s F (around -6°C) for short periods.

A small sunny border of plants that require only minimal weekly water might feature the 4–5 ft (1.3–1.5 m) evergreen *Cistus libanotis* from Portugal and Spain. It is early blooming, and at the center of the white-petaled flowers are heavy, golden yellow stamens. You could flank this evergreen with several plants of the *Salvia hierosolymitana*, whose wine-red flowers will provide a good contrast. The native California poppy *Eschscholzia californica*, with its brilliant orange petals, is just the plant to give pizzazz to the composition. To enliven this combination even further, sow poppy seed in the border in late autumn so that all these plants make a bold floral statement welcoming spring. California poppies are accommodating plants that respond well to whatever amount of water might be available.

Salvia hirtella Vahl

A long-blooming perennial herb, *Salvia hirtella* is found in Ecuador, both north and south of the equator, in the province of Cotopaxi. The distribution of *S. hirtella* is limited to high elevations in the Andes Mountains, and collections have been made in the range of 12,000 ft (3600 m). My plants come from seed collected in Valle del Rio Mestizo by Jim and Jenny Archibald in July 1993, which they made available the same year through their enticing seed list.

In my garden *Salvia hirtella* is an evergreen, branching herb that grows just under 2 ft (60 cm) in height. When the weight of its stems and inflorescences bend it to the ground it will root at the node if the soil is loose and friable. It is not unusual for a single plant to cover 3 ft (1 m) in two years. The salvia is very erect in spite of its mat-forming growth habit. The glossy, grass-green, triangular leaves are graduated in size. The average leaf is about 2 in (5 cm) wide at the base and 2 in (5 cm) long. Inflorescences, which are usually about 1 ft (30 cm) in length, are held upright. Richly colored orange-red flowers are 1.5 in (4 cm) long and in verticils of six. Even though a whorl has 12 flowers, only a few bloom at the same time. The calyx and stem of the inflorescence are covered with conspicuous dark purple hairs with glands that enhance the beauty of the plant. The calyces remain after the flowers have bloomed and dropped, giving the plant an additional attractive feature. The specific epithet, *hirtella*, means "rather hairy." Blooming begins in early summer and continues until the days are noticeably shorter.

The long-blooming, evergreen *Salvia hirtella*. (Ginny Hunt)

Place *Salvia hirtella* in the garden where it receives direct sun for a half day but has the protection of surrounding plants. Well-draining, friable soil amended with compost for a good root run is recommended as is deep watering on a weekly basis. Seed is usually produced in small amounts by garden plants and is easy to germinate. Cuttings taken during the active growing season are virtually sure to strike roots. Layering is another means of propagation. *Salvia hirtella* has remained evergreen and unharmed when temperatures have dropped into the high 20°s F (around -2°C) in my garden. Its high elevation habitat implies hardiness to an even lower temperature as well as tolerance of light frosts.

Planted along the edge of a woodland border that receives filtered light, the evergreen *Viburnum japonicum* or *V. cinnamonifolium*, both about 9 ft (3 m) in height, will in time make an impressive background. While the viburnums mature, the blue-flowered *Salvia cacaliifolia* and bright red-flowered *S. hirtella* provide excellent patches of summer color. If there is space, consider adding the evergreen *V. davidii*, which is 3 ft (1 m) tall, and the creeping *S. blepharophylla*, which is 1 ft (30 cm) tall and has orange-red flowers. These three salvias are colonizers and make fine fillers in the border. All plants require high or light shade and regular deep watering.

Salvia holwayi is a useful winter blooming plant. (Christine Andrews)

Salvia holwayi Blake

Throughout Guatemala, *Salvia holwayi* is found at elevations of 3000–9000 ft (900–2800 m). Prevalent at similar elevations in the Mexican province of Chiapas, it frequently makes an understory in thickets and mixed forests of pine and oak. Flowering in abundance in November at the end of the rainy season, it is regarded by Guatemalans as among the most attractive plants of their western highlands. It was named to honor the plant and fungi collector, Edward Willet Dorland Holway of Michigan, who made four collecting trips to Mexico at the turn of the 19th century.

A herbaceous perennial 3–5 ft (1–1.5 m) tall, *Salvia holwayi* grows profusely and will easily cover 8–10 ft (2.5–3 m) in a year. Its long lax stems look beautiful in its native habitat when they grow over and are supported by other shrubs. Many inflorescences are produced along each stem. After the inflorescences expand they measure about 8 in (20 cm) in length, creating a sea of subtle color. Whorls of cardinal-red flowers almost 1 in (2.5 cm) long and inflated in the center are spaced closely together and make a splendid show as large numbers of flowers expand and open at the same time.

SALVIA HOLWAYI

Blooming begins in late autumn or early winter and will usually continue through February and March. Established plants in mild climates bloom earlier and for a longer period. Leaves are yellow-green, deltoid in shape, and have pronounced veining. They vary in size, the average being about 2 in (5 cm) long by 1 in (2.5 cm) wide. The overall effect of the plant is one of luxuriousness.

Some shade, good drainage, and soil enriched with humus are needed for *Salvia holwayi*. Deep watering once every two to three weeks is advisable. If temperatures dip below 20°F (-7°C) much of the top growth may be damaged, but the plant will come back from its strong roots, possibly because the heavy top growth protects the base of the plant. After the blooming season is over and the danger of frost is past, prune the plant hard in order to keep it in bounds during the coming growing season. It is vigorous, and 8–10 ft (2.5–3 m) of growth each summer is usual for a mature plant.

After *Salvia holwayi* becomes well established, you may find small plants under or near it that are the result of adventitious roots. These plants may be removed and shared with other gardeners. Layering also frequently occurs when a lax stem becomes covered with soil. This promotes rooting at the nodes. Both forms of propagation produce desirable offspring. Cuttings taken in summer root quite readily. This salvia's rampant growth during each season necessitates the removal of additional plants.

Here is a wonderful winter-blooming plant with many uses. *Salvia holwayi* will camouflage fences that are 5–6 ft (1.5–2 m) high and hide unsightly rough and weedy places. It makes a fine background for other plants when placed at the back of the border with something it can climb. Flowering stems hold well in flower arrangements and are handsome in winter bouquets. Hummingbirds find its nectar a fine food source at the time of year when little food is available.

Salvia indica Linnaeus

An early-flowering and dramatic plant in the garden, *Salvia indica* has a wide native habitat that includes Palestine, Iraq, Iran, and Turkey but not, surprisingly, India. The specific epithet, *indica*, indicates that the species is from India but this is not the case, and it is unclear why Linnaeus gave it that epithet when he described and named the plant in 1753. Classified as a perennial herb, *S. indica* in the wild tends to grow on rocky limestone slopes between 350 and 5000 ft (100 and 1500 m) and shows a preference for sharp drainage.

Sow seeds of *Salvia indica* in late summer to ensure this unusual salvia will bloom in the spring border. (Ginny Hunt)

Both erect and stately, *Salvia indica* forms a beautiful clump of broadly ovate, egg-shaped leaves that have a scalloped and wavy edge. They are a rich, grassy green color and covered with long, soft, straight hairs. Blooming begins in spring, and one or more flowering stems 2–4 ft (60–120 cm) long rise from the center of the plant. Four to six flowers are in widely spaced whorls that open slowly to show the unique two-lipped flower. The upper lip is falcate and a shiny bright lilac color. It is about 1 in (2.5 cm) in length. The short and stubby lower lip forms a central trough that has purple and brown spots on a white background. Each flower is held in a calyx that is viscid and densely glandular. Buds of flowers begin to emerge as soon as the flowering stem starts its upward growth, and plants tend to stay in bloom for a long period, almost a month. Although it is classified as a perennial it is short-lived, frequently lasting for a mere two years. It will bloom its first spring if seed is sown in August or September. Seeds are the customary means of propagation, and it is not unusual to find seedlings near the mother plant.

Easy to situate in the garden, this salvia prefers full sun, good garden loam, and fast drainage. If there is only a little spring sunshine the plant will take longer to come into bloom. After seed has matured and been gathered, remove the flowering stalk to give the plant a rest period until the following spring. Plants require very little water during this dormant period. *Salvia indica* tends to be short-lived so I try to always have a few new plants each season. Tolerant of light frost, it can survive temperatures in the 20°s F (around -6°C) for brief periods.

For many years the familiarly known ornamental, Japanese, or flowering quince, *Chaenomeles*, has been the star of the early flowering spring border.

Kerria too has been a favored early blooming shrub since Victorian days. A large border combining these excellent shrubs would be enhanced when inter-planted with *Salvia indica*. Plants you could choose for the background include C. 'Nivalis', a 6 ft (2 m) tall, white-flowering shrub, and C. 'Enchantress', which is the same size but with shell-pink flowers. You could also plant the arching, 8 ft (2.5 m) tall *K. japonica* with single or double yellow flowers or single orange or white flowers. *Kerria japonica* can be sighted at the end of the border, and the spaces in between the shrubs filled with plants of *S. indica*. Both shrubs should be pruned after they flower. With the promise of flowering bulbs and trees still to come, an area such as this will cheer the gardener through unpre-dictable spring weather.

Salvia 'Indigo Spires'

Rapidly growing into a large shrub 4 ft (1.3 m) tall and equally as wide, *Salvia* 'Indigo Spires' is a spontaneous garden hybrid. It was found growing near *S. longispicata* and *S. farinacea* at the Huntington Botanical Gardens by the hor-ticulturist John MacGregor and was introduced to gardeners in 1979. MacGregor refers to this chance seedling as a "sterile hybrid, courtesy of the bees." (pers. comm.).

Blooming begins in early summer and continues until frost. The long, 10–12 in (25–30 cm) inflorescence is spikelike and crowded with rich violet flowers. Individual flowers are small, 0.5 in (1.3 cm) in length, closely spaced together in whorls, and a fine violet-blue color that does not fade in the hot summer sunlight. The upper lip has two very narrow white beelines leading insects to nectar, and the lower lip is covered with small violet-blue hairs. The 0.5 in (1.3 cm) long calyx is dark purple and remains intact on its violet stem after the flowers have dropped. The mid-green leaves appear slick and are pri-marily ovate and widely spaced along the branches. The margins are serrated and dark.

Full sun and fast-draining soil enriched with humus are essential for this salvia, which develops and blooms for such a long period. Deep weekly water is advisable too. Pinching and pruning throughout the growing season is vital in order to keep the plant shapely. Be sure to remove inflorescences when most of the flowers have dropped. This kind of grooming will take excess weight off the shrub and encourage repeated flowering. Propagation is by cuttings.

Salvia 'Indigo Spires' is a long-blooming and reliable border plant. *Stipa ramosissima* is on the right. (Ginny Hunt)

Probably hardy to the mid-20°s F (around -4°C), *Salvia* 'Indigo Spires' slowly came back from its rootstock when temperatures in my garden dipped to 11°F (-12°C) one December. It is wise to have cuttings in the greenhouse in case of a sudden drop in temperature. After all danger of frost has passed, prune the shrub heavily. When the earth has been warmed by the sun in late spring, a thick, 2–4 in (5–10 cm) mulch of humus at the base of the plant will provide food and help prevent water evaporation.

To take advantage of a salvia that blooms continually, plant *Salvia* 'Indigo Spires' in a herbaceous border designed for leaf texture and summer bloom. The back of the border might include several plants of 'Indigo Spires' inter-planted with a few *Gaura lindheimeri*, the graceful white and pink, 3–4 ft (1–1.3 m) tall Louisiana and Texas native. In front, drifts of *Artemisia absinthium* 'Lambrook Silver', which has silver-gray foliage, and the pink-flowered soap-wort, *Saponaria ocymoides* 'Splendens', would round out the composition. All require the same culture, including similar amounts of water. For a cottage gar-den border, plant over-wintered cuttings of 'Indigo Spires' in the background with masses of annuals in the foreground. In situ, sow seed of cosmos, cleome, zinnia, and *Salvia viridis*. All these annuals are more or less the same size and will develop concurrently. At any stage of growth, unwanted seedlings may be easily thinned.

SALVIA 'INDIGO SPIRES'

Salvia interrupta Schousboe

A perennial with some wood at the base, *Salvia interrupta* occurs throughout the range of the Atlas Mountains in Morocco. When in bloom, it is a dignified and beautiful plant. It grows at elevations of 1300–5000 ft (400–1500 m) on rock-covered limestone slopes and in lightly shaded forests. Described botanically in 1801, it was introduced to horticulture before 1870 and has become a favorite of gardeners on both sides of the Atlantic since the 1970s.

Salvia interrupta appears to grow in a basal rosette. It has apple-green leaves of varying sizes that are covered with short white hairs on the under-side. The leaf is three lobed, and the lobes can be situated at different angles at the base of the leaf. Flower-

Salvia interrupta blooms throughout the summer and will continue to throw flowering stalks in a mild autumn. It has handsome divided leaves. (David Madison)

ing is usually in late spring or early summer and frequently repeats quite heavily in October. At that time, the flowering stalk elongates approximately 2 ft (60 cm). Verticils of five to ten flowers are held on small stems called peduncles and are widely spaced along the stalk. This spacing is the reason for the plant's specific name, *interrupta*, and contributes to the plant's elegance. Large, fat, violet flowers, slightly less than 1.5 in (4 cm) long, come into bloom a few at a time. The lower lip of the flower is wide, and in its center are two distinct white lines that lead insects to pollen and nectar glands. Flowering stalks last well as cut

flowers if first conditioned by being cut under water. Interestingly, the stalks of this salvia are square when they are young, but with age they become round. At maturity they have two distinct, dark purple-brown lines that run the length of the stalk. This salvia is sometimes confused with *S.*

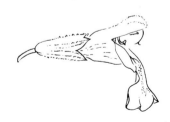

Salvia interrupta

Salvia interrupta

candelabrum from Spain because the inflorescences are similar. The leaves of *S. candelabrum*, however, are not divided. *Salvia ringens* too can be confused with *S. interrupta* as they look alike in the garden. However, *S. ringens* has longer petioles and repeats bloom more frequently.

Salvia interrupta thrives best in full sun but will survive with less direct light. Loamy, friable soil that has good drainage is necessary, and a small handful of ground oyster shells worked thoroughly into the soil when preparing a place for each plant is desirable. Fertilizer is not required but I recommend a deep weekly watering. This salvia is a tender plant and will probably not survive temperatures that fall below 25°F (-4°C) for long periods. It is a short-lived perennial that should be replaced every third year. Propagation is usually by seed, although cuttings can be taken.

Though described by William Robinson (1933) as among the most beautiful border plants, *Salvia interrupta* is difficult to place in a herbaceous border because its tall and dramatic flowering stalks tend to get lost in a sea of flowers and leaves. Since its tidy foliage stays in a loose and low mound, it can be planted at the front of a border. Matting ground cover, such as the silver-leaved *Achillea ageratifolia* with its white flowers, allows a good view of the salvia. For background, the rich, green-leaved sweet nancy, *A. ageratum* 'W. G. Childs', with its large flat heads of white flowers is a substantial but not a fussy possibility. This grouping can be planted alone or alongside other combinations. All plants flower at more or less the same time and require the same simple cultural conditions. As a single specimen in a large pot, *S. interrupta* makes a dramatic presence when in bloom. Sunny garden steps and a sun-filled terrace provide an appropriate and striking setting for pots or containers during the full month the salvia blooms.

Salvia involucrata Cavanilles
roseleaf sage

A perennial herb that builds some wood at its base, *Salvia involucrata* is not usually deciduous in a mild climate. Sometimes called roseleaf sage, the common name refers to the specific epithet, *involucrata*, which means "having an involucre." Involucre is a botanical term for bracts—those leafy parts that are situated under the flowers. In this case, the involucres that surround the flowers are large and colorful, and they contribute greatly to the plant's charm and attractiveness. Roseleaf sage has been collected in its native habitat in at least

The rich and deeply colored flowers of *Salvia involucrata* 'El Cielo' in autumn. (Christine Andrews)

three Mexican provinces, Puebla, Tamaulipas, and Veracruz. It usually establishes itself in shady places, such as the edges of forests.

Growing consistently throughout the late spring and early summer, *Salvia involucrata* will reach 5 ft (1.5 m) or more before it starts blooming in late summer. Both the flowers and bracts are a beetroot color. The colorful bracts occur in pairs and usually envelop three flowers. As the flowers expand, the bracts fall away. The leaves are a flat mid-green, and the petiole and veins reflect the beetroot color of the flowers and bracts. Flower stems hold well in arrangements.

Individual plants of *Salvia involucrata* that merit attention have been collected in the wild, and after evaluation have been given cultivar names. For example, 'Bethellii', introduced in 1881, was praised for having a compact habit and large ovate, cordate leaves. 'Deschampsiana' was selected in 1869 for the bright rose color of its inflated flowers. These cultivars are more common in France and Britain than in the United States, where nurseries seldom include them on their lists. Other selections of roseleaf sage that have been made in the wild for hardiness and flower color are being distributed in the United States. These particular selections usually carry the name of the place in Mexico where the cultivar was collected: 'Hidalgo', 'El Butano', and 'El Cielo' are three examples.

Salvia involucrata is known for its propensity to cross freely with other *Salvia* species, and hybrids have occurred at the University of California Botanical Garden, Berkeley. These plants show hybrid vigor, attaining approximately 6 ft (2 m) in height, and have a long blooming period. They are being evaluated as garden subjects. In the summer of 1991, a 4 ft (1.3 m) tall spontaneous hybrid of *S. involucrata* bloomed in my garden. Smaller in stature than the species, this hybrid is well suited for a small garden. The plant holds itself upright because its stems are thin and woody. A well-behaved and handsome addition to the summer and autumn borders, it was introduced in the fall of 1995 as 'Mulberry Jam'.

Roseleaf sage performs best when given good drainage, humus-enriched soil, half to three-quarters of a day of

'Mulberry Jam' is a hybrid of *Salvia involucrata* that has an upright habit and is in continuous bloom from summer to frost. (Christine Andrews)

sun, and deep watering at least once a week. Half-strength liquid fertilizer given every two weeks when the plant starts making active growth is often helpful. Flowering begins in mid- to late summer and continues until frost. If you remove old inflorescences throughout the blooming season, the tall flowering stems will stay erect. Propagation is by division of the rootstock or by cuttings. Cuttings taken in late summer or early autumn will strike roots rapidly. In my garden roseleaf sage has come back from its rootstock after light freezes of 25°F (-4°C). In early spring, cut the plant back to active nodes a few inches above the crown.

Salvia involucrata or one of its cultivars planted with a tall clumping grass such as *Miscanthus sinensis* 'Condensatus', a purple-blooming Japanese silver grass that is dark green through the growing season and a reddish purple in autumn, makes a very dramatic combination. Roseleaf sage benefits from the protection of other plants and, due to its stature, combines well with roses. The threesome of *S. involucrata* planted between the old-fashioned, pink-flowered tea rose 'Duchesse de Brabant' and the white sport of that rose, 'Mrs. Joseph Schwartz', gives pleasure in summer and autumn. Consider the new hybrid musk 'Ballerina', which is of medium size and repeats bloom almost without pause, as an additional companion.

Salvia iodantha Fernald

Generally found in the mountainous region of central Mexico, *Salvia iodantha* usually grows at altitudes of 2600–10,500 ft (800–3200 m). Even at such high altitudes, these mountains rarely experience low temperatures. *Salvia iodantha* has a wide distribution and occurs in seven or more provinces.

Described by Fernald in 1900, *Salvia iodantha* has come to the attention of gardeners only since the 1980s. Mature plants may be seen at Strybing Arboretum, the University of California Botanical Garden, Berkeley, and the Arboretum at the University of California at Santa Cruz. Conejo Valley Botanic Garden in Thousand Oaks, California, also has a large salvia collection where *S. iodantha* flourishes.

A herbaceous perennial, *Salvia iodantha* grows robustly to 10 ft (3 m) or more in height and 6 ft (2 m) or so in width. It tends to be scandent, and I have seen it supported by a deciduous tree with its flowering branches hanging from the tree's limbs in the late winter and early spring. Many branches rise from the base and are covered with mistletoe-green leaves that are ovate or lanceolate in shape. Leaves can vary greatly in size as well as shape; the average is 2–3 in (5–8 cm) long by 1–1.5 in (2.5–4 cm) wide. The cyclamen-purple flowers have a velvety appearance due to the many small hairs that closely cover them. As the flowers are less than 1 in (2.5 cm) long, it is their quantity that makes the colorful, 6 in (15 cm) long inflorescence so showy. The flowers, which are tightly packed in whorls, sometimes number as many as 12. The whorls too are tightly packed on short inflorescences. Flowering begins in autumn with peak bloom coming during a mild, sunny spell in December or January.

In my own garden this salvia tends to be shrublike and around 5–6 ft (1.5–2 m) tall. Even in a mild winter it seldom flowers. Though it can survive temperatures in the 20°s F (around -6°C), low temperatures most certainly prohibit flowering. In a warmer area where frost never or seldom occurs, the plant becomes scandent, and many racemes of vivid flowers are produced over a long period.

A position sheltered from cool air and wind is essential in siting this salvia. Sun for at least half the day throughout the year and a deep weekly watering are

A spectacular winter-blooming plant, *Salvia iodantha* is scandent and floriferous in a mild climate. (Sonja Wilcomer)

vital. It should be planted in good garden soil with fast drainage, and you can add humus each summer to keep the root-run of this salvia friable and cool. Propagation is by cuttings.

In a benign climate, *Salvia iodantha* can be the focal point of a subtle winter garden. Place it to grow on a wall or into a tree, and on either side of the salvia plant an early winter-blooming *Arctostaphylos stanfordiana* subsp. *bakeri* 'Louis Edmunds'. Clusters of urn-shaped, pink flowers remain attractively displayed against the manzanita's purple-brown trunk for over a month. Another combination of plants features *S. iodantha* grown as a shrub with the 3 ft (1 m) tall, evergreen *Ceanothus maritimus* 'Roger's Dark'. This wild lilac has textured leaves and clusters of violet-blue flowers that persist for about a month. The blooming periods of all three plants overlap. Both the manzanita and the wild lilac, though they are native California plants, will tolerate occasional summer water.

Salvia ×jamensis Compton

A hybrid swarm of colorful salvias from Mexico, *Salvia ×jamensis*, was described by the English botanist James Compton (1994a) in the early 1990s.

Naturally occurring selections of *Salvia* ×*jamensis* collected from the wild. In the foreground is the pale yellow 'Cienega de Oro', with the peach and yellow 'Sierra San Antonio' in the background. (Robert Kourik)

Collected in 1991 near the village of Jame in the province of Coahuila, *S.* ×*jamensis* grows in the Sierra Madre Oriental at elevations of 6500–9800 ft (2000–3000 m). Plants also occur in the adjoining provinces of Nuevo León and San Luis Potosí.

The parents of these hybrid salvias are *Salvia greggii* and *S. microphylla*, and the hybrids are found where the habitats of the two parent species coincide. Usually *S. greggii* grows in more open and sunnier spots than *S. microphylla*. At the collection site, a bank alongside a road furnishes the shade and exposure that *S. microphylla* requires, while the more open habitat preferred by *S. greggii* is close by.

Salvia ×*jamensis* is a shrub, usually under 3 ft (1 m) in height and width. Some plants are more rounded in shape than others. Small, glossy green, ovate leaves, usually less than 1 in (2.5 cm) long, lightly cover the shrub. The corollas vary in size and color, as do the calyces. Flowers may be found in many shades of red, rose, rose-pink, orange, salmon, or pale yellow, and some are bicolored.

Easy to grow in a climate with low humidity, *Salvia* ×*jamensis* requires full sun, good drainage, friable garden soil, and deep weekly water. Plants will tolerate overhead irrigation. Temperatures in my garden have not fallen below 20°F (-7°C) in the years that I have been growing these plants, but I suspect that because of their high altitude habitat, established plants would probably survive a lower temperature for a short period. Flowering begins in early summer and continues until frost. Some pruning is needed throughout the growing season in order to promote repeat bloom. In early spring, remove old wood and shape the plant to a compact form. Propagation is by seed or cuttings. Seedlings germinate around these hybrids throughout the growing season—a few resemble the parent plant, whereas others introduce flowers of different colors.

In 1988, Yucca Do Nursery found plants of what is now known as *Salvia* ×*jamensis* in the wild. Selections were made and introduced in their 1991 catalog as 'Cienega de Oro', which is pale yellow; 'Sierra San Antonio', which is peach-rose with a yellow lower lip; and 'San Isidro Moon', which is pale creamy pink with a dark purple calyx. These cultivars are popular on the West Coast. Many seedling cultivars are available in England, such as the peach-flowered 'El Duranzo' and 'La Luna', which is creamy yellow with the upper lip covered with reddish brown hairs.

A sunny south- or west-facing slope can be filled with these long-blooming and well-shaped small shrubs. Their delicate colors combine beautifully with one another and with other plants. Dot one or two dasylirions or yuccas among the salvias for a sharp contrast in habit and foliage. Another plant that complements these colorful salvias is *Carex buchananii*, brown sedge. About 2 ft (60 cm) or a little more in height, its very narrow, glossy, light brown leaves grow in delicate arches. All respond well to the same culture.

Salvia jurisicii Košanin

Salvia jurisicii is a petite herbaceous perennial whose native habitat includes the southern regions of the former Yugoslavia, Bulgaria, and Albania. Its high mountainous home is reflected in its hardiness to 0°F (-18°C).

Small and compact with pinnate leaves that have linear segments, *Salvia jurisicii* grows about 1 ft (30 cm) tall and wide. Reported to develop into a 2 ft (60 cm) tall plant, it has never attained this height in my garden. The pinnate leaves are much branched, and the hairs on the back of each rib and vein give the leaf a frothy effect. Olive-green in color, the leaves are eye-catching whether the plant is in bloom or not. Flowers appear in whorls that are closely spaced and turned upside down. They are small, usually 0.5 in (1.3 cm) in length, and covered with hairs. Flower color is variable but in the violet range. A white-flowered form, 'Alba', comes true from seed.

Easy to grow, *Salvia jurisicii* needs sun for half a day at the very least, good drainage, soil enriched with humus, and weekly water. Propagation is usually by seed but

Salvia jurisicii

The small upside-down flowers of *Salvia jurisicii* are clearly visible on a white-flowered form. (Robert Kourik)

cuttings will strike roots. Seedlings appear sporadically in the garden near the mother plant.

Salvia jurisicii is one of very few salvias that are appropriate for rock gardens since it is small, compact, and hardy. Plants with these characteristics are often sought for rock gardens or other small or contained areas. Well known to European gardeners, this salvia remains evergreen in a mild climate and also has a delightful appearance. *Salvia jurisicii* can be observed more easily in a bed that is raised because it is so small. A group of plants chosen for complimentary foliage texture includes the silky, tufted, low-growing *Achillea clavenae*, which has gray leaves and white flowers. *Artemisia schmidtiana* 'Nana' adds gray-white foliage with linear leaves, and *Geranium sanguineum* 'Minutum' has small dark green leaves and, unexpectedly, tiny magenta flowers. All plants are either smaller than a *S. jurisicii* specimen or in proportion to it. This salvia also makes a very good container plant.

Salvia karwinskii Bentham
Karwinski's sage

From moist mountain forests in southern Mexico, Guatemala, El Salvador, Honduras, and Nicaragua comes *Salvia karwinskii*. Grown as a garden plant throughout its native habitat, *S. karwinskii* is a stout, winter-blooming shrub that is found in abundance in the wild, usually in or near oak or pine forests at 4000–8000 ft (1200–2500 m). As a garden plant in its native habitat it is known as a honey producing plant. Rarely seen in private gardens, specimens may be seen at Strybing Arboretum, the University of California Botanical Garden, Berkeley, and Huntington Botanical Gardens.

A tall shrub with handsome foliage and form, *Salvia karwinskii* blooms prodigiously in winter. (Christine Andrews)

In mild California gardens during a long growing period, *Salvia karwinskii* usually attains 8 ft (2.5 m) in height and 4 ft (1.3 m) in width. In the wild it reaches anywhere from 3 to 12 ft (1 to 4 m). Sometimes Karwinski's sage comes into bloom before Christmas, developing a few short inflorescences. In January these elongate, and by February the shrub carries many 15 in (37 cm) racemes of brick-red, rose-red, or scarlet flowers. The two-lipped flower is inflated and about 1 in (2.5 cm) long. It is held in a long, showy, dark red, 0.5 in (1.3 cm) calyx. The stems and petioles of the leaves are covered with short woolly hairs, giving them a grayish appearance. The evergreen leaves are large, often 6 in (15 cm) long, and look rough on the surface. On the underside, the veining is prominent and covered with light, cream-colored hairs.

It is a good idea to remove some of this sage's flowering branches or to shorten them periodically because of its luxuriant growth. Branches of flowers hold well in flower arrangements if they are conditioned by cutting the stems under water. To encourage a more upright and compact habit, prune the shrub almost to the ground as it nears the end of its flowering period once the danger of frost has passed. April or May is the usual pruning time in the San Francisco Bay area. Propagation is usually by cuttings taken at this time, and rooting is rapid. *Salvia karwinskii* will produce viable seed, though pruning of course precludes it. This salvia is known to hybridize with other Mexican autumn-flowering salvias in the Berkeley, California, area.

A warm protected spot in the garden is a necessity for Karwinski's sage. Be sure it receives full sun in winter. Over the years I have noticed that it flowers more profusely in mild winters but on quite a few occasions it has withstood temperatures in the low 20°s F (around -6°C) and still produced a few flowers. A rooted cutting in the greenhouse is wise insurance against low temperatures.

Salvia karwinskii is a plant that, because of its uncommon blooming period, depends heavily on the background to provide protection and enhance its appearance. A south-facing wall or hedge is therefore an ideal location. A green hedge would certainly highlight its unusual reddish flowers. At the base of the salvia, a carpet of the dark green foliage of *Iberis sempervirens* 'Purity' would complete the composition. This perennial candytuft, with its sea of white flowers, blooms in very early spring, often at the same time as the salvia. A large and sunny shrub border of winter-blooming plants could feature *S. karwinskii* and *Chimonanthus praecox*, the fragrant and beloved wintersweet. Supposedly deciduous, wintersweet's tattered leaves sometimes refuse to drop, obscuring its pale yellow flowers. They can easily be removed, however. Undisturbed shrub areas are excellent places to establish drifts of bulbs. *Narcissus jonquilla*, known and prized as a winter cut flower, could be established between the large shrubs.

Salvia koyamae Makino
shinano-akigiri

Rarely found in the wild, *Salvia koyamae* comes from a limited habitat on the largest island of Japan, Honshu. It has affinities with two other salvias that occur on Honshu, *S. glabrescens* and *S. nipponica.*

Beautiful in both leaf and flower, *Salvia koyamae* has trailing stems that weave gracefully between other plants. (Christine Andrews)

A lax perennial with decumbent stems sometimes reaching 2 ft (60 cm) or more, *Salvia koyamae* appears to creep through beds or borders, forming a loose ground cover. Roughly 1 ft (30 cm) tall, this salvia has large cordate leaves. They measure 6 in (15 cm) in length and 5 in (13 cm) in width and have a 5 in (13 cm) long petiole. Yellow-green in color, the leaves are lightly covered with fine hairs. Whorls of pale yellow flowers are spaced along an inflorescence that sometimes reaches almost 1 ft (30 cm) in length but is usually half that. Blooming occurs in late summer and autumn. There are so few flowers in bloom at a given time the plant seldom commands attention; however, the heart-shaped leaves are luscious looking and a perfect foil for the subtle, pale yellow flowers. Leaves and flowers are attractive in bouquets.

Easy to grow, *Salvia koyamae* needs deep, rich soil, good drainage,

Salvia koyamae

shade, and a generous supply of water. When well established, this sage will climb through shrubs and between low-growing plants, easily filling a woodland border with handsome leaves. Propagation is by seed or cuttings taken after active spring growth or in late summer.

Sometime around 1990 *Salvia koyamae* was grown at the University of California Botanical Garden, Berkeley, and subsequently introduced to gardeners. At about that time its name appeared in nursery catalogs. In my garden it certainly withstands short periods of light freezes.

Here is a plant that can easily be tucked into an existing shaded border. In time it will weave itself through and around established plants, making a handsome cover throughout the growing season. Leaves tend to be evergreen in a mild climate. In a new border with filtered light, the 5 ft (1.5 m) tall, semievergreen *Viburnum* 'Anne Russell', combined with clumps of the 4 ft (1.3 m) tall *Miscanthus sinensis* 'Morning Light', which has a narrow band of white on the leaf margins, make a splendid pair. *Salvia koyamae* weaving around these two taller plants unifies the composition.

Salvia lanceolata Lamarck

In its native habitat in South Africa, *Salvia lanceolata* is confined to a small area along the coast of the Cape of Good Hope. Found at sea level on sandy ground, this salvia may also be observed on dry hills and flat areas up to 1000 ft (400 m). First described and named *lanceolata* in 1791 by the famous French botanist Jean Baptiste Lamarck, whose brilliant theory of evolution has long since been discarded, this salvia was well known by the epithet *nivea*. Between 1772 and 1775, the Swedish botanist Carl Peter Thunberg was in South Africa, where he was delayed from reaching his destination of Japan. While there he collected 3000 plants that he later described. It was in 1800 that he gave the name *nivea* to the salvia we know as *lanceolata*. Thunberg named the salvia to honor James Niven, a Scottish gardener who collected plants in South Africa. According to the botanical rules of nomenclature, Lamarck's name of *lanceolata* takes precedence.

Good-looking and precisely named, *Salvia lanceolata* is a handsome addition to our gardens. Described as a much-branched shrub, it stands 3 ft (1 m) high and is 2–4 ft (60–120 cm) wide, which are about the same dimensions that it attains in the wild. The stems appear rounded, and as they age they become

A water-conserving plant with gray foliage, *Salvia lanceolata* is a handsome addition to the dry border. (Ginny Hunt)

quite woody and light tan. Lanceolate, evergreen leaves lightly clothe the shrub. Some leaves have a short petiole and others have none, but all are thick textured and dove gray with a green undertone. In South Africa the leaves are used in cooking, particularly with fish. When crushed, the oil globules release a light odor reminiscent of lemon pepper. The calyx is just over 0.5 in (1.3 cm) long when in flower. After the flower is fertilized and the seeds begin to develop, the calyx turns pink and expands to more than 1 in (2.5 cm) in length. The flowers are 1.5 in (4 cm) long and an unusual but attractive, dull, rosy brownish color. There are never many flowers in bloom at any one time although there is a long blooming period from May through November.

This is another salvia from South Africa that is well behaved and quite easy to grow in a garden. Given full sun, good drainage, and soil that is not rich with nutrients, *Salvia lanceolata* is a stalwart in the border. Little pruning is needed to keep its attractive upright shape because its growth is modest. Weekly water is required, though more is recommended during hot spells. Some of my plants are out of reach of the watering system, and because they receive very little water they just idle, maintaining life but nothing more. Temperatures that dip

Salvia lanceolata

into the mid-20°s F (around -4°C) for a few hours cause this salvia no problems. *Salvia lanceolata* produces some seed but the usual method of propagation is by cuttings taken in late summer. It is also possible to tease away a rooted stem from the plant. By safely tucking away rooted cuttings in the greenhouse you will insure a plant for the garden if winter temperatures fall into the teens (-10°C).

A south- or west-facing border that is designed for interesting year-round foliage might feature the evergreen *Acacia boormanii*, which reaches about 9 ft (3 m) in height and width, at one end. Sweet-scented, globular yellow flowers come into bloom in early spring. To balance the height of the *A. boormanii*, place the huge perennial cardoon, *Cynara cardunculus*, with its silvery-gray, architectural leaves at the other end of this bold border. In between these two spectacular plants, fill the area with the upright *Salvia lanceolata* and the low-mounding perennial *Ballota pseudodictamnus*. All require good drainage, plenty of sunlight, and, because they are water-thrifty plants, irrigation on a weekly basis.

Salvia lanigera Poiret

A remarkable plant for several different reasons, *Salvia lanigera* is a small herbaceous perennial whose unique and unusual appearance immediately catches one's attention. Its specific name, *lanigera*, is from Latin meaning "wool-bearing" or "fleecy" and refers to the hairs found on all parts of the plant. Although this salvia was described botanically by Jean Louis Marie Poiret in 1817, I doubt it has been grown in gardens in California until 1998. Its native habitat ranges from northern Egypt and Arabia to the south of Turkey and Iran, where it grows in low altitude desert regions that are on sandy loam or chalky sandstone. I was very surprised to find that this plant, being of hot and dry regions, self-seeds in the clay soil of my frequently fog-filled garden.

A small salvia that in my garden varies in height from 4 to 8 in (10 to 20 cm), *Salvia lanigera* is reported to reach 1 ft (30 cm) in its native habitat. The entire plant is a soft, pale gray-green, and when brushed it has a pleasant, pungent odor. It is also completely covered with short, erect hairs that make the plant appear radiant. The leaves are quite narrow and are deeply divided with linear segments. Violet flowers, which are held in a tiny calyx that is covered with long white hairs, are in whorls of six to eight. The flowers are so small that I must remove one from the plant in order to see it. The entire growth cycle of this plant is rapid, and because the flowers are difficult to see it is a challenge to know when the calyces dry and it is time to collect seed. More often than not I find the plant has dispersed its seed and that seedlings have germinated near the mother plant in a very short time. Even though the plant is classified as a perennial it has never lived through the winter in my garden. Its seed apparently over-winters in the ground since seedlings appear in spring after the weather moderates and the soil has warmed.

Appearing frosty and radiant, *Salvia lanigera* performs best when treated as an annual. (Sonja Wilcomer)

Treated as an annual, *Salvia lanigera* is a delightful, ephemeral plant that will adapt itself to small spaces in among other perennials. Requirements for a healthy, seed-producing plant are full sun, lean soil, moderate irrigation, and good drainage. Conversely, to keep the plant a perennial, you must deadhead its inflorescences. This salvia's proclivity to grow and produce seed rapidly means that you can encourage such traits by placing them in a border where it will seed itself freely. Begin with seeds that are sown in situ among already established small plants such as pansies and violas. Many low-growing and mat-forming achilleas would make appropriate companions: *Achillea ageratifolia*, with leaves in rosettes, *A. clavenae*, which is tufted and has frosty white

Salvia lanigera

foliage, and *A. tomentosa*, with gray-green matting foliage and bright gold flowers. Erodiums too would make fine companions. Once the salvia seeds have germinated and the plants have begun to grow, make sure the companion plants do not crowd or make shadows on the salvias. All the companion plants I suggest require the same cultural conditions as *S. lanigera*.

Salvia lavandulifolia Vahl
Spanish sage

A small woody-based herbaceous plant with gray-white foliage, *Salvia lavandulifolia* is native to central, southern, and eastern Spain, extending into southern France. It is well known for succeeding on rocky soil, where it is frequently found growing with rosemary, *Lavandula lanata*, and *Genista cinerea* in a habitat that is dry in summer and wet in winter. This kind of habitat in California is referred to as chaparral. Seldom seen in gardens in America, gardeners in England discovered the salvia's charm many years ago. Harold Bawden wrote in the 1970s that it "is most desirable for its low carpet of grey downy leaves."

Usually 1.5 ft (45 cm) in height and width, Spanish sage is more or less reclining in habit. The narrow, whitish gray, lanceolate leaves, less than 2 in (5 cm) long, are evergreen. They are arranged opposite one another along the stem and appear to be in bunches. The leaves are small, which gives the plant an airy appearance. When rubbed, the oils in the leaves release a scent similar to rosemary. These oils are of economic value and are used to scent soaps. Flowering for about one month in late spring and early summer, *Salvia lavandulifolia* has many short inflorescences of pale, rather washed-out lavender-blue flowers that are less than 1 in (2.5 cm) long. These leafless flowering stems have but a very few flowers in widely spaced whorls. Clones with a dark calyx are frequently found. Propagation is by cuttings taken either before or after flowering, or by seed.

Full sun, friable clay soil with fast drainage, and good air circulation are the cultural needs of Spanish sage. Occasional deep watering throughout the summer is advisable. Given perfect drainage, this salvia has successfully weathered over 60 in (1.5 m) of rain in my garden in an El Niño winter. In areas of high humidity and heat, this salvia seldom succeeds. However, it is tolerant of temperatures as low as 20°F (-7°C), possibly to 10°F (-12°C).

The preceding description of *Salvia lavandulifolia* might lead one to think the salvia uninteresting, even dull, but that is not the case. When this plant comes into bloom, insects and hummingbirds immediately find its nectar. Its leaves alone create texture and sparkle in areas of the garden that are hot and dry. In a dry and difficult border that is filled with plants with rich green foliage, such as rosemary and myrtle, the whitish gray leaves of Spanish sage planted in groups will lighten the foreground. In a rock-filled, sunny border, its ability to fit into nooks and crannies because of its reclining habit is a great advantage in filling a difficult site. I always look forward to its long period of flowering as spring warms and slowly turns into summer.

Salvia leucantha Cavanilles
Mexican bush sage

Reported to occur in tropical and subtropical conifer forests in central and eastern Mexico, *Salvia leucantha* is a small shrub or herbaceous perennial. It grows about 4 ft (1.3 m) tall in a season and develops many flowering stems from its rootstock. In several years the plant may quickly spread from 3 ft to 6 ft (1 m to 2 m) in width.

The linear-lanceolate leaves of *Salvia leucantha* are a soft mid-green with a grayish cast. The underside is white and hairy, making the leaves very attractive. The inflorescence, which is 6–12 in (15–30 cm) in length, extends well beyond the foliage. Individual flowers are white and project from a purple calyx. They are arranged in whorls, and many come into bloom at the same time. Fine hairs covering both flower and calyx give the look and feel of velvet. The specific epithet, *leucantha*, means "white flowered." Flowering begins in summer and continues until frost.

Salvia leucantha

To promote flowering, remove inflorescences as they show signs of fading. This procedure takes excess weight off the tops of stems and allows the extension of more inflorescences. Deadheading of this kind, practiced throughout

Salvia leucantha 'Midnight', a purple-flowered form of the species. (Ginny Hunt)

the long flowering period, will enable the plant to stay more upright. Both flowers and leaves are useful in flower arrangements. When dried, the flowers and calyces retain their color.

Mexican bush sage prefers full sun, ordinary garden soil, good drainage, and infrequent water during the summer. It has proved to be cold tolerant to about 25°F (-4°C). Prune it to the ground in late February or early March. This is also a good time to remove excess rooted stems for gardening friends. In cultivation since 1846, *Salvia leucantha* has probably been shared more frequently than it has been purchased because of its ease of propagation and prolific flower display. It is commonly grown in the United States, Britain, and mainland Europe.

One form of *Salvia leucantha* has deep violet flowers and calyces. It differs from the typical form only in the different violet color of the flowers. It is quite common in cultivation and can be seen in gardens and nurseries in California and Arizona. For a number of years it has been listed in catalogs as *S. leucantha* 'Midnight'.

In early 1999, a compact form of *Salvia leucantha* came to the attention of Randy Baldwin of San Marcos Growers. Kathy Ann Brown had found it in her Santa Barbara garden, and it now has the cultivar name, 'Santa Barbara.' It has been grown in many locations, and although it resembles *Salvia leucantha* 'Midnight' in all other aspects, it is a more compact plant. A mature two-year-

Salvia leucantha 'Santa Barbara' looks similar to *S. leucantha* 'Midnight' but is more compact. (Ginny Hunt)

old plant is 2.5 ft (0.8 m) tall and 4 ft (1.3 m) wide. 'Santa Barbara' is in the process of being patented; in the meantime, several wholesale nurseries are offering the plant to growers under a licensing agreement.

The autumn-blooming 'Anthony Parker' was introduced to horticulture in the late 1990s. This sturdy and vigorous hybrid originated in 1994 in a garden designer's South Carolina garden. One parent is *Salvia leucantha* 'Midnight' and the other is believed to be *S. elegans*. The leaves of 'Anthony Parker' reflect both parents, the upper surface like that of *S. leucantha*, and the lower surface like *S. elegans* but without the glands that give pineapple sage its fragrance. It has been grown in the East and in the southern states for about five years, where it makes a compact plant 3 ft (1 m) tall and equally as wide. In California it displays great hybrid vitality and easily reaches 4–5 ft (1.3–1.5 m) in height and width. Flowering begins in early autumn and continues until frost. Inflorescences are 6–12 in (15–30 cm) long with whorls of dark purple flowers that are held in purplish calyces.

Easy to establish, Mexican bush sage is also able to survive where choicer but choosier plants would fail, and it is helpful to keep this in mind when placing *Salvia leucantha* in the garden. It combines well with the thin, dark green foliage of rosemary and the gray foliage of lavender. A border of good, tough, drought-tolerant plants giving successive bloom consists of rosemary, which

An offspring of *Salvia leucantha*, *S.* 'Anthony Parker' blooms in autumn with *S. confertiflora*. (Sonja Wilcomer)

flowers in winter, lavender, which flowers in early summer, and Mexican bush sage, which continues flowering until frost. In a large border of summer flowering plants, *Gaura lindheimeri*, with its wonderful wands of almost pink flowers, can be interplanted with either form of Mexican bush sage. The upright, summer-blooming *Verbascum olympicum* has a 6 ft (2 m) high candelabra of bright, golden yellow flowers that appear imbedded in white wool. The verbascum, together with the beautiful, bright blue *Linum narbonense*, would add an intriguing touch to the composition. All plants will adjust to similar cultural conditions.

Salvia leucophylla Greene
purple sage, gray sage

An extraordinarily beautiful California native shrub, *Salvia leucophylla* grows in the wild in the southern coast ranges from Santa Barbara to Orange County. Hot, dry hillsides and gravelly soil seem to determine its habitat. It has two appropriate common names: purple sage reflects the pale purple flowers seen in swatches on slopes in the wild, and gray sage reflects the color of the evergreen leaves. The specific epithet, *leucophylla*, refers to the plant's whitish

SALVIA LEUCOPHYLLA

A handsome plant throughout the year, *Salvia leucophylla* is particularly appealing in spring with its myriad of flowers arranged in verticils. (Ginny Hunt)

leaves. David Douglas, the ardent Scottish plant explorer, collected the herbarium specimen from the vicinity of Santa Barbara, and the species was named from this plant by the botanist Edward Lee Greene in 1892.

Reaching 3–5 ft (1–1.5 m) in both height and width, gray sage begins its blooming period in early March and continues for a solid month or more. Tight whorls of many flowers open gradually on an inflorescence that elongates to 6–8 in (15–20 cm). The short flowering stem is usually pinkish purple and adds intensity to the color of the flowers. Pinkish purple flowers, about 1 in (2.5 cm) in length, are held in a 0.5 in (1.3 cm) gray calyx tinged with purple. Leaves are an apple green in spring, becoming grayer and whiter as the days get hotter. The habit of growth of purple sage is graceful, with the uppermost branches swooping downward. When limbs touch the ground they frequently root, expanding the volume of the plant. Propagation is usually by cuttings, since branches strike roots so readily, though the salvia does set viable seed. Reputed to be frost sensitive, it took blasts of 11°F (-12°C) in my garden on one occasion and has frequently withstood 20°F (-7°C).

Carl Epling (1939) writes of purple sage growing so densely that it gives a velvety texture to the rounded coastal hills of southern California, noting that it frequently occurs with *Salvia mellifera* and *S. apiana*. It is indeed a choice plant whether in the wild or in the garden.

In the 1970s, James Roof, former director of the Regional Parks Botanic Garden in Berkeley, California, visited many of the native habitats of *Salvia leucophylla*, and on his return to Berkeley cultivated the species in the garden. Although he was concerned about the tendency of the plant to decline and die after five or six years in cultivation, the *S. leucophylla* plant he collected at Point Sal in Santa Barbara County, California, remained healthy for a number of years. My own experience is that *S. leucophylla* and its hybrids and cultivars live much longer, perhaps because of the influence of the ocean storms, winds, and heat on my garden. All the plants of *S. leucophylla* that I planted between 1980 and 1990 remain vigorous and handsome.

Purple sage is easy to care for if given full sun, fast drainage, and water as it is becoming established. A sloping hillside with two or three 15 ft (4.5 m) tall western redbuds (*Cercis occidentalis*) interplanted with three or more plants of *Salvia leucophylla* will make a flowering display for almost a two-month period. The silvery bark of the redbuds in winter will be complemented by the gray-green foliage of the salvias. All the varieties of *S. leucophylla* I describe are substantial plants that are handsome and easy to place in a dry garden. Their care is minimal. Purple sage is not only beautiful, but it is also an important nectar source for hummingbirds. Its canopy of attractive, aromatic foliage can provide a refuge for small animals.

Over time, many selections of *Salvia leucophylla* have been made, each chosen for a unique characteristic. The tendency to use the collection site as a cultivar name, however, has sometimes made it confusing and difficult for nursery people and gardeners to keep cultivars clearly defined. Hybridization in the wild and in the garden has given rise to a number of plants with *S. leucophylla* as one parent, making matters even more complicated. Incidentally, the seed-bearing parent of these promiscuous hybrids cannot usually be determined even with expensive laboratory work. Consequently, when the two parents are cited they are given alphabetically. The list that follows will demonstrate how confusing the situation has become:

Salvia leucophylla: A low coastal form from Point Sal. Introduced by East Bay Regional Parks Botanic Garden in the early 1950s, it is without a cultivar designation.

Salvia leucophylla: A large pink-flowered shrub form. Introduced by Saratoga Horticultural Research Foundation in the 1970s, it is probably the most hardy and most beautiful of all the selections. It may reach 7–8 ft (2.3–2.5 m) in width and height.

'Bee's Bliss', a beautiful hybrid of *Salvia leucophylla* with an attractive spreading habit, is in the background. In the foreground is a graceful, low-growing coastal form of the same species. (Christine Andrews)

Salvia leucophylla 'Point Sal': Selected by Dale Smith of the University of California in Santa Barbara for Santa Barbara Botanic Garden and introduced by Randy Baldwin through San Marcos Growers in 1986. Commonly referred to as "Point Sal Spreader" because of its draping habit, it is notable for its broader and grayer foliage.

Salvia leucophylla 'Point Sal': The name signifies the collection site. This selection was made by David Fross of Native Sons Nursery in Arroyo Grande in the 1990s. It is remarkable for its 6 ft (2 m) by 12 ft (4 m) height and spread.

Salvia leucophylla 'Figueroa': A selection from Figueroa Mountain made by Nevin Smith for hardiness and introduced through his Wintergreen Nursery in the 1980s.

Salvia 'Bee's Bliss' (*S. leucophylla* × *S. clevelandii* or *S. sonomensis*): A selection made in 1989 by Roger Raiche of the University of California Botanical Garden, Berkeley, for its low growth and beautiful spreading habit. Its rich gray foliage and prolific spring flowering make it an unusually handsome garden subject. Long spikes, 1 ft (30 cm) or more in length, of large lavender-pink flowers adorn the plant for a full month.

The lustrous magenta flowers of *Salvia littae*, which bloom from autumn to winter.
(Don Mahoney)

Salvia littae Visiani

A late-blooming herbaceous perennial, *Salvia littae* is native to the Mexican province of Oaxaca and is found at altitudes of 8000–10,000 ft (2500–3100 m). Plants are usually established in groups growing at the edge of wet oak forests in some shade, areas that are referred to as cloud forest habitats.

Reaching 4–5 ft (1.3–1.5 m) in height and frequently 6 ft (2 m) across, *Salvia littae* becomes thicketlike when left untended. Many leafy stems rise from the base, and when they touch the ground they often root. The plant is generously clothed with 1–3 in (2.5–8 cm) long, medium green leaves that are glabrous and rounded. Flowers in tight verticils elongate, and some inflorescences are 1 ft (30 cm) or more in length. Brilliant magenta flowers covered with hairs are just less than 1 in (2.5 cm) long. When open, the upper lip is upright and the lower lip is opened wide and gaping. The two-parted lower lip appears to be curled and turned under. (I know of no other salvia flower that has this curled-back lower lip.) The calyx is small and a bright lime green that heightens the colorful inflorescence.

Plant *Salvia littae* where it will receive a half day of sun in well-draining garden soil amended with humus. Use humus regularly as a mulch, not only to retain moisture but to improve the soil. Simple cultural requirements involve watering on a regular basis throughout the growing season. This autumn-blooming salvia is hardy to

Salvia littae

about 25°F (-4°C) and propagation is by cuttings. In case of frosty weather, take cuttings in late August and winter them over in the greenhouse. In early spring, prune stems to more or less 3 ft (1 m) in order to achieve a shapely and controlled plant during the coming season. Blooming branches last well as cut flowers if stems are cut under water and displayed in a cool place.

To help control the plant's lax growth, place a piece of wire fencing 3 ft by 3 ft (1 m by 1 m) over the plant in late spring. The fencing should be parallel to the ground at a height of about 2 ft (60 cm). Drive four stakes in the ground and secure the fencing with staples in each stake. As the plant develops, it can be trained up and through the wire.

Salvia littae produces abundant foliage and flowers, and it combines beautifully with the 6 ft (2 m) evergreen *Viburnum tinus* 'Spring Bouquet'. The handsome, mulberry-colored buds of the spring-blooming viburnum appear as the salvia reaches the end of its blooming period. Another fine companion is the 3–4 ft (1–1.3 m) shrub rose 'Lyda Rose', which produces continuous large, white, single flowers edged in lavender-pink. Penstemon cultivars that repeat bloom, such as 'Garnet', 'Midnight', and 'Sour Grapes', would also make colorful partners.

Salvia longispicata Martius & Galeotti

Salvia longispicata is found in southwestern Mexico, usually at elevations of 1000–6500 ft (400–2000 m). Even though classified as a perennial, it has the size and stature of a small shrub. In one season it grows 4–5 ft (1.3–1.5 m) in height and a good 3–4 ft (1–1.3 m) across. Regardless of its size, this salvia cannot be described as a showy plant for the garden, but it has interesting, dark purple flowers and a splendid upright habit—two characteristics that hybridizers seek and value.

The specific epithet, *longispicata*, would suggest that the plant has long spikes. As a matter of fact, this is not the case, and the word refers to the plant's many projecting or extending clusters of short flowering spikes, which resemble small ears of corn.

Leaves are many different sizes, mid-green, ovate, and connected to the petiole at the broader end, giving the plant a bumpy look. Small dark purple flowers less than 0.5 in (1.3 cm) in length start appearing in summer and continue to bloom until late autumn. The calyces are a pale green and about the same length as the flower. Tight whorls of flowers elongate on inflorescences to 6–8 in (15–20 cm) but do not stand erect above the foliage. Hardy to 20°F (-7°C), *Salvia longispicata*, if struck by a freeze, will eventually come back from its rootstock.

Cultural requirements are a half to full day of sun, regular garden soil amended with humus, quick drainage, and water once every week or two. Propagation is by seed or cuttings. In early spring, prune all stems to two active nodes just above ground level to encourage healthy and uniform growth during the coming growing season.

Salvia longispicata is thought to be a pollen parent and *S. farinacea* the seed parent of a spontaneous sterile hybrid that was found at the Huntington Botanical Gardens in 1979. This hybrid was introduced as *S.* 'Indigo Spires' and has proved to be quite ornamental in the garden.

Salvia longispicata is rarely seen in gardens or in nurseries in the United States, but it may be found in the national collections of salvias in both Britain and France. It is clearly a plant for the collector or hybridizer. In a garden setting it attracts little attention and could easily be overlooked. However, when placed as a filler between large shrub roses such as the rugosa 'Roseraie de l'Hay', which has violet-red flowers, or the hybrid rugosa 'Blanc Double de Coubert', which has almost pure white flowers, its most noteworthy attributes are emphasized—namely, its sturdy upright habit and deep purple flowers.

Salvia lycioides Gray
canyon sage

A small shrublike plant that builds wood at its base, *Salvia lycioides* was described botanically by Carl Epling (1939) as a perennial herb. Found in a wide

Salvia lycioides blooms in spring and again in autumn. It is well suited for a rock garden. (Ginny Hunt)

territory from west Texas to New Mexico and south through Mexico to the province of San Luis Potosí, canyon sage is reported to be established on dry limestone hills and canyons at high elevations, usually 5000 ft (1500 m) or more.

Canyon sage fairly twinkles with bright cornflower-blue flowers in the spring and again in the fall. A few flowers appear from time to time during the summer, but it tends to bloom best when nights are cool. Usually reaching 1–1.5 ft (30–45 cm) in height and width, the plant has a graceful sprawl. From its base, many small branches grow up and then out. Little mistletoe-green leaves less than 1 in (2.5 cm) long and 0.5 in (1.3 cm) wide cover the plant well and tend to be evergreen in a mild climate. Its hardiness is reported to be around 10°F (around -12°C).

A selection of *Salvia lycioides* was made by nurseryman Pat McNeal of Austin, Texas, and introduced as

Salvia lycioides

'Guadalupe Mountain Form'. It is similar to *S. lycioides* except its flowers and leaves are smaller. The flowers are a deep and vibrant delphinium blue.

Situated in ordinary garden soil with good drainage and in full sun, this drought-tolerant salvia needs little, if any, additional summer water. I have found regular dressings of humus to be helpful in conserving water and furnishing food for the plant. Also, light dressings of lime on a yearly basis will keep the soil sweet. *Salvia lycioides* is usually propagated by seed and cuttings.

Named by Asa Gray in 1886, canyon sage is relatively unknown and rarely seen in gardens and nurseries. It has been cultivated at the Texas Agricultural Experiment Station since 1976, however. It is not known when it was introduced to horticulture. The specific epithet, *lycioides*, from the Greek, refers to the plant's resemblance to *Lycium*, a genus called boxthorn in the nightshade family.

This is a plant made to order for the rock garden, where it can climb or nestle among rocks and other plants. The neat growing habit of *Salvia lycioides* allows for many possible placements in the garden. One planting might include groups of *S. lycioides* along with 'Dark Dancer', a hybrid of *S. greggii* that has dark raspberry flowers. These two salvias are more or less equal in size and produce quantities of flowers during late summer and autumn. A composition eminently suited for siting on a mound includes the prostrate and spreading evergreen shore juniper, *Juniperus conferta*, and canyon sage. *Teucrium lucidum*, the clumping, evergreen, 4–6 in (10–15 cm) germander, adds a little dark green foliage that anchors the planting very well. Canyon sage does very well as a container plant or on the perimeter of a dry border, and the texture of the foliage is eye-catching year-round.

Salvia madrensis Seemann
forsythia sage

A slow developing and late-blooming perennial from the Sierra Madre Oriental in Mexico, *Salvia madrensis* has been given the common name forsythia sage, which refers to the rich yellow color of its flowers. The specific epithet, *madrensis*, describes the plant's origin, highlighting the plant's high mountain habitat. Occurring at 4000–5000 ft (1200–1500 m) in warm and often wet areas, it is reported to be hardy to 25°F (-4°C). In my garden it has come back from its rootstock after withstanding 11°F (-12°C) for very short periods.

The rich butter-yellow flowers of *Salvia madrensis* are enhanced by the fire-engine red flowers of *S. fulgens*. (Ginny Hunt)

To watch *Salvia madrensis* push up its square stems and heart-shaped leaves from underground rhizomes is to see a marvel in slow motion. All summer the plant builds, and by early September, stems measure 4–7 ft (1.3–2.3 m) tall and are 2 in (5 cm) wide on each of their square sides. A ridge at each corner of the stem emphasizes the squareness. Rough-textured, heart-shaped, spinach-green leaves are graduated in size from large at the bottom to small at the top. In spite of being widely spaced along the stem, the leaves give a lush covering to the plant. Many 12 in (30 cm) inflorescences develop and are covered with softly colored, butter-yellow flowers. These splendid flowers are held in calyces that are aromatic and sticky with glands. Blooming begins in late August and continues until frost. The flowers are arranged in whorls and hold well as cut flowers.

Salvia madrensis prefers a warm growing season, light to medium shade, and soil mixed with humus. Even though it will tolerate high humidity, this salvia must have good drainage as well as regular water. It

Salvia madrensis

will take full sun but will need more water and the protection of other plants. I have never found fertilizer necessary, but regular mulching increases the plant's food supply and preserves water. In a few years plants will multiply by spreading rootstock into a colony and may easily be divided. In the wild, fertile seed is set but this occurs only occasionally in cultivation. Divisions and cuttings are the usual methods of propagation. Cut the plants back to 6–8 in (15–20 cm) above the ground after flowering for good air circulation and a tidy border.

The upright, orange-red, autumn-blooming *Salvia regla* makes a striking companion for *S. madrensis*. Also, the old-fashioned snowball *Viburnum opulus* 'Roseum', which colors wonderfully in the autumn, brings a range of reds to complement the soft yellow flowers of *S. madrensis*. The repeat-blooming *S. elegans* 'Honey Melon', with its lush green foliage and bright scarlet-red flowers, makes a fine ground cover at the base of all these plants.

Salvia melissodora Lagasca
grape-scented sage

At elevations ranging from 4000 to 8000 ft (1200 to 2500 m) in the Sierra Madre Occidental, *Salvia melissodora* is found in the Mexican provinces of Chihuahua in the north all the way to Oaxaca in the south. Both leaves and seed of grape-scented sage have been used by the Tarahumara Indians for medicinal purposes for several hundred years.

A woody shrub 6 ft (2 m) high and 4 ft (1.3 m) wide, *Salvia melissodora* has an upright and graceful habit. Ovate leaves 1–1.5 in (2.5–4 cm) in length cover the shrub lightly and tend to be evergreen in a mild winter. The upper surface is mid-green in color, and the veins on the lower surface stand out because of the chamois-colored pubescence that covers them. When partially dry the leaves emit a pleasant fragrance. The flowers are frequently described as grape-scented. Blooming continually from late spring until frost, *S. melissodora* attracts bees, insects, butterflies, and hummingbirds because of its dependable nectar supply. Short inflorescences hold several whorls of flowers with upper lips of violet-lavender. The lower lip is pale lavender, as is the back of the upper lip. This light lavender color probably lures and directs insects to the nectary. The specific epithet, *melissodora*, comes from two Greek words, *melissa*, meaning honeybee, and *odora*, meaning fragrant. Melissa is also the name of a

A graceful, shrublike garden plant with a pleasing scent, *Salvia melissodora* attracts insects and hummingbirds. (Ginny Hunt)

Cretan nymph who discovered how to collect honey. It is a fitting name for an appealing and useful plant.

Undemanding in culture, *Salvia melissodora* likes full sun, quick drainage, good air circulation, and regular watering on a 10-day basis. Once established it will produce viable seed and, occasionally, seedlings. Propagation is also by cuttings. Pruning and pinching of new growth will help in shaping the plant. If entire branches need to be removed, the best time to do this heavy pruning is during the active growing season. I have found grape-scented sage to be hardy to 20°F (-7°C). On one occasion when the temperature fell to 11°F (-12°C) in December, the mother plant was killed but the following spring we found seedlings had germinated at the base of the original plant.

A delight to have in a border, *Salvia melissodora*, together with *Aloysia triphylla*, lemon verbena, will form the backbone of a border designed for fragrance. These plants are similar in size and stature. The small and compact shrub rose 'Wise Portia' is strongly scented and a lovely magenta color. This rose reaches 3 ft (1 m) in height and width and makes a floriferous filler. Several groups of the white *Dianthus* 'Jealousy' and *D.* 'Danielle Pink', both about 1 ft (30 cm) tall and very fragrant, would help in unifying the scented border.

Salvia mellifera Greene
black sage

Commonly found on dry slopes under 2000 ft (600 m), *Salvia mellifera* has a lengthy coastal distribution in California that stretches from Contra Costa County south into Baja. It is among the chief components of the coastal sage scrub plant community. Both in the wild and in gardens, *S. mellifera* hybridizes freely with *S. apiana, S. columbariae,* and *S. leucophylla,* and sometimes with *S. carduacea* and *S. clevelandii.* The specific epithet, *mellifera,* means "honey producing." Beekeepers have long been aware of this nectar and pollen source and often place their hives in chaparral where large stands of black sage thrive.

Relatively unknown to gardeners until the early 1950s, black sage is rarely seen even today outside nurseries that specialize in California native plants. However, there are fine specimens at the University of California Botanical Garden, Berkeley, and the Arboretum of the University of California, Santa Cruz, as well as Strybing Arboretum, East Bay Regional Parks Botanic Garden, Santa Barbara Botanic Garden, and the Rancho Santa Ana Botanic Garden.

With water shortages occurring frequently on the West Coast and elsewhere, designers are searching for tough, drought-tolerant plants to bring into dry garden settings. California native salvias and their hybrids provide many examples of such plants, with *Salvia mellifera* prominent among them. A 3–6 ft (1–2 m) evergreen shrub that sometimes mounds 3–5 ft (1–1.5 m) across, black sage has an overall look in keeping with a Mediterranean or dry garden setting. Its small leaves clothe the shrub but do not give it a predominantly leafy look. The leaves are a strong mid-green color, 1–2 in (2.5–5 cm) in length, with indented veins giving the surface a textured appearance. If stroked, the leaves release a pleasant scent. Blooming takes place in late spring, with tight whorls of flowers that hardly attract attention but do attract bees. The small flowers are whitish or pale lavender.

Usually placed in full sun in the garden, black sage will also succeed with some shade. A gritty soil with a light texture is needed for quick drainage, and fertilizer is not recommended. Additional water is not necessary once the plant becomes established. It is reliably reported that deer never browse *Salvia mellifera,* its hybrids, or its cultivars.

Many California native plants make inestimable companions for black sage. *Rhus ovata,* sugar bush, with its slick and shiny dark evergreen leaves, is about the same size as *Salvia mellifera*. The sugar bush's fat, eye-catching buds and flowers emerge before the sage comes into bloom. Various species of evergreen *Ceanothus* are other good partners. In areas with relatively cool summers, the 2–3 ft (60–90 cm) tall *C. gloriosus* var. *porrectus*, with its narrow, hollylike leaves and lavender-blue flowers, does well. *Ceanothus* 'Dark Star', which has masses of cobalt-blue flowers, tolerates more heat and is usually under 6 ft (2 m) in height. Both are drought tolerant.

Several selections of the prostrate form of *Salvia mellifera* have been made. In the 1990s David Amme, a nurseryman specializing in California native plants, made the selection 'Little Sur' from the mouth

Salvia mellifera blooming in May on the south-facing slope of Mount Baldy, southern California. (Betsy Clebsch)

of the Little Sur River. It is prostrate in growth and notable for draping over walls or among rocks. 'Terra Seca' was introduced in the 1970s by the Saratoga Horticultural Research Foundation from a plant from the University of California Botanical Garden, Berkeley. This selection was made in the 1950s by the California nurseryman Louis Edmunds. Sold by some nurseries as 'Prostrata', it is hoped that name will be abandoned in favor of its correct name, 'Terra Seca'. Reaching 2 ft (60 cm) in height and over 6 ft (2 m) in width, 'Terra Seca' will endure the toughest conditions. An early spring-blooming plant with tiny white flowers, its mid-green leaves appear rough and are both aromatic and shiny. Drought tolerant when established, the plant should have its upright growth regularly pruned or pinched as it develops so that it remains both prostrate and leafy. A good ground cover, it is particularly attractive at the base of the upright, 8–12 ft (2.5–4 m) *Fremontodendron californicum* subsp. *crassifolium*, a small evergreen tree with primrose-yellow flowers.

Salvia 'Mrs. Beard', a hybrid of *S. mellifera* and *S. sonomensis*, is described under *S. sonomensis* because of its strong resemblance to that parent.

Salvia merjamie Forsskål

An extremely variable herbaceous plant, *Salvia merjamie* has a habitat in the East African highlands from Ethiopia to Tanzania. Specimens have also been collected across the Red Sea in Yemen. Occurring at altitudes between 6000 and 13,000 ft (1800 and 4000 m), its habitat includes grasslands, the edge of forests, rocky outcrops, basalt slopes, waysides, and fallow fields. It is reported to be perennial in some areas and biennial in others. Plants that I have grown are short-lived, usually flowering and producing seed for about three years. Described by the Finnish plant collector Peter Forsskål in 1775 (both he and his family have spelled his name many different ways), this salvia's specific epithet, *merjamie*, is derived from the Arabian common name for the plant. *Salvia lanigera* is a distant relative of *S. merjamie*, and its common name, 'meryamiye', is similar sounding. In fact, several salvias have this same common name. The native Masai name for *S. merjamie* is *Naingungundeu*, which means that the plant smells of rats! Although *S. merjamie* has a similar distribution to *S. nilotica*, the two species apparently do not hybridize.

An erect plant that varies in height from just 2 in to 3 ft (5–90 cm), *Salvia merjamie* produces mostly basal leaves that are covered with oil globules and sometimes lightly hairy on both surfaces. Forming a rosette, the dark green leaves are oblong and faintly scalloped along the edge. The largest leaf measures about 6 in (15 cm) long and 2 in (5 cm) wide with a petiole about 1.5 in (4 cm) long. The plant's entire inflorescence tends to be short with a central flowering stem that has alternate pairs of flowering stems projecting at right angles to each other (*decussate* is the botanical term for such an arrangement). The plant is quite beautiful in its precise and mathematically arranged flowering structure. Flowers are in whorls and are small, usually under 1 in (2.5 cm) in length. They can vary in color but the plants I have grown all have very pale blue flowers verging on a cream color with an upper lip that is falcate. Calyces are small and often violet-purple in color. Flowering occurs in early summer and continues for about a three-week period during which time pollinators such as bees and hummingbirds are busy visiting the flowers. Seed, the usual method for propagating this salvia, is typically produced in moderate amounts.

The cultural requirements for growing *Salvia merjamie* are few and simple. It should receive a half to full day of sun, good drainage, friable garden soil, and a moderate amount of water on a regular basis. Its high elevation habitat reflects its ability to withstand temperatures into the 20°s F (around -4°C) for very short periods. Its modest growing habit means that pruning can be accomplished when seed is ripe and dry enough for gathering. When you are pruning, remove the entire inflorescence to prepare the plant for a time of rest.

A small bed or border in a sunny spot that is designed for early summer bloom and interesting foliage throughout the growing season might feature three plants each of *Salvia merjamie* and *Scabiosa farinosa*. Scabiosa flowers are pale lavender and its leaves are dark green, and the plant's small rounded shape would make a good contrast to the more uniformly branched salvia. Several plants of the California native *Dudleya caespitosa* would bring a dramatic shape and a cool gray-green color to the combina-

A short-lived perennial, *Salvia merjamie* will often flower and produce seed for three years. (Ginny Hunt)

tion. If you have space, add a couple of clumps of *Elymus magellanicus*, a lovely blue-gray grass that hardly reaches 1 ft (30 cm) in height. All these plants are less than 2 ft (60 cm) tall, and although they have very different habits of growth or structures, they all require the same culture.

Salvia mexicana Linnaeus
Mexican sage

A highly variable plant in the wild, *Salvia mexicana* is distributed over a wide area throughout central Mexico. Its habitat includes arid subtropical regions in the north and tropical areas in the south. Growing at elevations ranging from 2600 to 8500 ft (800 to 2600 m), Mexican sage is frequently found at the edge of forests where it receives some protection from the elements.

Described as a shrubby perennial, Mexican sage grows 3–9 ft (1–3 m) tall and 3–4 ft (1–1.3 m) wide in cultivation. Leaves are variable in size and color—

Salvia mexicana 'Limelight'

some plants have mid-green, glabrous leaves, and others have gray-green leaves with short hairs covering the surface. Leaves are sufficient in number to give the plant a clothed look. Inflorescences are variable, both in length and size of flowers. The size and color of the calyces and flowers vary as well, ranging from purple-blue to midnight-purple. Beginning in late summer, midnight-purplish flowers in whorls are abundantly produced for several months. Flowering branches are beautiful and long lasting in bouquets. Stems can be conditioned by cutting them under water.

The large-flowered 'Lollie Jackson' is a 4 ft (1.3 m) tall selection of *Salvia mexicana*. (Christine Andrews)

Salvia mexicana is best grown in a climate where temperatures do not fall below 20°F (-7°C). In my garden this sage came back from its rootstock after temperatures dropped to 11°F (-12°C), but it took two summers for it to regain its former vigor and stature. Situate plants so they receive a half to full day of sun and have fast drainage. Occasional deep watering is necessary but excessive watering stimulates the plant to produce lots of branches that break quite easily. In spring, after the danger of frost has passed, prune *S. mexicana* to a pleasing shape approximately 2 ft (60 cm) in height and width to prepare for the coming season's growth. Prune plants throughout the flowering season by removing spent inflorescences, as this will reduce the plant's bulk and weight. Remove crossed or weighted branches to encourage upright growth. Propagation is by seed and cuttings.

I am unable to find a record of when *Salvia mexicana* came into cultivation, but collection records from

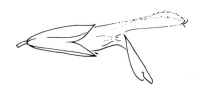

Salvia mexicana

several botanic gardens show that it was grown in these gardens in the early 1970s. Distinctive plants without cultivar names are being propagated by nurseries and gardeners. One plant collected in Mexico by the Huntington Botanical Gardens has gray leaves and attracts several species of butterfly. Another undesignated plant, collected in Guanajuato province by the University of California Botanical Garden, Berkeley, has short, showy, chartreuse-green calyces. Still another plant was collected in 1978 by botanist Robert Ornduff for the University of California Botanical Garden, Berkeley. Found in the province of Quertaro at the edge of a fir and oak woodland in abundant litter, it has large chartreuse-green calyces and vibrant violet-blue flowers. It was designated a cultivar and given the name 'Limelight'. Two additional cultivars appear frequently on nursery lists: 'Lollie Jackson' is a compact, 4 ft (1.3 m) plant, and 'Ocampo' is upright in growth to 7 ft (2.3 m) and survives low temperatures for short periods. All these cultivars grow well under high tree canopies, making them fine understory plants.

For continued autumn bloom, *Salvia mexicana* is among the most reliable plants for the border. It is a nectar source for many insects, butterflies, and hummingbirds. It needs wind protection and some pruning throughout the summer because its branches are brittle. Try growing it next to upright trees or shrubs. By chance I planted it between *Magnolia dawsoniana* and a 4 ft (1.3 m) tall fence and found it had no choice but to grow upward in this wind-protected position. A border of evergreen shrubs interplanted with *S. mexicana* gives the gardener subtle color to enjoy until the end of the season.

Salvia microphylla Kunth

Covering an immense geographical area, *Salvia microphylla* may be found in the wild both in southeastern Arizona and in the mountains of eastern, western, and southern Mexico. It is a complex and variable species, and its propensity to hybridize further complicates matters. Carl Epling (1939) considers *S. microphylla* to consist of three geographical races that are difficult to define because even in 2002 they are in the process of emerging. Known to show great variation, this species could conceivably have more than three variants. James Compton (1994a) devised a key to varieties of *S. microphylla* using leaves and bracts as characteristics. I find his key to be most helpful in looking more closely at the large number of plants that have been brought into horticulture as cultivars since the 1990s. John Sutton (1999) calls attention to these same

The shrubby *Salvia microphylla* 'Graham's Sage' is dazzling all summer. To the right is *S. chamaedryoides*. (Christine Andrews)

nomenclature problems and describes named cultivars and hybrids of both *S. microphylla* and *S. greggii* that are notable garden plants. To further complicate matters, *S. greggii* is frequently confused with *S. microphylla*. Epling (1939) distinguishes between the two by a pair of papillae inside the *S. microphylla* corolla near the base of the flower tube and by its leaves, which have obvious serrate margins. The narrow, elliptic leaves of *S. greggii* have smooth margins. Reinforcing the complexity of this nomenclature matter is the fact that *S. greggii* and *S. microphylla* are the parents of *S. ×jamensis*.

Salvia microphylla, along with its hybrids and cultivars, usually comes into full bloom in late spring and again in autumn. In mild areas it throws a few sporadic flowers practically year-round. Flowering ends only with the onset of cold weather and short days. Standing 3–4 ft (1–1.3 m) tall and wide, this sage has ovate green leaves of differing sizes that are smooth or very lightly covered with hairs. The plant produces flowers its first year and grows rapidly, attaining full size in its second year. Some plants spread underground and make attractive, dense patches. A pronounced, pleasing fragrance is released when the leaves are crushed. The specific epithet, *microphylla*, is from the Greek and means "small leaved." Flowers are arranged in whorls, and there is great variation in color—pink, rose, magenta, and many shades of red.

Salvia microphylla 'Forever Red' is never without flowers from early summer through autumn. (Christine Andrews)

'Red Velvet' is a lustrous, red-flowered selection of *Salvia microphylla*. (Don Mahoney)

Called *mirto de montes*, meaning "myrtle of the mountains," this salvia is sometimes used for making tea. It is a tough, much-branched shrub that tends to become woody. It grows in full sun or part shade, and although drought tolerant, it will take regular water if it has good drainage. *Salvia microphylla* is usually ignored by deer but is adored by hummingbirds and insects. It has escaped from gardens in the San Francisco Bay area and become naturalized in many small pockets in that benign climate. During the growing season, deadheading will stimulate flower production. In late winter, remove all woody stems as close to the ground as possible to encourage new and more succulent growth. You can propagate plants using seeds, cuttings, or a rooted stem teased from the clump. It is likely that, because of the plant's wide distribution in the wild, some strains are more frost tolerant than others. In my garden, many different clones have withstood temperatures into the teens (-10°C) for short periods.

There has been and remains some confusion about the salvia known in the United States as *Salvia microphylla*, whose common name is Graham's Sage. It

SALVIA MICROPHYLLA

was previously called *S. grahami* and *S. neurepia* in Britain. Graham's Sage, *S. grahami*, was described by George Bentham who did not know an earlier description had already been published. Similarly, *S. neurepia* with the same identity was described by Fernald. According to the rules of nomenclature, however, this salvia is correctly known as *S. microphylla*. The addition of the cultivar name 'Graham's Sage' to the clone being grown in the United States will distinguish it from other salvias. Even in 2002, it is relatively obscure to gardeners and remains rare in horticulture. A selection that has been grown in Britain since the 1880s as a prized ornamental plant now has the cultivar name 'Kew Red'.

Salvia microphylla var. *wislizenii* is described by botanists as a perennial plant. It grows quickly, building wood at its base and appearing shrublike. Found at high elevations of 6000–8000 ft (1800–2500 m) in the mountains of southern Arizona and northern Mexico, it probably came into cultivation in Arizona and California in the late 1980s. Asa Gray described it and named it for John Gill Lemmon, the pioneer California botanist, who had collected it in Arizona in 1885. For many years this plant was referred to as *S. lemmonii* because Gray named it for Lemmon when he first looked at the dried Arizona specimens. Later, when examining specimens from Mexico, Gray called the plant *S. microphylla* var. *wislizenii* because it differed from *S. microphylla*. From the beginning there have been botanical problems in dealing with both *S. microphylla* var. *wislizenii* and *S. lemmonii* as these plants are not distinguishable one from the other in the original material. In addition, gardeners have quite naturally attempted to segregate these salvias, which has led to more confusion. James Compton suggested to me in 2001 that a broad species approach be taken and that all material be lumped under *S. microphylla*. (pers. comm.). His suggestion solves many problems and at the same time allows gardeners to distinguish one plant from another by giving it a cultivar name. This is the approach I have taken.

There are dozens of garden-worthy cultivars of *Salvia microphylla* that have been selected from the wild. A brief list follows:

'Cerro Potosí', from Nuevo León, has large, vibrant, magenta flowers.
'Hoja Grande', from Nuevo León, has magenta-red flowers and dark
    green leaves.
'La Trinidad Pink', from Nuevo León, has persistent, bright pink
    flowers.

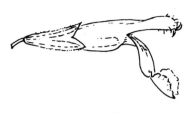

Salvia microphylla 'Rosita'

'Rosita', from Nuevo León, blooms repeatedly with bright candy-pink flowers. 'San Carlos Festival', from Tamaulipas, has magenta-scarlet flowers and gray-green leaves.

Other selections and hybrids include:

'Desert Blaze' has bright red flowers and variegated green and yellow leaves.

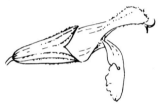

Salvia microphylla 'Forever Red'

'Forever Red' is shrublike and long blooming with scarlet flowers.

'Graham's Sage' has many red flowers that come into bloom simultaneously.

'Kew Red' grows vigorously and has vivid red flowers.

'La Foux', originating in France, has deep crimson flowers with dark calyces.

'Newby Hall' is a robust plant with bright scarlet flowers.

'Pink Blush' has a good habit with free-flowering, rose-magenta flowers.

'Red Velvet' is a lustrous, red-flowered selection.

'Wild Watermelon' has large pink flowers on arching stems with dark calyces.

Salvia miltiorrhiza Bunge

A very beautiful plant that comes from both China and Japan, *Salvia miltiorrhiza* is widely distributed in its native habitat. Growing between elevations of 300–4000 ft (90–1200 m), it occurs in grassy places in forests as well as on hillsides and along streambanks. For centuries the outside of the salvia's taproot, which is red, has been used medicinally to treat coronary diseases in the countries where it naturally occurs. The specific name, *miltiorrhiza*, means "red juice extracted from a root." Described and named by the Russian botanist Alexander Andrejewitsch Bunge in 1833, it has become known to western horticulture through herbalists in the 1990s primarily because of its medicinal qualities.

A gracefully spreading plant, *Salvia miltiorrhiza* is a perennial with a thickened and succulent taproot. It is deciduous in winter but in very early spring it begins to show signs of life and growth. By late spring or early summer, branching stems that are 1–2 ft (30–60 cm) in height begin to flower, and both simple and divided leaves that are widely spaced cover the stems. Inflorescences are about 1 ft (30 cm) long, and their weight causes the stems to bend downward. They are

The roots of *Salvia miltiorrhiza* have been used for centuries to treat coronary diseases in countries where it naturally occurs. (Sonja Wilcomer)

hairy and covered with sticky glands that release a light and pleasant odor when brushed. Whorls of light purple or lavender-blue flowers about 1 in (2.5 cm) long and with a handsome falcate upper lip are held in a dark purple calyx. Flowering continues off and on all summer. I have been reluctant to deadhead this salvia because I was hoping for seed, and although two species of hummingbirds and many different insects visit the flowers, no seed has formed. Seed, if available, is reputed to be difficult to germinate unless it is fresh. I do remove spent inflorescences from time to time to keep the plant in bounds. Cuttings taken in August can be held in the greenhouse until the following spring. These cuttings will remain evergreen.

Similar in cultural needs to all its close relatives, *Salvia miltiorrhiza*

Salvia miltiorrhiza

needs good drainage. Planted in a light clay soil with some humus, it should receive about a half day of sunlight. Weekly irrigation is recommended in the spring, but as the days lengthen and temperatures rise, this salvia needs frequent watering. My experience with the hardiness of this plant is limited, but based on its native habitat, I would expect it to survive temperatures in the teens (-10°C).

Salvia miltiorrhiza likes shade in summer so can easily be worked into a border with other plants. Medium-sized shrubs that are deciduous would furnish shade for this salvia when it is needed. Several plants at the base of *Rosa* 'Ballerina' or *R.* 'Mevrouw Nathalie Nypels' would add to a color scheme of pink and lavender-blue. *Pimpinella major* 'Rosea', which is hard to find, is worth the extra effort to locate as its several clumps of the less than 3 ft (1 m) tall stems and lovely umbels of soft pink flowers would complement the combination handsomely.

Salvia miniata Fernald

From Belize and the Mexican province of Chiapas comes the handsome and luxuriant *Salvia miniata*. In the wild it grows on shaded mountain hillsides at elevations of around 2000 ft (600 m). These are warm, moist mountains with precipitation in the form of rain or fog occurring throughout the year, the winter months being the driest.

The specific epithet, *miniata*, means "red," "vermilion," or "scarlet," in particular the red used in illuminating or decorating letters in a manuscript. The salvia's flowers reflect this name, being clear red with an orange undertone. The glossy green foliage intensifies the rich vermilion flower color.

A herbaceous perennial, *Salvia miniata* is quite tender and will not survive a light freeze. In the ground it grows robustly, reaching 3 ft (1 m) in height and width during the summer. It is well branched from the base, and the myrtle-green leaves, which are glistening and hairless, amply clothe the plant. The glossy leaves reflect light, which in turn brightens the shaded plant. The largest leaves measure about 5 in (13

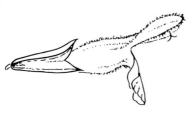

Salvia miniata

cm) long and 2 in (5 cm) wide and are the perfect foil for the 1 in (2.5 cm) long, signal-red flowers. Flowers are loosely spaced in whorls on an inflorescence that will reach a good 12 in (30 cm) in length. Many flowers elongate simultaneously, making a visual treat. Flowering begins in midsummer and tapers off as the days grow shorter. If autumn weather is warm, however, the plant will persist in producing flowers. Flowering branches last well in bouquets if stems are conditioned by first cutting them under water. A frost-free and mild climate will permit *S. miniata* to persist in the garden throughout the winter. To obtain a nicely shaped plant, wait until just before active growth begins and then cut stems to two active nodes about 6 in (15 cm) above the ground.

Salvia miniata is a well-proportioned salvia that requires high shade and moisture. The soil must have good drainage and be prepared with humus. A half day of sun is needed along with weekly deep watering. *Salvia miniata* will not succeed in a hot and dry climate. Like many salvias that produce a lot of growth, it needs protection from winds. Easily propagated by cuttings, it may be over-wintered by this method.

It is not known when *Salvia miniata* was introduced to horticulture, but Fernald described it in 1900. Few people have seen it in gardens although it is an excellent garden plant—in spite of having to be lifted for the greenhouse or have cuttings taken each autumn. It has been grown outdoors at Strybing Arboretum for many years and is propagated regularly for their plant sales. Since the early 1990s, quite a few nurseries have offered it on their lists. Gardeners in the southern part of the United States and England find it worth the effort of wintering cuttings in a greenhouse in order to enjoy it in the garden.

A group of *Salvia miniata* plants, growing with clumps of *Chasmanthium latifolium* (sea oats), the handsome grass from the eastern United States, will reach the same height. These two plants make remarkable partners, and their profuse and contrasting foliages have a rich and plentiful look. Both require high shade and similar cultural conditions.

Salvia moorcroftiana Wallich ex Bentham

Found throughout the Himalayan mountains from Pakistan to western Nepal, *Salvia moorcroftiana* is particularly common in the Kashmir valley area of

A plant of high altitudes, *Salvia moorcroftiana* is a wise choice for gardens that experience cold winters. (Ginny Hunt)

India. Not fussy as to habitat, it grows on open slopes and disturbed areas between 5000 and 9000 ft (1500 and 2800 m). The leaves of *S. moorcroftiana* are reported to be used medicinally in Kashmir.

A robust herbaceous perennial, *Salvia moorcroftiana* builds mostly basal leaves to 2.5 ft (0.8 m) in height and a little less in width. They are long-stalked, covered with white wool, and have a toothed margin. The inflorescence rises just above the foliage, making a mass of pale lilac or nearly white flowers. Individual flowers are about 1 in (2.5 cm) long and are held in a hairy calyx. Showy, green-veined bracts add to the plant's charm. Flowering takes place during early summer and usually lasts for a solid four-week period.

Easy to situate in a border, *Salvia moorcroftiana* prefers full sun, friable garden soil, good drainage, and regular water. Large leaves make a damp and attractive haunt for snails and should be inspected occasionally. Little attention is required to keep this salvia in good condition because its needs are simple—only the removal of spent inflorescences and tattered leaves is needed. Reflecting its high mountain habitat, *S. moorcroftiana* is hardy to 0°F (-18°C). Propagation is by seed.

This salvia's blooming period, which is from late spring into early summer, allows it to combine beautifully with the fragrant, one-time blooming, pale pink rose 'Baltimore Belle'. This rose is a vigorous climber, and when covered with flowers on a high trellis, the flowering salvia echoes that effect but at a lower height. Another rose, 'Kathleen', a hybrid musk that repeat blooms, is also a desirable companion. Fragrant, almost single flowers of soft pink to pale yellow bloom repeatedly and are followed in autumn by outstanding hips that are the color of the flesh of a perfectly ripe cantaloupe. In a mild climate there is an additional reward—the large, woolly, soft gray leaves of *Salvia moorcroftiana* are evergreen, so enhancing the winter garden.

SALVIA MOORCROFTIANA

The small and colorful royal purple sage alongside *Origanum dictamnus*. (Robert Kourik)

"*Salvia muelleri*" Epling
royal purple sage

Salvia muelleri has a very limited natural range and distribution in the Mexican province of Nuevo León in the mountains near Monterrey. To my knowledge there have been no other sightings or habitats reported. Almost never seen in nurseries or gardens before 1987, the plant known as royal purple sage is popular in California but remains scarcely known to gardeners elsewhere. At the time of this book's publication, it was determined that this plant is not the true *Salvia muelleri*. However, royal purple sage will surely find a place in gardens.

When Carl Epling described and named *Salvia muelleri*, he called it a perennial herb. In my garden it builds up light wood very rapidly and looks shrubby by the end of the growing season. In late winter when pruning takes place, however, one can see many underground runners with wiry stems. About 2.5 ft (0.8 m) tall and 4 ft (1.3 m) wide, royal purple sage blooms from spring through autumn, doing so more freely when the days are short. The royal purple flowers are less than 1 in (2.5 cm) long and two-lipped, with the lower lip 0.5 in (1.3 cm) wide and showy. The small calyx is dark purple and intensifies the color of the royal purple flower. Small, shiny, grassy green leaves lightly cover the plant, allowing its woody structure to be visible. They measure less than 1 in (2.5 cm) in length and 0.5 in (1.3 cm) in width and are ovate. In small flower arrangements, the leaves and inflorescences are a rich addition.

The culture of royal purple sage includes full sun, fast drainage, and soil enriched with humus. It is drought tolerant and needs little water to survive. If you want constant bloom, however, you should water deeply every week during hot weather. A top dressing of humus once a year helps with moisture retention and nourishment. Some pruning throughout the growing season will keep the plant's growth in check. Propagation is by seed, cuttings, or division of the rootstock. Once established, the roots of the plant will send out fresh. stems. These new plants can be divided from the mother plant and shared with other gardeners or simply removed in order to maintain a well-shaped plant. Royal purple sage is hardy to 10°F (-12°C).

Royal purple sages is eminently well suited for a drought-tolerant garden. Placed among rocks, it looks natural and fills niches freely. A sunny rock garden might include clumps of *Helictotrichon sempervirens*, a grass with evergreen, blue-gray foliage from southwestern Europe, patches of the native California *Eriogonum grande* var. *rubescens*, red buckwheat, with its rosy balls of flowers, and the Eastern European *Limonium latifolium*, sea lavender, with its basal rosettes of dark green leaves and sprays of lavender flowers. Several or more royal purple sages would complete a picture of harmonious flower color and varying leaf textures.

Salvia muirii Bolus

Known as a stiffly erect, small shrub in its native habitat, *Salvia muirii* occurs frequently in limited areas of South Africa east of the Cape of Good Hope and Mossel Bay. This habitat has rolling hills that are about 200 ft (60 m) to 1000 ft

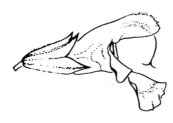

Salvia muirii

(400 m) above sea level and a climate that is strongly influenced by the Indian Ocean. *Salvia muirii* was discovered by John Muir in the late 1920s. Muir wrote to Harriet Margaret Louise Bolus, the botanist who described and named the plant for him, about several locations of the

Salvia muirii produces many small and brilliant violet-blue flowers with a pronounced white bee-line. Flowers appear sporadically from late April to November. (Ginny Hunt)

salvia and also noted, "Its flowering period is from April to June but it is very fine in May." (Hedge 1974).

A small evergreen shrub with olive green leaves, *Salvia muirii* attains 2 ft (60 cm) in height in its native habitat but less in my California garden, where it is usually slightly more than 1 ft (30 cm) tall and about 2 ft (60 cm) wide. Shrubs are also not as stiffly erect as they are in South Africa. The small branches sweep the ground, and over time, the plant expands modestly on underground runners. The largest leaves are tiny, about 0.75 in (2 cm) in length and 0.25 in (0.6 cm) in width. Thickly textured, they appear to be even smaller because each leaf is slightly folded along its middle vein. When stroked, the leaves release an odor that is reminiscent of a medicine cabinet. The entire plant has a petite, tidy look. Inflorescences are short and have violet-blue flowers in whorls of two or three. There is a prominent white splash or beeline on the lower lip of the flower. The lower lip is wider, longer, and more showy than the short, straight, and singly colored upper lip. Like Muir, I have noted that flowering is very fine from April to June. In my garden, more flowers appear in summer, although flowering continues well into November. In the Southern Hemisphere, April to June correspond to autumn in the United States, but I cannot account for the plant flowering in more or less identical months.

This salvia is well suited for areas with mild winters. It died one December when temperatures held at 19°F (-7°C) for four days and nights. Although it did not come back from its roots, the plant was not lost to me forever because nursery people had cuttings in their greenhouses. Propagation is by cuttings taken in September or by teasing away a rooted stem from the mother plant. Seed is seldom produced in California.

Very easy to place in the garden, *Salvia muirii* will make a light and airy plant for the front of a sunny border. *Artemisia pycnocephala* 'David's Choice', a California native plant, is an outstanding companion with silvery gray foliage. California native plants do not usually tolerate summer water, but 'David's Choice' has received regular overhead irrigation in my garden for at least 10 years. *Dianthus* 'Devon Dove', which has wonderfully scented, double white flowers, would add texture to this combination with its mound of gray foliage. There are several cistus all in the range of 3 ft (1 m) in height that would make handsome, early flowering background plants. One such plant is *Cistus* ×skanbergii, which has gray leaves and pink flowers. *Cistus* 'Peggy Sammons' is another pink-flowered possibility. Larger plants, such as the light pink- to almost white-flowered *Lavatera thuringiaca* 'Barnsley', can be placed behind the grouping. The handsome, old-fashioned but reliable *Hibiscus syriacus* 'Diana', rose of Sharon, would be a noteworthy white-flowered companion. Full sun, regular watering, and a good friable soil that drains well are the cultural requirements for all these plants.

Salvia namaensis Schinz

An evergreen shrub with leaves that are aromatic and have an unusual shape, *Salvia namaensis* has a limited habitat in Namibia in southwest Africa but covers a wide area in South Africa. Plants are found on rocky slopes, shales, limestone hills, and sandy soils between 1000 and 5000 ft (400 and 1500 m). The name of this salvia probably derives from Nama, one of the Hottentot tribes of Great Namaland or Namaqualand, a region of Namibia where the plant occurs.

This slightly woody shrub forms an upright plant about 3 ft (1 m) tall and wide. The leaves of this salvia are irregular and very small, less than 0.75 in (2 cm) in length, and as they are also pinnatifid, the plant's appearance is light and airy. The new stems and calyx are the same yellow-green color as the foliage. Inflorescences are short, usually about 4 in (10 cm) in length, with flowers numbering two to six in each whorl. Flowering is never heavy, but there are more flowers when the days and nights are warm. Corollas are white or very pale blue and measure about 0.6 in (1.6 cm). This salvia is also reported to have mauve flowers. My plant came from seed from Silverhill Seed in South Africa, and I look forward to seeing seedlings that have mauve flowers. As it is, my plant is reluctant to set seed even though there are abundant pollinators in the garden, but perhaps in time and with prolonged, warm summer weather, seed will be produced. Propagation is by seed or cuttings taken in midsummer.

It is essential to site *Salvia namaensis* in full sun with good drainage. You can prune the plant to keep it in good shape whenever necessary, but as the plants produce only a modest amount of new foliage, a little shaping rather than pruning may be all that is required. Little, if any, deadheading is necessary, and you should provide regular weekly water. I have not grown this salvia long enough to find out what low temperature it will tolerate. However, the other salvias from the region from which *S. namaensis* comes will all survive 25°F (-4°C) and a little lower. Propagation is usually by cuttings taken in September, but plants may be started by sowing seed in the spring.

The unusual foliage of *Salvia namaensis* gives the plant a frothy appearance. It remains evergreen in a mild climate. (Sonja Wilcomer)

The lovely frothy appearance of *Salvia namaensis*, as well as its spicy aroma, makes it suitable for placement towards the front of the border. To give you some idea of the overall look of the salvia, some garden visitors say it looks similar to *Pelargonium crispum*. If you strive towards simplicity in your garden, you might design a South African border by combining several plants of *S. namaensis* with *S. chamelaeagnea*, which has dark and handsome evergreen foliage. Behind the salvias, the deciduous *Agapanthus inapertus*, which blooms at 5 ft (1.5 m) and has clusters of beautiful drooping, deep blue-violet flowers, would make a striking companion. In front of the salvias, *Diascia* 'Ruby Field', which has bright green mats and 8 in (20 cm) stems of deep coral flowers, will bloom in spring. This collection of South African plants emphasizes the texture of the foliage, and all require the same culture as *S. namaensis*.

Salvia napifolia Jacquin

A perennial herb with understated form and quiet beauty, *Salvia napifolia* was described by Nicholas Joseph de Jacquin in 1773. This salvia grows on islands off the coast of western Turkey and the mainland at elevations near sea level to 3000 ft (900 m). Its habitat is one of rocky slopes and disturbed roadsides as well as maquis, a plant community that is characterized by dense, spiny thickets that have often been browsed and trampled on by grazing animals. The holly-leaved, shrubby oak *Quercus coccifera* is among the dominant components of this particular community. *Salvia napifolia* has been grown abroad since the 1950s but since the 1990s is becoming known to American gardeners.

Reported to be hardy and to survive temperatures in the teens (-10°C), *Salvia napifolia* is a small, herbaceous, clumping plant with many erect stems. It is well covered with simple leaves that are hastate to ovate, occasionally lyrate, in shape, and that frequently have one or two pairs of lateral segments. The leaves are soft, lightly covered with hairs, and its undersides have pronounced veining. The specific epithet, *napifolia*, refers to the leaves being shaped like a turnip, but I must admit that even with a bit of imagination, I find the similarity hard to see. The glands on the leaves are sessile, and little if any scent can be associated with this salvia. Flowering begins in summer, and if the plant is deadheaded it will repeat bloom until late autumn. Inflorescences are about 1 ft (30 cm) in length with dense whorls of flowers that are widely spaced. Several to many inflorescences come into bloom at the same time, and the pale lavender to purplish violet flowers are tiny. The calyx and the corolla are about equal in length, and together they measure roughly 0.5 in (1.3 cm). The plant is not showy but is consistently good-looking throughout the long growing season.

Salvia napifolia will produce lavender to violet flowers in crowded whorls over a long period if it is regularly deadheaded. (Ginny Hunt)

Good drainage, ordinary garden soil, and a half to full day of sun are required for this salvia, as is moderate water on a regular schedule. In a cold climate this salvia is dormant in winter, but in a Mediterranean climate its leaves are persistent. After signs of life return in early spring, apply a 3–4 in (8–10 cm) layer of humus to the plant for summer feeding. The plant's needs are simple, and if you remove the spent inflorescences, it will flower for four or five months.

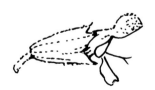

Salvia napifolia

Gardens often have an area, such as along a well-traveled path or passageway, that the gardener looks forward to quickly viewing while moving on to other sections of the garden. This salvia is a perfect candidate for a small sunny area of the garden that the gardener sees on a daily or regular basis. Such an area is one that does not need to call attention to itself with bright flowers but instead includes subtle colors that are revealed in summer as well as year-round good foliage. During the growing season and even in winter, this area could display a combination of handsome foliage. I envision a raised bed about 2 ft (60 cm) high with a fence or wall behind it in a location that receives at least a half day of sunlight. If the bed is very small, you could fill it amply with several plants of *Salvia napifolia* and the evergreen *Berberis stenophylla* 'Irwinii'. Handsome and compact, the graceful 2 ft (60 cm) tall and wide berberis has orange-yellow flowers in spring and glossy, dark green leaves that are white on the underside. If this raised bed or well-traveled area is large enough to accommodate several berberis, you could plant *S. napifolia* and *Sedum cauticola*, which has thick gray leaves that are edged in rose, as both species will form drifts that soon cover the bare ground with healthy and vigorous foliage. These plants all require the same culture.

Salvia nemorosa Linnaeus

A hardy salvia with a wide distribution in central Europe and western Asia, *Salvia nemorosa* was described by Linnaeus in 1762. Attractive, hardy, and easy to grow, the plant has, unsurprisingly, been passed around by gardeners ever since. The specific epithet, *nemorosa*, refers to its habitat in groves and woods. Its long history of cultivation has contributed to problems in identifying and distinguishing species of salvias that have hybridized with *S. nemorosa*, both in the wild and in cultivation, making it exceedingly difficult to define or establish relationships. In John Sutton's (1999) most helpful work *The Gardener's Guide to Growing Salvias*, he lays out the problem and goes toward solving it by describing the cultivars of *S. nemorosa* as well as cultivars of *S.* ×*superba* and *S.*

Salvia nemorosa

The dark purple spikes of *Salvia nemorosa* 'Ostfriesland' in the foreground along with *Penstemon* 'Huntington Pink'. Behind is a purple
hybrid penstemon. (Christine Andrews)

×*sylvestris*. These two hybrids originated in cultivation, and *S. nemorosa* is either a direct parent or a close relative. James Compton (2000) points to the same problem with these salvias in *The European Garden Flora* and suggests a similar solution in order to identify and distinguish clones.

The following list of *Salvia nemorosa* cultivars are very hardy and will easily withstand temperatures well below 0°F (-18°C): 'Amethyst', purple-rose; 'Blauhügel', dark blue; 'Blaukönigin', violet; 'Lubecca', royal blue; 'Lye End', lavender-blue; 'Mainacht', violet; 'Ostfriesland', deep blue-violet; 'Plumosa', a series of purple bracts; 'Rose Queen', rose-pink; 'Rubin', bicolored, pink, and purple; 'Schneehügel', white; 'Superba', deep blue with reddish purple bracts; and 'Tänzerin', violet.

All are perennial and produce many leafy stems that elongate from the base as spring turns into summer. Blooming begins in early summer. Flowers are usually a shade of violet or violet-blue, but there are rosy pinks as well as white-flowered forms. Each plant produces many inflorescences of closely spaced whorls of small flowers held in tiny calyces that are subtended by small but colorful bracts. After the flowers are fertilized and seeds begin to mature, you should prune stems to two active leaf nodes to encourage branching and repeat blooming. In areas with mild climates that extend into October, you can induce flowering for three periods if you regularly dead-head the plants.

This salvia and its cultivars require a sunny position in the garden with well-draining, friable soil and moderate weekly water throughout the growing season. Plants may be pruned to the crown before winter comes, and if temperatures fall to the teens (-10°C) or below, protect them with conifer boughs to prevent heaving. When propagating cultivars, you should take cuttings in late July or August.

Gardeners will find the *Salvia nemorosa* cultivars I list to be choice plants for the herbaceous border. They will flourish when combined with other plants, and they are also good plants for attracting butterflies, bees, and other insects. The parentage of these cultivars remains in a state of confusion; they could be hybrids of *nemorosa*, *pratensis*, *virgata*, ×*superba*, and ×*sylvestris*, or a combination of any of these. Whatever the parentage of these cultivars, their performance has proven them dependable, undemanding, and excellent repeat bloomers.

I would like to call special attention to the white-flowered 'Schneehügel', which is reported to be a cultivar of *Salvia nemorosa*. It has never failed to repeat bloom three times in a long season in my garden. I confess that it flops a bit, but its fresh green foliage and pure white flowers give an understated sparkle to the border.

Ernst Pagels of Germany, who has been called the paradigm of plantsmen, worked for Karl Foerster, a famous German nurseryman and author. Foerster gave the young Pagels a packet of salvia seed in 1949, counseling "seek and you will find." In 1955 Pagels introduced the widely and deservedly popular selection 'Ostfriesland', named for East Friesland. Its abundant, rich violet-blue flowers are held above the crown of the plant. It repeats bloom several times if cut back. Subsequently, Pagels introduced six additional salvia selections. In 1997 the Perennial Plant Association chose Pagels' 1956 introduction 'Mainacht' ('May Night') as their plant of the year.

All the *Salvia nemorosa* cultivars I list are tough, healthy plants that easily adapt to many garden situations. They also make long-lasting cut flowers. I am surprised that these plants are absent from California gardens given their dependable traits. Try tucking these plants in around the base of shrub roses, where a tendency to sprawl becomes an asset. An old-fashioned border that contains spring-flowering clumps of iris, with its swordlike foliage, and peonies, which have divided leaves that turn beautiful colors in autumn, will be enhanced with drifts of the intense violet-blue flowers of 'Blauhügel', a very compact plant that reaches 2 ft (60 cm) tall and wide. *Salvia nemorosa* and its cultivars are excellent fillers for odd-shaped spaces. They also look handsome and healthy in raised beds with gray-foliaged plants, such as the California native *Artemisia pycnocephala* 'David's Choice' or the old tried and true hybrid *Artemisia* 'Powis Castle'.

Salvia nilotica Jacquin

Growing in the eastern part of the African highlands, *Salvia nilotica* extends from Ethiopia to Zimbabwe. Sometimes described as an understory plant, it apparently has many different kinds of habitats and occurs at elevations between 3000 and 12,000 ft (900 and 3600 m). Found on the margins and in the clearings of forests, this salvia grows in waste grounds and burnt grasslands, among low-growing vegetation, and along roadsides, canals, and streams. It is reported to be a rare plant of shaded and disturbed ground in Yemen. Described by Nicolaus Joseph von Jacquin in 1776, the plant's epithet, *nilotica*, refers to regions of the Nile River where the plant may be found in situ.

Salvia nilotica will flourish with only small amounts of water. The dusky green foliage makes it a good companion for other water-conserving plants. (Ginny Hunt)

A salvia with many creeping rhizomes and stems that reach about 2–3 ft (60–90 cm) in height, *Salvia nilotica* is a perennial herb that is strongly aromatic. Despite its custom of creeping, plants tend to stay in clumps 2 ft (60 cm) wide in my garden. Lyrate leaves in mostly basal clumps are mid-green and heavily rugose with short hairs on both surfaces. The largest leaves are 7 in (18 cm) long and 2.5 in (6 cm) wide. The inflorescence is branched and short, usually about 10 in (25 cm) in length. The campanulate calyx is sometimes brownish or purplish and measures up to 0.375 in (1 cm). The upper lip has three teeth and the lower lip has two. Flowers are small, a mere 0.5 in (1.3 cm) long. They are held in whorls of six to eight and range in color from purple to rose to white. Flowering occurs over a lengthy period from early spring to autumn. Removal of spent inflorescences will encourage continued flowering. Even though this salvia produces lots of flowers, it is its overall appearance that makes it attractive to gardeners. Temperatures to 25°F (-4°C) do not harm *S. nilotica*; in fact, it has come back from roots after temperatures registered 19°F (-7°C) in my garden for four days and nights.

This is a water conserving salvia; a small amount of water on a weekly basis is all that it requires. Easy to care for, it needs full sun, sharp drainage, and

SALVIA NILOTICA

medium clay soil that is moisture retentive. This last requirement—moisture retentive soil with sharp drainage—appears paradoxical. I think gardeners understand this kind of contradiction, however, and are able to prepare a well-draining soil that is lean in nutrients. Propagation is by seed or removal of creeping rootstocks.

A bed in the driest, sunniest spot in the garden may appear inhospitable, but it is an amenable and agreeable siting for a group of attractive plants with low water requirements. At the back of such a bed you could place the dark red New Zealand *Phormium tenax* 'Atropurpureum', which will attain 6 ft (2 m) in height and become a strong focal point. Several plants of *Salvia nilotica* will gradually fill the midground, while *Origanum dictamnus* or *Geranium incanum* will billow and soften the edge of the border. Also appropriate is the charming and free-flowering *Erigeron karvinskianus* with its dainty, daisylike, white and pink blossoms. However, because of its tendency to become invasive, the erigeron must be watched and its seedlings periodically removed. All these plants are hardy when temperatures drop to the teens (-10°C) for short periods and they all require a similar culture.

Salvia nubicola Wallich ex Sweet

A full-leaved, summer-blooming herbaceous perennial, *Salvia nubicola* has a wide distribution that includes Afghanistan, Bhutan, India, Pakistan, southwest Asia, and Europe. Found at elevations of 7000 ft (2100 m) or higher, it has been collected many times and grown frequently as a garden subject. In 1993, botanists from Quarryhill Botanical Garden, Glen Ellen, California, and the Royal Botanic Gardens, Kew, collected seed at 9200 ft (2850 m) on a heavily grazed hillside in northern India, where it grew in full sun on light loam along with *Agrimonia*, a *Polygonum* ground cover, and a giant thistle.

Holding its stems erect, *Salvia nubicola* reaches 3 ft (1 m) in height and close to the same in width. The leaves have a fresh green color and are triangular. The largest grow at the base of the plant and measure about 5 in (13 cm) in length. The petiole is more or less the same length as the

Salvia nubicola

Salvia nubicola

leaf blade. Inflorescences are numerous and about 10 in (25 cm) long. Pale yellow flowers with finely spotted maroon markings on the upper lip appear in whorls of two to six. They are held in a bright green, hairy calyx that is glandular and sticky. A light medicinal odor is released when the calyx is rubbed. Flowering is in summer, and seed frequently matures in autumn. Propagation is by seed or cuttings. This salvia superficially resembles the early summer-blooming Jupiter's distaff, *S. glutinosa.*

The specific epithet, *nubicola,* means "dweller among clouds", which underlines the plant's high mountainous home. Hardy to 0°F (-18°C), *Salvia nubicola* also performs well at low elevations in warm climates. Regular, fast-draining garden soil and

Salvia nubicola is a fine filler for a summer border. Here it nestles between an unknown plant of *Agastache* and *Tanacetum parthenium,* feverfew. (Robert Kourik)

protection and some shade from other plants are the main requirements of this salvia. Regular water will insure flowering and seed production. In a cold climate, the plant is dormant, but in a mild climate, it will frequently retain a few leaves.

Salvia nubicola makes a fine filler in a border of summer-blooming perennials. The lax, 4–5 ft (1.3–1.5 m) tall and spreading *Buddleja davidii* 'Nanho Purple', which has dark red-purple flowers with an orange eye, would make a focal point at the back of the border. Several of the 4 ft (1.3 m) tall *S.* 'Purple Majesty', along with the butter-yellow *S. madrensis,* would fill in the back and middle of the border. Mix plants of *S. nubicola* in groups of three with the 2 ft (60 cm) tall *Agastache barberi,* which has red-purple flowers. The *Agastache barberi* plants will fill the front and probably overflow. If you can find some extra space in the front of the border, try the matting, pale yellow yarrow *Achillea* 'King Edward' as it grows quickly and would soon cover the bare spots.

Salvia officinalis Linnaeus
garden sage, common sage

Described in 1753 by Carl Linnaeus, *Salvia officinalis* has long been known and grown. Old herbal books tell of the miraculous properties attributed to it:

> *He who would live for aye*
> *Must eat sage in May.*

Called sage or garden sage in early times, the specific epithet, *officinalis*, refers to the plant being sold in shops for its medicinal virtues. Found in the wild on the northern shores of the Mediterranean, including in Asia Minor, it is renowned for its culinary and medicinal properties. Cultivated for centuries in England, France, Germany, Spain, and Italy for these attributes, it is also valued throughout the temperate world as a handsome and well-tested garden subject. Through widespread cultivation it has become naturalized in a few benign climates.

Described by botanists as a shrub because of the woody stems at the base, it appears to gardeners more like a well-branched, evergreen, herbaceous perennial. With a height and width of 2 ft (60 cm), the handsome gray-green leaves have a rugose surface and are almost white underneath because of the short, soft hairs. Oblong in shape, the leaves vary in size, the largest being about 2.5 in (6 cm) long and 1 in (2.5 cm) wide. The leaves give the sage a well-covered look in both summer and winter. Flowering occurs in late spring or summer. *Salvia officinalis* is exceedingly variable in flower and leaf color. You may find white, pink, purple, or lavender flowers, the latter being the most common. Highly variable in size, the foliage color and pattern are also variable. Leaves can be variegated with yellow, cream, purple, or rose in different patterns.

These varied characteristics have given rise to many different cultivars. The weak 'Aurea' has gold-colored leaves. 'Berggarten', meaning mountain garden, was introduced by Herrenhausen Grosser Garten in Hannover, Germany, and has wide, rounded leaves and few flowers. 'Compacta' is a narrow-leaved and compact form. 'Icterina' has green leaves with a wide golden yellow margin. 'Purpurascens', the favored sage of medieval times, has purple-red leaves and was commonly called red sage. 'Tricolor' has gray-green leaves that are zoned creamy yellow and rose. 'Holt's Mammoth' has long, wide, gray-green leaves and is a compact form. All these cultivars hold their foliage and flowers well in bouquets. Other cultivars that are more familiar in Britain and Europe than in the United States are: 'Albiflora', which has long leaves and white flowers; 'Crispa', which has variegated leaves with wavy margins; 'Grete Stolze', which has pointed, pale gray leaves; 'Milleri', which has spotted red leaves; 'Salicifolia', which has long narrow leaves; and 'Sturnina', which has white-green leaves.

Salvia officinalis is hardy and reputed to withstand temperatures of 0°F (-18°C) or less. All cultivars are much less hardy and need protection from freezing and thawing. Quick-draining garden soil and full sun are necessities for these sages. Some kind of grit or coarse sand can be incorporated in the soil and the plant elevated on a small mound in order to ensure fast drainage. Somewhat drought tolerant, garden sage needs moderate additional summer watering and will withstand overhead irri-

The lavender blooms of *Salvia officinalis* together with both white-flowered and rose-flowered valerian, *Centranthus ruber*. In the midground are the irislike leaves of *Sisyrinchium striatum*, and behind them is the yellow-flowering *Euphorbia characias* subsp. *wulfenii*. (Robert Kourik)

gation if given fast drainage. Though perennial, these sages are short-lived plants—they usually look good for only three to four years. Propagation is by cuttings or divisions in late spring or early autumn. Seeds germinate readily, but because of the plant's variability, vegetative propagation is advised. Leaves have the highest concentration of volatile oils just before the plant comes into bloom, and this is the most advantageous time to gather leaves for drying. A saying from the Middle Ages is, "Why should a man die whilst sage grows in his garden?"

Garden sage and its many cultivars need little if any attention when well placed in the garden. I frequently squeeze *Salvia officinalis* 'Purpurascens' into the front of my border or into spots where its purple-gray leaves bring out the color of other plants. I find this plant indispensable. Trevor Nottle (1984), an

Foliage that is rich purple year-round makes *Salvia officinalis* 'Purpurascens' a notable garden companion. (Christine Andrews)

The bright yellow, variegated foliage of *Salvia officinalis* 'Icterina' is seen here above the golden foliage of *Origanum vulgare* 'Aureum'. (Mark Kane)

Australian garden writer, advocates its placement in the front of the border combined with a plant or two of *Geranium sanguineum*, bloody cranesbill, which has finely divided, dark green leaves and magenta flowers. The cultivar 'Berggarten' is choice for the border too. Its large, rounded, gray-green leaves make a quiet pool of color, and it is longer lived than the species or any cultivars that I have grown. 'Icterina' is also especially useful. Penelope Hobhouse (1985) laments that 'Icterina' is typically described as having variegated green and golden yellow foliage because she insists that the green is yellowish and

SALVIA OFFICINALIS

the golden yellow almost honey colored. This gives the plant a subtlety of hue which is softer than gold. A good choice for small tight spaces is the cultivar 'Compacta'. Its small gray-green leaves look good throughout the year. All these plants add color and texture to garden designs and they also provide short-term reliability.

Salvia oppositiflora Ruiz & Pavón

Although a very tender plant, *Salvia oppositiflora* is a most pleasing perennial plant, and when in bloom it is a delight. It grows in Peru at many high elevation sites from 7000 to 12,000 ft (2100 to 3600 m). Extremely frost sensitive, it has been grown and wintered in greenhouses on both sides of the Atlantic since the early 1800s. In 1798, Hipolito Ruiz and José Pavón collected a plant in Peru and later described it in *Flora of Peru* (Steele 1964).

Of medium size, *Salvia oppositiflora* will reach 2 ft (60 cm)—even 3 ft (1 m) or more in a mild climate—in both height and width. A bit lax in habit, it is nevertheless a good choice for a container and will spill gracefully over its sides. Mid-green leaves are ovate, almost triangular in shape, and the largest measure about 1.5 in (4 cm) long and wide. Leaves are smooth or lightly covered with hairs, and the margin is serrate. The multiple stems of the plant are well covered with leaves, which make a fine background for the long, slim, orange-red flowers. The two-lipped

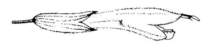

Salvia oppositiflora

flower appears tubelike and measures over 1 in (2.5 cm) in length with showy reddish stamens that protrude from the upper lip. The inflorescence tends to be short, and flowers are in opposite pairs, giving the plant its specific name. The flower is an unusually soft and mellow orange-red. The calyces are lime green and covered with short hairs and glands, as are the plant's stems. Leaves, calyces, and flowers make a beautiful combination of color. Even though hummingbirds and many insects visit the flowers, I have never found seed on *S. oppositiflora*. Fortunately, it is easy to propagate plants by cuttings. This salvia is exceedingly tender so you should hold over rooted cuttings or plants in pots in a protected place.

When warm temperatures during both the day and night return, *Salvia oppositiflora* can be moved outdoors. A half day of sunlight, regular water, and

Favored for more than 100 years as a greenhouse plant, *Salvia oppositiflora* can be grown in a garden in a mild climate. Its tubular flowers attract hummingbirds and insects. (Ginny Hunt)

good drainage are its cultural needs. In midsummer when plants show signs of starting to bloom, I give them half-strength, nitrogen-free, liquid fertilizer about every two weeks. Its blooming period begins in midsummer, and if you can take the plants into a sunny greenhouse, flowering will continue through November.

Salvia palaestina Bentham

Known as an Asiatic species, *Salvia palaestina* is commonly found in a large area that includes Turkey, Syria, Iraq, Iran, Israel, the Sinai Peninsula, and northeastern Egypt. Its habitat consists of rocky slopes, cliffs of limestone and volcanic rock, oak woodlands, vineyards, and fallow fields. Occurring at elevations between 1000 and 4000 ft (400 and 1200 m), this salvia has proven to be frost tolerant to the low 20°s F (around -6°C). It was introduced to horticulture in California and elsewhere in 1997 by seed that Seedhunt distributed.

An erect perennial herb, *Salvia palaestina* is about 1–2 ft (30–60 cm) tall and has a habit and size that are perfectly suited for a herbaceous border of

A plant that repeats bloom, *Salvia palaestina* is a water-conserving plant that performs well in a dry border. (Ginny Hunt)

water conserving plants. Many quadrangular stems emerge from basal roots with leaves that vary in both shape and size. Some leaves are deeply cut while others are lyrate. All are a mid-green color and rugose with light hairs on both surfaces. When the leaves are rubbed, the glands release a scent reminiscent of newly crushed green leaves. Inflorescences are about 12 in (30 cm) long and in a candelabra-like position at the top of the stems. Four to six flowers are set in clearly distinct whorls and subtended by large leafy bracts. The straight, tubular flowers are white or whitish lilac and just over 0.5 in (1.3 cm) long. Hummingbirds obligingly pollinate the plants in my garden and there is always an adequate crop of seed. Seed is an easy means of propagating *S. palaestina* but you can also propagate this salvia by taking cuttings in August or September.

A border on a hillside with good drainage and full sun is the ideal setting for a group of plants with low water requirements. Rosemary is a natural choice for such a location and there are several cultivars that attain about 5 ft (1.5 m) in height and are upright in habit, including *Rosmarinus officinalis* 'Tuscan Blue', 'Miss Jessopp's Upright', and 'Spice Islands'. Mounds of the tough, 2 ft (60 cm) tall rockrose, *Cistus ×skanbergii*, with soft gray-green foliage and small coral-pink flowers will bloom after the rosemary. Drifts of *Salvia palaestina* will bloom off and on from early spring until frost or until the days become short. *Salvia algeriensis* has the same long blooming period as *S. palaestina*, and drifts of the light lavender-flowered annual would make handsome companions. Another worthy companion is the dwarf sageleaf rockrose, *Cistus salviifolius* 'Prostratus', which makes a gentle mound 1 ft (30 cm) high and occasionally 6 ft (2 m) wide. In spring it is covered with small, spotless white blossoms. Some of the salvias from Mexico with showy flowers that repeat bloom quite heavily in spring and autumn make fine additions to the border. Two selections of *S. greggii* that would be colorful partners with *S. palaestina* are 'Purple Pastel' or 'Furman's Red'. All these plants require the same culture.

Salvia patens Cavanilles
gentian sage

Since being introduced to horticulture in 1838, *Salvia patens* has been extensively grown and deservedly praised. William Robinson (1933) says that without question, *S. patens* is among the best plants in cultivation. Many gardeners wholeheartedly agree with him.

Found in the wild over a large section of central Mexico, *Salvia patens* is a herbaceous perennial that will overwinter with protection in areas where the temperature dips down into the 20°s F (around -6°C). Beth Chatto (1988) confirms the plant's hardiness in her Essex garden but cautions that cuttings should be kept under cover as insurance. It is frequently treated as an annual, and new plants can be bedded out in midspring. A few color selections, such as 'Alba', white, 'Cambridge Blue', light blue, 'Chilcombe', lilac, and 'Oxford Blue', dark blue, are periodically offered on seed lists and at nurseries. Seeds of special selections with large and richly colored flowers have been available from Holland since the 1990s. In 1991 a party of botanists and plant enthusiasts from England and Texas embarked upon an exciting expedition in northern and central Mexico. During that trip James Compton found and collected seed of *S. patens* in Sierra de Guanajuato. The unusually deep blue flowers were large, more than 2 in (5 cm) in length, and were on plants that grew to 6 ft (2 m). He calls this beautiful variant 'Guanajuato'.

Salvia patens is tuberous and easy to lift for greenhouse protection if winters are cold and unpredictable. Mature plants reach 1–2 ft (30–60 cm) in height and width and are generously covered with mistletoe-green leaves that are has-

tate in shape. The inflorescence rises
well above the foliage, extending 6–12
in (15–30 cm), sometimes more. Rich,
cornflower-blue flowers over 1 in (2.5
cm) long are spaced along the inflorescence. On close examination, the
hood of the flower is a lighter color
(probably because of the hairs that

Salvia patens

cover it) than the wide, two-parted lip. Both parts are violet-blue. The specific
epithet, *patens*, refers to the two spreading parts of the flower, which make it
easily accessible to pollinators. The calyx is green, about 0.5 in (1.3 cm) long,
with an upper and lower lip. It is a graceful appendage and adds to the beauty
of each flower. Propagation is by seed and cuttings. Established plants can be
carefully divided from the rootstock.

    Salvia patens needs some shade and good garden soil that drains well and
is enriched with humus. Deep weekly watering and a monthly application of
fertilizer will stimulate reblooming if spent inflorescences are removed. Peak
bloom is in early summer and lasts close to a month. A 2–4 in (5–10 cm) layer
of mulch will conserve water and improve the soil around the plants.

    A versatile plant because of its neat growing habit, gentian sage planted in
groups looks good when coupled with the wonderful dark red Gallica roses
'Tuscany' or 'Tuscany Superb'. An alternative rose to consider is *Rosa rugosa*
'Rubra', which frequently produces violet-red hips. An effective planting is
Salvia patens massed in formal beds or areas that are edged with clipped box-
wood. Another fine edging plant is the handsome, low-growing *Tanacetum
haradjanii*. Its silver-white, feathery foliage contrasts well with the blue flowers
of the sage, and together these plants make a striking combination.

Salvia penstemonoides Kunth & Bouché
big red sage

Salvia penstemonoides is a rare plant in nature, occurring in only three locations
in Texas, including the Edwards Plateau in central Texas. It was first sighted and
documented in 1849 growing along the Salado Creek near San Antonio. In 1946
it was thought to be extinct, but it was rediscovered in 1987 by Marshall
Enquist, a botanist who was taking photographs for his book *Wildflowers of the*

Texas Hill Country. He found a large colony at that time but the plant remains endangered and on the verge of extinction because of destruction of its habitat and browsing by deer. There is speculation that a severe drought in Texas in the early 1950s contributed to its decline.

A herbaceous perennial, big red sage grows to 5 ft (1.5 m) tall in its native habitat of limestone rock along seeps or creeks. This habitat information provides a good clue as to its requirements in the garden. In a mild climate, the flowering stalks will reach a mere 3 ft (1 m) and have a tendency to be lax. It has a slick and healthy-looking basal rosette of leaves that are lancelike in outline and mistletoe-green in color. From the rosette, numerous stalks arise bearing flowers 1 in (2.5 cm) in length and beetroot-purple in color. The calyx is 0.5 in (1.3 cm) long and the color of red wine. Whorls of loosely packed flowers are spaced along an inflorescence that sometimes measures 8–12 in (20–30 cm). As its name suggests, *Salvia penstemonoides* resembles a penstemon. Flowering can begin in early summer but more frequently starts in August. Quite hardy to the low 20°s F (around -6°C), big red sage is most easily propagated by seed. Cuttings are possible, and large clumps can, with care, be divided. Plants and seed are available from a limited number of sources.

Before planting *Salvia penstemonoides*, you should incorporate humus and ground oyster shells or lime into the soil. The plant requires fast drainage and enough space for the roots to develop deeply. A half day of morning sun with the protection of high shade is desirable. Deep weekly watering will encourage good growth. It is reported to grow in full sun in areas where the humidity is high. I have seen big red sage in gardens in Austin, Texas, where it thrives in full sun.

If you are fortunate enough to have limestone rocks in your garden, this is the perfect salvia to plant among them. Other rocks are suitable if the soil is adjusted. A possible companion plant for *Salvia penstemonoides* is the cotoneaster, all of which are notable for their preference for sweet soil. There are many cotoneaster species to choose from as they come in a wide array of habits and sizes. For example, *Cotoneaster horizontalis*, which prefers north or east light and deep weekly watering, is known for its low-growing and spreading habit. Ferns are also an interesting group of plants to grow with big red sage, particularly in a border. One possible combination is *Cyrtomium falcatum* (Japanese holly fern) and *Pteris cretica*; both enjoy the same cultural conditions as *S. penstemonoides*. Whether or not you plant them among rocks, the contrast in foliage makes a pleasing and graceful combination.

Considered a weed in its native Mexico, *Salvia polystachya* is a charming addition to an autumn border. (Christine Andrews)

Salvia polystachya Ortega

A tall perennial herb, *Salvia polystachya* has a wide distribution from central Mexico south through Guatemala into Panama. It is found at altitudes of 3000–10,000 ft (900–3100 m) where the climate is mild and there is some summer rain. Rarely seen in gardens or on nursery lists, this salvia deserves to become better known.

Salvia polystachya, which is shrublike, grows 3–9 ft (1–3 m) in a season. As is the case with so many of the late-blooming Mexican salvias, it is brittle and needs the protection of other plants. By late September, *S. polystachya* begins to show a few violet-blue flowers less than 0.5 in (1.3 cm) long, but it does not come into full bloom until the middle of October. It is then that many short and slender spikes composed of verticils of tightly held flowers provide a burst of color. The specific epithet, *polystachya*, refers to the many flowered branches or spikes. Yellow-green leaves are small, barely 1 in (2.5 cm) long and wide, and are held in little clusters. They clothe the stems of the plant without obstructing the spikes of sparkling flowers, which are violet blue at the edge, gradually fading to white in the center.

The flowering of this salvia came as a delightful surprise to me for it had been in my garden two years before it began its autumnal display. Before it will flower, the plant must build a strong root system. Once such a root system is in place, leafy stems about 5 ft (1.5 m) in height and 4 ft (1.3 m) in width develop during the summer. A few flowers appear in September, but as October gradually rolls into November, the plant continues flowering through rainy autumn days and nights of light frost. I recommend taking cuttings for the greenhouse in early autumn as the plant is hardy only to 20°F (-7°C). Propagation is by cuttings.

Place *Salvia polystachya* in the border so that it receives half to three-quarters of a day's sun. Well-draining soil amended with humus is advised, as is a mulch of humus during the summer months. The additional humus helps keep the soil friable and moist. Deep watering is required once or twice a week throughout the growing and flowering periods. More water may be needed if temperatures are high. Prune the plant back to two active nodes about 1 ft (30 cm) from the ground in early spring to encourage shapeliness during the coming season of growth. Cut flowers are a disappointment because once they are brought inside they loose their brilliant sparkle and merely look gray.

This salvia complements many herbaceous perennials and shrubs. For example, its height and sparkling flowers add an additional touch to an autumn-blooming border of asters and penstemons. A fine companion for shrub roses, *Salvia polystachya* will hardly be noticed until it comes into bloom late in the season, complementing reblooming roses such as the single, buff-yellow 'Mrs. Oakley Fisher', the warm pink 'Mary Rose', or the clear, light pink 'Duchesse de Brabant'. In my garden it grows behind the handsome, shrublike *S. microphylla* 'Forever Red'. The combination of red and blue flowers on two dissimilar salvia plants is impressive.

Salvia pratensis Linnaeus
meadow sage

A widely scattered species, *Salvia pratensis* is found throughout Europe, including the United Kingdom. It is also reported to occur in North Africa. An erect perennial, it grows in sunny meadows together with other wild flowers and grasses. The epithet, *pratensis*, is from Latin and means "growing in meadows."

Making a basal clump of rich green leaves, meadow sage has a leafy, herbaceous look. The margins of the leaves are slightly ruffled and toothed and the wrinkled surface is rugose. The upper leaves clasp the stem and twist in an attractive way. Flowering spikes are usually branched, with four to six flowers held in each verticil. Rich violet flowers, less than 1 in (2.5 cm) long, open from the base of the inflorescence as it elongates to about 12 in (30 cm). Each flower is held in a tiny dark brown calyx that sits on a platter of small green bracts. The seedlings of *Salvia pratensis* vary in flower color from violet-blue to bluish white and from pure white to pink. The plant is usually in bloom for three or four weeks if early spring weather stays moderate. The selection 'Tenorii' has especially fine, rich blue flowers.

Salvia pratensis grows rapidly and blooms in early spring. (Christine Andrews)

Salvia pratensis subsp. *haematodes* is widely grown and admired for its erect sprays of large, summer-blooming, lilac-blue flowers. Flower arrangers in particular prize its endurance as a cut flower. It is not apparent why it is called *haematodes*, which means "bloody-veined." Some botanists regard it as a separate species. John Sutton (1999) reports that this subspecies was introduced from Greece.

Indigenous to areas with hard winters as well as to frost-free areas, the deciduous meadow sage can be tried in all kinds of climates. Full sun and good garden loam that drains readily are needed, as is occasional water throughout the year. In a very mild climate, meadow sage comes into bloom in March and makes a wonderful display of rich purple spikes. Plants growing in the north or in areas with hard winters may not bloom until June or even July. If the plant is cut back before it makes seed, it will probably rebloom if summer temperatures are warm and the autumn long. Meadow sage makes a long-lasting and handsome cut flower.

As long ago as 1968, the seed of *Salvia pratensis* was not permitted to be shipped to California because it was thought to have naturalized in the wild in three locations. In 1983 this naturalized salvia was correctly identified as *S. virgata*, another widely distributed European native. Botanists at the California

Department of Food and Agriculture have decided that *S. virgata* is no longer a threat. Seed catalogs for 1995 from other countries still warn that seed of *S. pratensis* may not be sent into California. It probably will take quite some time to unravel this tangle.

A meadowlike border in full sun might include *Leucanthemum vulgare*, the single, white, ox-eye daisy, along with clumps of meadow sage and quantities of *Stipa pulchra* (purple needlegrass). *Stipa pulchra* is the grass that gives California the name "the Golden State." By midspring its green foliage begins to recede and its beautiful and delicate flower panicles rise 2 ft (60 cm) or more. The entire plant dries to a rich tawny color. Even though it is considered drought tolerant, some additional summer water may be necessary, even in its dormant state. Another grass that can be interplanted with meadow sage and ox-eye daisy is *Koeleria cristata*. It is a clumping evergreen perennial under 2 ft (60 cm) tall with rich green foliage and flowering stems that rise 12 in (30 cm) above the foliage. Sweet vernal grass, *Anthoxanthum odoratum*, is another possibility. About 6–8 in (15–20 cm) in height, its flowers rise 12 in (30 cm) above the clump. In June it turns a warm gold color. These grasses are particularly effective visually because they respond so gracefully to the movement of the wind.

Salvia prunelloides Kunth

Reported to come from a limited geographical area in Mexico, *Salvia prunelloides* is found in the wild in the provinces of both Mexico and Puebla. Described and named by Karl Sigismund Kunth in 1817, this salvia had been known previously by another epithet. It was given the name *prunelloides* to reflect a similarity to *Prunella vulgaris*, sometimes called "all heal" or "salt of the earth." *Prunella vulgaris* is another common mint that has spread from Great Britain over all of Europe and across the United States to California.

Not a common plant either in the wild or in cultivation, *Salvia prunelloides* is a small herbaceous and procumbent plant with nodules on its roots. It is not a clumping plant but is one that instead increases by making underground runners that appear singly and erratically. Stems are lax, under 1 ft (30 cm) in length, and lightly covered with small trowel-shaped leaves. The largest measure about 1.25 in (3 cm) long and 0.75 in (2 cm) wide with a petiole that is 0.5 in (1.3 cm) in length. A faint, haylike odor is released when the

With good grassy green foliage, *Salvia prunelloides* produces stems that multiply and develop into a fine ground cover. (Ginny Hunt)

foliage is brushed. Flowering occurs in summer and is both limited and sporadic. Periwinkle-blue flowers are small, barely 0.5 in (1.3 cm) long, and held in tiny calyces that are arranged in tight whorls at the very tip of the inflorescence. There is no space between the smattering of whorls. The upper lip of the flower is hooded and quite small, the lower lip being three times as long and wide. There are faint white markings on the lower lip to guide pollinators to the nectary.

Given a half to full day of sun, *Salvia prunelloides* will produce tiny flowers sporadically for several months. It needs adequate drainage and a friable soil that contains plenty of humus. Water is needed on a regular basis, and a liquid fertilizer at half strength can be used to good advantage in spring, when the plant starts active growth. Plants in a mild climate tend to be evergreen. In my garden, if temperatures drop to the low 20°s F (around -6°C), plants come back from the roots with the return of warm spring weather. You do not need to prune or deadhead this salvia, but you should spread an additional layer of mulch each year at the beginning or end of spring.

Not a showy or a compelling plant, *Salvia prunelloides* is nevertheless interesting and useful in the garden. It makes a light ground cover around the feet of small evergreen or deciduous shrubs. A border that receives only a half day of sunlight might feature the beautiful and slow-growing, 5 ft (1.5 m) tall *Osmanthus heterophyllus* 'Goshiki', which has foliage with intense yellow blotches that will lighten the area in summer and winter. The deciduous *Philadelphus* 'Avalanche' or 'Bouquet Blanc', which are Lemoine hybrids, are also in the same height range and would add a lovely fragrance to the border. Consider *Helleborus argutifolius*, which blooms heavily from winter into spring, as a companion plant, and *S. prunelloides* as a light ground cover. All these plants will benefit from water on a regular basis and a spring application of humus or mulch of wood chips.

Salvia przewalskii Maximowicz

In the wild, *Salvia przewalskii* grows in China in the provinces of Gansu, Hubei, Sichuan, Xizang, and Yunnan. A freely seeding herbaceous perennial, this salvia establishes itself along streambanks and forest margins, among shrubs, and on granitic hillsides. Described and named in 1881 by the indefatigable Russian botanist Carl Johann Maximowicz, it has been collected in China by many famous plantspeople on a number of occasions. In naming the salvia, Maximowicz honored the Russian zoological and botanical explorer Nicolai M. Przwalski, who made four collecting trips to China between 1872 and 1884. Botanists have specified four varieties that are based primarily on leaf covering and shape. *Salvia przewalskii* has a wide distribution and is known throughout its native habitat for its medicinal properties. Its leaves have very long petioles. *Salvia przewalskii* is usually seen growing only in botanic gardens but since the 1980s it has appeared on seed lists that are available to gardeners.

From a clump of basal leaves between 1 and 2 ft (30 and 60 cm) in width and height, flowering stalks of 3 ft (1 m) rise above yellow-green foliage in midsummer. Leaves are 6–12 in (15–30 cm) long with veins clearly delineated on the underside. On the tall, branched inflorescence, widely spaced whorls of flowers open a few at a time. The flowers are about 1 in (2.5 cm) long, fat, and an unusual purple-red or red-brown color. The hairy and glandular calyx is red-brown and two-lipped. These handsome flowering stems are subtle in color and make fine cut flowers if you condition them by cutting them under water. The blooming period usually lasts for well over three weeks. Propagation is by seed. Self-seeding becomes evident when plants are established.

Salvia przewalskii

Salvia przewalskii

Salvia przewalskii needs well-draining, friable garden soil. Plants will bloom liberally if situated in full sun, and they will bloom fairly well with a half day of sun. Deep weekly watering is also necessary. Mulching with compost provides food and helps with water retention. Established plants are hardy to 10°F (-12°C).

This plant is a handsome addition to a high-summer flowering bed of purple-red and pink cut flowers, including both annuals and perennials. *Perilla frutescens*, which has purple-red leaves, can be interplanted in threes or fives with *Datura wrightii* (formerly known as *Datura meteloides*), with its handsome gray leaves and a trumpet flower of soft white tinged with purple. Both make harmonious companions for *Salvia przewalskii*. This subtly colored composition would be brightened with a few pastel pink zinnias. To further enliven the color combination, add one or two plants of wispy, white flowering cosmos. If there is space, try the continually blooming *S. microphylla* 'Rosita', which has candy-pink flowers, as it would add both substance and uninterrupted color. All require the same culture and some cutting-back in order to encourage repeat bloom.

Salvia puberula Fernald

Rarely seen in the wild, *Salvia puberula* has been reported growing in the Mexican provinces of San Luis Potosí, Tamaulipas, Hidalgo, and Nuevo León. It is usually found in small colonies near oaks, yews, liquidambers, lindens, and dogwoods at elevations that vary from 4500 to 8000 ft (1400 to 2500 m). Some authorities consider *S. puberula* to be a variety of *S. involucrata* Cavanilles.

Growing 3–5 ft (1–1.5 m) tall, this shrublike herbaceous perennial comes into glorious bloom in autumn. From October until frost, terminal clusters of bright magenta flowers are displayed at the top of long stems. The inflated flowers are about 1 in (2.5 cm) in length and are two-lipped. The upper lip is heavily covered with magenta hairs that fairly sparkle in sunlight. The 0.5 in (1.3 cm) calyx, which is also magenta, adds to the colorful display. Leaflike bracts surround the expanding flowers and soon drop. The leaves are hastate in shape, the largest being 4 in (10 cm) long and 2.5 in (6 cm) wide. The pea-green leaves are widely spaced along the stems. Short, soft hairs cover the stems and leaves, and the upper lip of each flower has magenta hairs. This characteristic probably led to the specific epithet, *puberula*, meaning soft and downy. *Salvia puberula* was described and named in 1900 by Fernald.

Fine specimens of *Salvia puberula* may be seen at the University of California Botanical Garden, Berkeley. Gardeners have quickly discovered its long autumn flowering season. Yucca Do Nursery has introduced plants collected in two different locations in the province of Nuevo León in Mexico.

Autumn-blooming *Salvia puberula* with large inflated flowers. (Christine Andrews)

One selection comes from an elevation of 4500 ft (1400 m), and the other comes from El Butano at an even higher elevation, 7000 ft (2100 m). Both clones grew in well-draining but moist soil in the company of dogwoods, yews, and oaks.

Cultural requirements are simple and include well-draining soil enriched with humus and at least a half day of sun. Deep watering on a one- to two-week basis is desirable. Depending on its collection site, *Salvia puberula* is probably hardy to 20°F (-7°C), but I recommend you take cuttings for the greenhouse in autumn. In early spring, prune the plant almost to the ground; it grows prolifically once the weather warms. Propagation is by seed or cuttings.

Salvia puberula likes close association with other plants. Small trees, such as cherries, redbuds, and arbutus, are fine companions and provide added protection from both wind and strong sunlight. A border of shrubs

Salvia puberula

interplanted with *S. puberula* is handsome as well as practical. Good companion shrubs with an upright-growing habit and dark green foliage include *Osmanthus heterophyllus*, *Rhamnus alaternus*, and *R. californicus*. The weight of foliage and flowers gives this salvia a tendency to lean, so the thick green foliage of these three shrubs acts not only as a foil for the yellow-green leaves and distinctive magenta flowers but also as a support.

Salvia 'Purple Majesty'

A large herbaceous shrub, the hybrid *Salvia* 'Purple Majesty' comes from an artificial cross made at the Huntington Botanical Gardens by Fred Boutin in 1977. The parents are *S. guaranitica* and *S. gesneriiflora* 'Tequila'. From that cross pollination, three seeds were produced, and from those seedlings, one plant was chosen for introduction because of its garden merit. *Salvia* 'Purple Majesty' was introduced to horticulture around 1980 and has proved to be a tireless bloomer with rich and colorful flowers.

Salvia 'Purple Majesty' reaches 3–4 ft (1–1.3 m) in a growing season and comes into bloom in midsummer, flowering until frost. Ovate, serrated, yellow-green leaves amply cover the plant. They measure about 3 in (8 cm) in length and 2 in (5 cm) in width. Spikelike inflorescences 8–10 in (20–25 cm) long form at the top of stems. Individual flowers are about 1 in (2.5 cm) long and a rich violet color. The calyx is 0.75 in (2 cm) long and an even darker purple than the flowers, adding to the beauty of the inflorescence. The inflorescences are handsome and make fine cut flowers that last for many days in an arrangement if they are conditioned by being cut under water. Their color remains when they are dried for winter bouquets.

Full sun, fast-draining soil, and regular dressings of humus are needed to keep this salvia flowering for a long period. I also recommend three applications of liquid fertilizer spread out over the growing season. Deep watering once every week or two is desirable. The frequent removal of spent flowering parts is necessary for two reasons: the weight of the spent inflorescences will break stems and branches if not removed, and new flowering is stimulated by this kind of pruning. Propagation is by cuttings so that identical plants can be obtained. When taken in late summer, cuttings strike roots readily. *Salvia* 'Purple Majesty' is reported to be hardy to 10°F (-12°C) when the crown is protected with straw or some other light mulch. In a moderate climate no protection is needed. When all danger of frost has passed, prune all stems back to the lowest active nodes. This procedure will assure a well-shaped plant for the coming season.

This is a fine plant for the summer into autumn border. *Salvia* 'Purple Majesty' combined with the 6 ft (2 m), yellow flowering *S. madrensis* makes an admirable background for drifts of the 4 ft (1.3 m) *Boltonia asteroides* 'Snowbank' and 3–4 ft (1–1.3 m) Michaelmas daisies. (Both *Aster novae-angliae* from New England and *A. novi-belgii* from New York have been used in hybridizing work, and the name Michaelmas daisy applies to their hybrids.) A selection of lavender-blue, violet, white, and purple Michaelmas daisies looks handsome in the border or in bouquets with this salvia.

The aptly named *Salvia* 'Purple Majesty'. (Christine Andrews)

Salvia purpurea Cavanilles

An autumn- into winter-blooming herbaceous perennial from Mesoamerica, *Salvia purpurea* is distributed from the province of Jalisco in Mexico south into Guatemala, El Salvador, and Honduras. It is widely spread through six Mexican provinces. Epling (1939) states that great variation in the length of the corolla is typical throughout the range of the species. The plant was described in 1793, though I can find no mention of it in horticultural literature. Huntington Botanical Gardens, Strybing Arboretum, and the University of California Botanical Garden in Berkeley have examples of the plant collected in Mexico. It is likely that its introduction to horticulture came from those institutions. This desirable salvia is rarely seen in nurseries or on seed lists.

The flowers of *Salvia purpurea* are truly lavender-violet, a color rarely seen in winter. Behind the salvia is the long-needled *Pinus oaxacana*. (Don Mahoney)

A striking plant because of the color of its flowers, *Salvia purpurea* is shrub like in stature, about 3–7 ft (1–2.3 m) in height, and a little less in width. Ovate, yellow-green leaves with serrated margins cover the plant well. Branched inflorescences begin to appear in the middle of autumn and the flowering period is usually two, even three months long. When the plant breaks into bloom it is a surprise to see pinkish purple-violet flowers, rather than the more common warm autumnal reds and yellows. Flowers are in tight verticils that appear to be swept to one side of the spike. Small individual flowers about 0.75 in (2 cm) long are crowded together at the ends of numerous branches. These inflorescences of pinkish purple flowers make a rich display. Flowering stems hold well as cut flowers if kept in a cool place.

Provided with a few basic conditions, *Salvia purpurea* is easy to establish in a garden. Place it so that it receives a half day of sun in both summer and winter in well-draining soil that has been amended with humus. A mulch of humus and regular weekly water are needed to imitate conditions in its native habitat. To ensure a shapely plant, prune stems back to active leaf nodes near the base in early spring. *Salvia purpurea* is tender but withstands temperatures of 25°F (-4°C) for very short periods. Propagation is generally by seed or cuttings.

An unusual plant because of its flowering period and flower color, *Salvia purpurea* is not easy to place in an autumn garden design. However, companion plants can be found for its pinkish purple flowers. *Osmanthus heterophyllus*, an evergreen shrub with dark green, shiny leaves, makes a splendid backdrop for the salvia. It too blooms in late autumn with tiny, fragrant, creamy white blossoms. The compact Australian shrub *Westringia* 'Wynyabbie Gem', growing to 3–4 ft (1–1.3 m) tall with silky, gray-green leaves and lavender flowers that appear periodically throughout the year, would complete the picture.

Salvia recognita Fischer & Meyer

Salvia recognita, an endemic from central Turkey, grows in light shade at the base of cliffs at an elevation usually of 4000 ft (1200 m) or less. It is described as a woody-based perennial with a mass of divided leaves that forms a small to medium basal clump. Leaves vary in size, ranging from 3 to 4 in (8 to 10 cm) to almost 1 ft (30 cm) in length with three or more leaflets. Light green leaves with a grayish cast appear thick in texture due to a covering of long, soft hairs. Each

The pink-flowering Turkish endemic *Salvia recognita*, with the foliage of *S. sclarea* in the foreground and the taller foliage of *S. guarantica* behind it on the left. (Betsy Clebsch)

leaf blade has a wine-colored petiole. The cyclamen-pink flowers appear in whorls and the calyces that hold them are covered with glands and hairs. These shaggy hairs and dewlike viscid glands add further interest to this handsome plant. Round flowering stalks elongate to 2–3 ft (60–90 cm) and hold many whorls of widely spaced flowers at the top. The long blooming period begins in spring and continues into warm weather, with an occasional inflorescence occurring throughout the growing season.

Reported to be hardy down to 0°F (-18°C), *Salvia recognita* has a springtime display that is something to look forward to. This salvia may be short-lived, but once established it seeds itself freely, and there are usually many seedlings of varying sizes around it. Cuttings are possible but propagation is usually by seed. Planted in full or partial sun, it needs fast drainage, good garden loam, and weekly water. A light dressing of lime in late winter may be added at its base.

Described by botanists in the 1800s, *Salvia recognita* has only come to the attention of gardeners since the early 1990s. It was in the 1980s that Jim and Jenny Archibald made seed they had collected in Turkey available through their seed list. My records show my seed germination was poor but one small plant survived and was planted in the garden in May 1986. It soon died. The follow-

Salvia recognita

ing spring, one plant again germinated and was planted in the garden in the early autumn of 1989. This plant did well from the start, and by late winter or early spring of 1990–1991, many seedlings were germinating all around the mother plant.

SALVIA RECOGNITA

Salvia recognita

A bed or border of small shrubby roses that are of similar size, such as the 2 ft (60 cm) tall and 3 ft (1 m) wide 'Little White Pet' along with the soft pink *Rosa* 'The Fairy', is enhanced by patches of *Salvia recognita*. To give depth of color to the composition, add drifts of *Nepeta ×faassenii*, which has gray foliage and rich lavender flowers. If there is space, a small 4–5 ft (1.3–1.5 m) shrub with wine-colored foliage, such as *Berberis thunbergii* 'Red Chief', would add substance to the composition. Requiring the same culture, all these plants except the berberis are remontant.

Salvia recurva Bentham

A very big and beautiful perennial, *Salvia recurva* comes from areas in Central America known as cloud forests. Its native habitat is somewhat confined to the protected northern slopes of Oaxaca, Chiapas, and Guatemala, where it is found at mountain elevations of 10,000 ft (3100 m). These mountains are noted for year-round warmth, and there is an abundance of moisture both in the humid air and in the damp forest floor. George Bentham described this salvia in 1848, and the specific epithet, *recurva*, refers to the plant's inflorescence, which is distinctly curved when it first emerges. All you see when the inflorescence first appears are the tightly packed, lime-green calyces, which later turn dark purple at maturity. As the inflorescence elongates, it becomes upright and full of large elegant flowers.

Blooming in late October and through November, *Salvia recurva* is a perennial that develops a woody base. In the wild it reaches 6 ft (2 m) in height and 4 ft (1.3 m) in width; in a mild garden habitat it will have the same dimensions. Plants are well covered with large ovate leaves that are 6 in (15 cm) long and equally as wide. The back of the leaf has pronounced veining. The petiole can be as long as the leaf itself and is the same dark purple color as the upper surface of the leaf. Inflorescences vary in length but frequently are 1 ft (30 cm) long. Flowers are in whorls of six to twelve, and many come into bloom at the same time. The showy dark purple flowers are frequently 2 in (5 cm) long, and the upper lip is lightly covered with hairs. The lower lip descends downward. The calyces are large and dark purple, as is the stem of the inflorescence. This salvia is easy to propagate by cuttings taken in July or August. I have not heard of plants setting seed as far north as California.

Salvia recurva requires a special climate to grow and flower satisfactorily. Coming into bloom late in the season, the plant reaches full bloom only well into November. The conditions that bring about this late blooming period are warmth, moisture in the air and ground, and low light. It is essential that you protect the plant from the wind as it is both heavy with foliage and brittle. Strybing Arboretum regularly brings *S. recurva* into full bloom year after year. I long ago found that the plants in my garden were not able to flower by November; by then, nighttime temperatures were in the low 40's F (around 5°C) and the salvia appeared dormant. *Salvia recurva* also needs well-draining soil that has a lot of humus in it, and an additional application of humus around the base of

With numerous inflorescences that bear large, dark purple flowers, *Salvia recurva* is a dynamic dazzler in the autumn garden. (Don Mahoney)

the plant in spring will furnish it with food for the long growing season ahead. I recommend you remove spent inflorescences to help reduce wind damage, and in late spring you should prune stems to two active nodes near the base of the plant. This pruning procedure prepares the plant for a long season of growth.

In a garden that has high shade, *Salvia recurva* can be combined with many other shade-loving plants. Its leaves are so large that it is difficult to find plants with contrasting foliage that make interesting partners. Although they do not bloom at the same time, the tall thalictrums with lacy foliage are good candidates. There are many selections of the 4 ft (1.3 m) tall *Thalictrum delavayi* from which to choose. Ferns, too, have distinctive foliage that would make memorable partners. The giant chain fern, *Woodwardia fimbriata*, is 3–6 ft (1–2 m) in height and is found in many western states. It requires exactly the same growing conditions as *S. recurva*.

Salvia regla sited on the southeast side of the house where it is protected from the wind and the sun during the hottest part of the day. (Christine Andrews)

Salvia regla Cavanilles
mountain sage

Salvia regla comes from a small area in the Chisos Mountains in western Texas and a large area in Mexico from Coahuila and Durango to Oaxaca. It is probably named after the town of Regla in the province of Hidalgo, though the specific epithet, *regla*, also means "a standard" or "a model." Mountain sage certainly is a model specimen—whether in the wild or in the garden. Called the queen of the Chisos Mountains, *S. regla* has been planted on the Texas flyway for migrating birds and has become an important food source for humming-birds making their return migration to the tropics in September and October.

A deciduous shrub, *Salvia regla* will reach 6 ft (2 m) or more in height and about 4–5 ft (1.3–1.5 m) in width over several years in the garden. It builds on upright woody stems that give it a regal appearance. Flowering begins in late summer or early autumn and continues until frost. Deeply veined, mistletoe-green leaves are deltoid and 1 in (2.5 cm) wide and long. The tube of the flower is usually 1 in (2.5 cm) long. Frequently, the calyx is 1 in (2.5 cm) long, signal-red on the side that is turned to the light, and chartreuse on the underside. It is a striking plant when in bloom.

Introduced into cultivation in 1839, it was rarely seen in gardens until the 1980s. Several cultivars of mountain sage are grown and distributed by nurseries. The selection *Salvia regla* 'Royal' was first introduced by a nursery in Texas and later in California by the Saratoga Horticultural Research Foundation. It resembles the species. 'Mount Emory' is a selection from the Chisos Mountains in Texas and was introduced in 1983 by the Texas A & M

Salvia regla

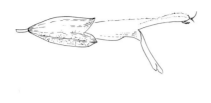

Salvia regla

University Research and Extension Center. 'Mount Emory' has large glossy leaves that are 2 in (5 cm) long and equally as wide. Its calyx is large—1 in (2.5 cm) long—and mostly signal-red in color. The tubular flowers are 2 in (5 cm) long and repeat the vivid orange-red color of the calyx. The overall plant is lush looking as it bends to the ground with the weight of its flowers and foliage. To prevent collapse, pinch and prune the plant judiciously throughout the growing season. Yucca Do Nursery has made another selection. Called 'Warnocks Choice', it grows 4–6 ft (1.3–2 m) in height, is woody and cold tolerant to 20°F (-7°C), and is very floriferous. Another selection collected in Coahuila by Yucca Do Nursery is being tested in Texas and California for introduction. In the wild it is treelike and reaches 12 ft (4 m) tall.

Planted on an east-facing wall or in dappled shade, mountain sage needs good drainage and ordinary garden soil. After it becomes established it is a drought-tolerant plant, requiring only occasional deep watering in long periods of drought. It is a woody and deciduous shrub so it should be pruned lightly by removing flowering branches or, occasionally, an entire stem from the base during its active growth period. Beware of heavy pruning during the dormant season; in my experience it does not bloom well with winter pruning. Mountain sage does not show any signs of life until late spring, when it seems the entire shrub breaks into leaf at once. It is hardy to 15°F (-9°C), and propagation is by cuttings.

Botanists and others who have seen its spectacular bloom on mountainsides in the wild agree that mountain sage is eminently worthy of cultivation. In garden settings it is an exciting, autumn-blooming plant that can be grouped with the compact form of the evergreen *Arbutus unedo*, which has red fruits and deep brown, shredding bark. Both require the same culture, including slightly sweet soil. For a smaller grouping, the graceful 3 ft (1 m) tall and wide *Bracteantha bracteata* 'Dargan Hill Monarch' (frequently called *Helichrysum bracteatum*), which has feltlike, gray-green leaves, makes a handsome companion. The gold-brown centers and glossy yellow bracts of the flowers of 'Dargan Hill Monarch' add more harmonizing colors to the grouping.

Salvia repens Bentham

A herbaceous perennial, *Salvia repens* is extremely variable in its native habitat. Found in the eastern part of South Africa from elevations of 1500 ft (460 m) to 8000 ft (2500 m), it is a common plant in open country and among shrubby vegetation. Widespread and adaptable, it may also be found on grass-covered land and slopes as well as bare or shale banks. It is closely related to four *Salvia* species, including *S. stenophylla*, that grow in the same areas where it occurs. Described by the botanist George Bentham in 1833, the plant was given the specific name *repens* because of its creeping rootstock.

Salvia repens is a charming plant that travels rapidly on underground runners. In a mild climate, the rough and sometimes deeply cut leaves are evergreen. (Ginny Hunt)

A small upright garden plant, *Salvia repens* is usually 2 ft (60 cm) in height. Its more or less erect stems are branched and lightly covered with slender oblong leaves. The margins of the leaves appear torn as they are lacerate and irregularly cut. The inflorescence, which measures about 1 ft (30 cm) in length, is simple or branched. Flowers are in spaced whorls of six to eight and can vary in color from purple or deep blue to white. The most common flower colors I have seen are pale lilac on the upper lip and white on the lower lip. There are oil glands on the calyx and leaves that, when stroked, release a light, herblike fragrance. Plants tend to produce lots of seed, but the usual method of propagation is through the removal of a rooted piece of rootstock. This salvia can invade a large patch of ground if allowed to run rampant so you should remove fruiting stems and allow the plant no more than an allotted space in the garden to keep it under control. In midsummer it blooms ceaselessly and makes a pretty picture, but beware of its reproductive powers.

Within the area of its native habitat in South Africa, *Salvia repens* has many traditional uses. It is added to the bath as a means of treating sores on the body, and a decoction of the root is taken before meals for stomachache and diarrhea.

It is also used to treat cattle for diarrhea. Smoke from the burning plant is used to disinfect a hut after sickness and to drive away unwanted bugs and insects. Plants are mixed with tobacco and smoked, I presume for pleasure. With so many practical uses, this is a plant whose proclivity to proliferate could be very advantageous.

Occasional water and sunshine is all this salvia needs to keep growing, flowering, and producing seed. It is certainly hardy to the low 20s°F (around -6°C) for short periods. In the San Francisco Bay area, where it is evergreen, I have seen it used successfully to control erosion on a steep bank. Its rapid growth rate and profuseness might cause problems if it is combined with other plants.

Salvia reptans Jacquin

A salvia with an unusual habit of growth, *Salvia reptans* produces numbers of lax or decumbent stems. It has a large distribution and is found in the mountains of the Trans-Pecos in Texas and also in Mexico and Guatemala. Dry washes and gravelly soils in stream beds are its usual habitat in the wild. Introduced to cultivation in the early 1800s, *S. reptans* was previously known as *S. angustifolia*, which means narrow leaved, or *S. leptophylla*, which means slender leaved. The specific epithet, *reptans*, refers to the plant's creeping habit and aptly describes a graceful salvia that has been grown in cultivation for many years.

Two distinct clones of *Salvia reptans* exist in nature. The clone that is typically grown in gardens is lax in habit, whereas the other clone is approximately 3 ft (1 m) tall and upright. This second clone is found in western Texas and has not been introduced as a garden subject. In addition, *S. reptans* var. *glabra* occurs naturally in Texas but is not grown horticulturally.

Salvia reptans

A perennial herb, *Salvia reptans* sprawls about 3 ft (1 m) or more in width and has handsome, thin, almost black stems. Most of the very narrow, mistletoe-green leaves measure less than 0.25 in (0.6 cm) in width and are sparsely set along the stem. The stems are abundant and virtually cover the ground. The flowers are a lovely wisteria-blue and about 0.5 in (1.3 cm) long. They are held in a tiny dark calyx that enhances the flowers' beauty. Blooming begins in summer, becoming sparse by October until frost. Hardy in the San Francisco Bay area, *S. reptans* dies to the ground when temperatures fall below 30°F (-1°C). In spring, new growth will emerge from the tuberous rootstock. Cut *S. reptans* back to its crown in early spring to encourage the growth of multiple stems and to prevent a woody base, which will prohibit plentiful new growth, from developing. A half day of sun, quick drainage, ordinary garden soil, and weekly water are its cultural needs. Propagation is easily achieved by seed, cuttings, or division.

Even though *Salvia reptans* has been grown as a garden subject for a long time, it is seldom seen outside botanic gardens. It makes an ideal plant for a warm, sloping rock garden in moderate shade or as a ground cover among shrubs. Its lax growth, which will spill over the side of a large container, means that you can successfully combine this species in planters with reliable space fillers, such as fancy-leaved lettuces, parsley, and basil. I have seen it in window boxes with stiff pink pelargoniums, where it added a note of grace to the planting. Another combination capitalizes on a red, white, and blue theme—*S.* 'Red Velvet' for the background, *S. reptans* to trail over the side, and a white-flowering filler such as petunias or *Chrysanthemum paludosum*. Elevating the plant in a container or planting it on top of a low wall is another way of taking advantage of its sprawl.

Salvia ringens Sibthorp & Smith

Grown in English gardens before 1913, *Salvia ringens* is one of those valuable horticultural plants that dropped out of sight for close to 100 years before being rediscovered in the late 1990s. The plant was described by English botanists John Sibthorp and James Edward Smith, but the description was only printed in 1806 after Sibthorp's death. By 1933, William Robinson was writing about the salvia in the twelfth edition of *The English Flower Garden*. A hardy, herbaceous perennial, this salvia occurs in the southern and eastern parts of the Balkan Peninsula. It is an endemic of that area with a high concentration on Mount Olympus, the inaccessible home of the gods, where it grows in colonies at altitudes as high as 6200 ft (1900 m). On the mainland, its habitat is in areas of scrub and coniferous woodland usually between 1600 and 4200 ft (500 and 1300 m).

A showy and first-rate plant for the herbaceous border, *Salvia ringens* repeats bloom from summer through autumn. (Sonja Wilcomer)

A remarkable herbaceous perennial, *Salvia ringens* makes a clump of
basal leaves that are pinnately divided. The leafy clump is generally less
than 1 ft (30 cm) high and wide, and
in my garden, plants are evergreen.
The leaves themselves are dark green
with a grayish cast, and in winter the
stems and petioles stand out because
of their noteworthy wine color. The

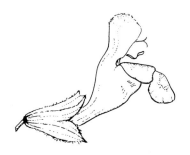

Salvia ringens

blooming period for *S. ringens* is summer through autumn. Over this long
time span the plant produces tall flowering stems that measure 2 ft (60 cm)
in height with widely spaced whorls of two to four flowers at the top. There
are usually only one or two stems—four or five at most—at any given time.
Individual violet-blue flowers are showy and large, about 1.5 in (4 cm) long,
and held in a small calyx that is covered with glands and hairs. The specific
name, *ringens* refers to the gaping, two lipped flowers. Propagation is by seed
or cuttings taken in August or September. This salvia is cold tolerant when
temperatures go to 25°F (-4°C) for only short periods. William Robinson
(1933) writes, "The plant will bear a mild winter in the south of Britain."

Needing both good drainage and soil that has humus, *Salvia ringens*
requires a warm spot with plenty of sun. I have found it thrives when planted
with other perennials. No pruning or staking is necessary, only the periodic
removal of spent inflorescences. A moderate amount of water is called for
throughout the growing and flowering season. It produces viable seed, which is
the usual way to propagate the plant. Every now and then seedlings appear in
my garden.

The tall inflorescences of *Salvia ringens* show up quite well when planted in groups of three with penstemons, asters, and silenes. Add the delightful
low-growing nepetas, santolinas, violas, and the carpeting thymes for a full
display of colorful summer flowers. *Salvia ringens* also shows particularly well
when planted between and in front of substantial shrubs of medium size,
such as the evergreen *Berberis darwinii* or *B. hookeri*. Hybrid musk shrub
roses of modest size like 'Ballerina' and 'Felicia' are also enhanced by this
salvia's presence.

Salvia roborowskii Maximowicz

Regarded as an annual or occasionally a biennial herb, *Salvia roborowskii* has a wide distribution that includes Tibet, Sikkim, and five provinces in China. This salvia's habitat is comprised of grasslands, hillsides, and wet streambanks at elevations that range from 8000 to 12,000 ft (2500 to 3600 m).

Salvia roborowskii is scarcely known in horticulture but merits the gardener's awareness and attention. My plants came from seed collected in China in 1991 by botanists from Quarryhill Botanical Garden and the Royal Botanic Gardens, Kew. Plants were growing at 10,000 ft (3100 m) on an east-facing meadow. Near this open hillside grew pines and dogwoods, as well as roses, clematis, and nepeta.

Small and upright, *Salvia roborowskii* usually reaches 1.5 ft (45 cm) tall in cultivation, but in the wild it has been recorded at 3 ft (1 m). Rosemary-green leaves are mainly triangular in shape and neatly cover the plant. The margins of the leaves are scalloped and the surface is hairy with indented veins. Flowering takes place in summer. Small lemon-yellow flowers about 0.25 in (0.6 cm) in length emerge from a rosemary-green calyx. Each whorl has eight to twelve flowers but only a few come into bloom at the same time. Far from being showy, *S. roborowskii* is nevertheless beautiful because of its precise erectness and fine green color. The miniature flowers hold well in arrangements.

A spot in the garden with at least a half day of sunlight and the protection of other plants is the ideal setting for a group of these salvias. Be sure to enrich the well-draining soil with liberal amounts of compost, and water the plants deeply every few days.

This annual is easy to grow and has the tendency to self sow once established. Sow seed of *Salvia roborowskii* in pots and then transplant young seedlings into the garden where you would like a colony to grow. After summer flowering, plants should be allowed to set and drop seed in situ. You should gather and save a few seeds in case the first attempt at establishing a colony fails. Another tactic is to prune inflorescences after seed production to encourage plants to live another year. Whichever approach you take, you may have to make several attempts before a colony will sustain itself, but this tidy salvia is worth the effort.

Salvia roborowskii is a perky filler for the front of the summer border. In my garden it grows next to the 1.5 ft (45 cm) high *S. elegans* 'Honey Melon'. Behind the salvias are long sweeping branches of *Cotoneaster horizontalis* 'Variegatus', which has cream-colored, variegated leaves that are suffused with red in the autumn. A dahlia with flat, dark red flowers the size of a small grapefruit completes the picture. The name of this dahlia has been long forgotten—it is one of those favored plants, passed from gardener to gardener.

Salvia roemeriana Scheele
cedar sage

Salvia roemeriana is found in the Edwards Plateau area of Texas, as well as in Arizona and several provinces in Mexico. Its specific epithet honors Ferdinand von Roemer, who became known as the "father of Texas geology." Born into a distinguished German family in 1818, he lived in Texas from 1845 to 1847. He was trained as a scientist and provided valuable reports to other scientists and to those who might immigrate to that distant land. On returning to Germany, he published his travelogue and notes in a book called *Texas*. The common name, cedar sage, refers to the cedar brakes where it grows in patches. It grows prolifically in oak woodlands and on rocky outcroppings.

Cedar sage has rounded leaflets of a good, grassy green color that wither and die to the ground in winter. Its flowering stalk is 8–10 in (20–25 cm) in length, with bright scarlet flowers in loose whorls rising one above the other over the foliage. Each plant has many inflorescences, and when a patch of sage comes into bloom it is a very pretty sight. Plants are hardy to 10°F (-12°C). Plants with larger leaves and flowers have been found in limestone areas of Sierra Chiquita, Tamaulipas, Mexico, by John Fairey and Carl Schoenfeld.

A small perennial that is less than 1 ft (30 cm) in height and width, *Salvia roemeriana* will quickly become established and make a nice colony of plants by freely seeding itself. New plants appear throughout the spring and summer. A half day of shade, good garden soil with humus, and weekly watering will encourage the multiplication of plants and prolong the blooming season from late spring to late autumn. Removal of spent flowering stalks during the summer is necessary for a long flowering period. Propagation is by seed or cuttings. Seedlings appear throughout the summer months once the parent plant is established and they may be replanted or shared with other gardeners. Both foliage and flowers hold well in arrangements.

Introduced into cultivation in 1852, *Salvia roemeriana* was grown and admired by William Robinson (1933), who commended its neatness to other gardeners for edgings or the front of the border. Cedar sage can brighten plantings in many parts of the garden. For example, the evergreen needles of mugo

Naturally occurring in a limestone habitat in the province of Tamaulipas, Mexico, *Salvia roemeriana* is a natural rock garden plant.
(Carl Schoenfeld)

pine or other conifers will look darker and greener when contrasted with the salvia's scarlet flowers. Since it needs some shade, *S. roemeriana* makes a fine ground cover for rhododendrons; it will cover the ground with green foliage when the rhododendrons are in bloom. Later, after the rhododendrons have flowered, the scarlet flowers will sparkle alone in a pool of green during the summer and autumn. *Hydrangea quercifolia*, which is native to the southeastern United States and has large, strongly lobed leaves that color well in the autumn, would be enhanced throughout the growing season by a large patch of cedar sage growing at its base, particularly if you plant the hydrangeas in a group. All these plants require the same culture.

Salvia rubescens Kunth

Stately and handsomely textured, *Salvia rubescens* has been grown in our California gardens only since the 1990s. It was found and collected in the state of Merida in Venezuela in 1993 by Robert Ornduff. At that time he wrote on a herbarium sheet that the salvia was a "striking plant," and it has certainly

SALVIA RUBESCENS

Autumn is the time to enjoy the rich red flowers of *Salvia rubescens*. The dark purple stem and calyx intensify the brilliant red flowers. (Sonja Wilcomer)

proven to be so in cultivation. It has been grown in the University of California Botanical Garden, Berkeley, since 1993, its only designation being that it was from Venezuela. Originally described by Reinhard Gustav Paul Kunth in 1817, it was again described by Carl Epling (1939) in his monumental work *A Revision of* Salvia, *subgenus* Calosphace. In the spring of 2001, James Compton was able to see herbarium specimens of the salvia and to identify it as *rubescens*. This salvia already had an excellent reputation, and with a legitimate name that describes its attractive flower color, its popularity is spreading rapidly.

Having an erect habit and excellent shape, this salvia is fully clothed with mid-green ovate leaves that have a saw-toothed edge. The largest measure 4.5 in (11 cm) in length and 3.5 in (9 cm) in width. Leaves are lightly covered with hairs on both surfaces, which gives them texture, and with the sunshine and heat of summer, they will slowly become a handsome gray-green. *Salvia rubescens* is 4–5 ft (1.3–1.5 m) tall, and the inflorescence rises 1–2

Salvia rubescens

ft (30–60 cm) above the foliage. Flowering begins in midsummer or later and continues until frost. The onset of flowering is probably triggered by shorter daylight hours, as it is with asters, chrysanthemums, and dahlias. The flowering stem, like the calyx, is dark purple, and both are lightly covered with fine hairs. Vibrant red-orange flowers that are just under 1 in (2.5 cm) long are in widely spaced whorls. A large number of flowers come into bloom at the same time, making quite an attractive and showy inflorescence.

Classified as herbaceous perennials, the *Salvia rubescens* plants in my garden live for many years, developing a little wood at the base. In a mild winter the plant is evergreen, but when temperatures fall below 25°F (-4°C) it will not survive. It is fortunate, then, that this salvia produces an ample supply of seed from which it can be renewed. As an additional safeguard against cold winter weather, cuttings that were made in August or September can be held in the greenhouse.

Salvia rubescens requires ordinary garden soil and excellent drainage. Be sure to site it where it will receive full sun throughout the year. Plants usually require deep watering twice a week depending on the intensity of summer and autumn heat. You should periodically remove spent inflorescences to keep the salvia in bloom for a very long time. Pruning does not seem to be necessary; you will need to only occasionally clip the spent inflorescences. In early spring after there is no danger of frost, cut the plant back to about 2 ft (60 cm) in order for fresh new growth to develop.

This is just the plant to give a flowering border a boost as summer slowly comes to an end and autumn approaches. *Salvia rubescens* can be placed among perennials and annuals that have bloomed early and are on the wane as days become noticeably shorter. Alternatively, it can grow and develop while other plants reach their peak of maturity late in the season. In early autumn it will provide substance to the border and rich color through its flowers. This salvia needs full sun, friable garden soil, good drainage, and regular water. I list a few large plants that bloom at the same time and require the same growing conditions.

> *Aster cordifolius* is 6 ft (2 m) tall. There are many selections of this lavender-flowered, northeastern American native.
> *Calamagrostis* ×*acutiflora* 'Stricta' has foliage that is 2–3 ft (60–90 cm) tall with flowering stalks that rise 3 ft (1 m) above the green foliage.

Ceratostigma willmottianum is 2–4 ft (60–120 cm) tall. The deciduous leaves turn yellow and red. Flowers are pale blue and do not stand out.

Coreopsis verticillata is 3 ft (1 m) in height and has cut leaves and large yellow flowers. It forms a colony.

Helenium autumnale is 4–5 ft (1.3–1.5 m) tall. Plants sold under this name are mostly hybrids. Flower colors are autumnal shades of gold and rusty red.

Helenium 'Moerheim Beauty' has coppery red petals with a brown center.

Three additional companion plants that require similar culture but less water include *Leonotis leonurus*, which is 4–5 ft (1.3–1.5 m) tall with textured green foliage and rich orange flowers in whorls; *Perovskia* 'Blue Spire', which is 3–4 ft (1–1.3 m) tall with grayish foliage and woolly calyces; and *Teucrium fruticans*, which is 4–6 ft (1.3–2 m) tall with small gray foliage. It blooms frequently with lavender-blue flowers.

Salvia rypara Briquet

A delightful and airy herbaceous perennial plant, *Salvia rypara* is a native of Argentina and Bolivia. It is an adaptable plant and reported to be naturalized in Mexico and possibly Central America. The specific epithet, *rypara*, reflects the plant's preference for streambank habitats. It also grows in weedy thickets. A plant of low altitudes, it thrives in habitats under 3000 ft (900 m). The eminent botanist John Isaac Briquet described it in 1896, but it is not well known horticulturally even though a few gardeners have been growing it ornamentally since the 1990s. It has gradually become known in England, France, Italy, and the United States because it is easy to grow and well suited for cultivation. Its good reputation will insure its spread.

A small and erect plant with many thin stems, *Salvia rypara* is about 2 ft (60 cm) tall and wide. Its medium green leaves cover the plant well and are ovate in shape, the largest measuring 2–3 in (5–8 cm) in length and 1.5–2.5 in (4–6 cm) in width. Long and slender 6–8 in (15–20 cm) inflorescences have spaced whorls of two to twelve flowers. Many come into bloom at the same time, giving the plant a light and lively look. The flowers are pale lavender, and

A delightful filler for the late summer and early autumn herbaceous border, *Salvia rypara* repeats bloom until short days and cool weather slow it down. (Ginny Hunt)

the lower lip is flaring and just over 0.5 in (1.3 cm) long. The upper lip is short and erect. Flowers are held in a greenish, purplish, two-lipped calyx that is tiny and measures only about 0.25 in (0.6 cm) long. Flowers come into bloom in midsummer and continue blooming until the days of autumn become dark and chilly.

Salvia rypara can be placed in a half to full day of sunlight. It requires good drainage and ordinary garden soil with weekly water. Very seldom has it set seed in my garden; consequently, propagation is by cuttings. After plants have been in the ground for several years its roots will spread on underground runners. These rooted stems can easily be transplanted. Plants are tolerant of temperatures into the high 20°s F (around -2°C) for short periods. When hard freezes occur and the entire plant dies back, you should wait until there has been a warm spell in spring to give the plant a chance to come back from its roots before removing it from the garden. A little deadheading throughout the growing season will keep flower production active. In spring, after warm temperatures have returned, you can prune the plant to two active nodes near the ground. This type of pruning insures a shapely plant for the season ahead.

This salvia is the epitome of a good garden filler. Its size, habit, and long blooming period are qualities that warrant its placement among other plants in the border. Plants that bloom from summer into fall are globe thistle, *Echinops bannaticus* 'Blue Globe', and the graceful *Lespedeza thunbergii* 'Alba'. Both are about 3 ft (1 m) tall and appropriate for the back of the border. The pink *Penstemon* 'Garden Star' and purple 'Sour Grapes', which are both 2 ft (60 cm) tall or less, could be spotted throughout the middle of the bed with *Salvia rypara*. For the front of the bed there is an array of low-growing verbenas from which to choose. Selections from *Verbena ×hybrida* include many shades of purple, lavender, pink, and white. All these plants enjoy the same culture.

Salvia sagittata Ruiz & Pavón

In the late 18th century, two young Spaniards who were trained in botany and pharmacology studied and recorded the natural history of Peru and Chile for over ten years. In 1798, Hipolito Ruiz and José Pavón were commissioned by the Spanish government to find pharmaceutical and agricultural plants in the New World. They were primarily plant hunters and collectors and they sent both seed and plants to Spain. In 1798 they collected and named *Salvia sagittata*. The specific name, *sagittata*, refers to the leaf's arrow-head shape. This salvia is native to the Cordillera de los Andes and is found at high elevations from 9500 to 10,500 ft (2900 to 3200 m).

Admired for the beauty of its stately habit and striking blue flowers, *Salvia sagittata* blooms more freely with warmth and light. It is a herbaceous perennial that in cultivation is usually 2.5 ft (0.8 m) high and a little less wide, but it is reported to reach 7.5 ft (2.5 m) in the wild. Well clothed with yellow-green leaves that are rugose on the surface, the back of the leaf is prominently ribbed and veined and is covered with short white hairs. The inflorescences, which are quite viscid, arise from the top of the leafy stems and are sometimes 2 ft (60 cm) in length, making them appear thin and wiry. The brilliant blue flowers are 1 in (2.5 cm) long with a widely spreading lower lip. A pistil and two yellow, pollen-covered stamens are projected from the upper hooded lip. Flowering takes place in summer and

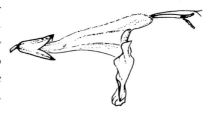

Salvia sagittata

The brilliant blue flowers of *Salvia sagittata* bloom repeatedly from late summer through autumn. It is a fine plant for sustained winter bloom in the greenhouse. (Ginny Hunt)

continues throughout autumn. Seed production is liberal, and the plant roots easily from cuttings taken in early summer. This salvia can also be propagated by division.

Plant *Salvia sagittata* in full sun or, at the very least, a half day of strong sunlight. Soil should have a high humus content and drain freely, and a mulch of humus will help the root-run remain cool. Regular garden water is necessary to keep the plant in active growth. If it is in a container, I recommend you apply a half-strength liquid fertilizer once or twice a month.

From her mild Australian climate, Sue Templeton writes that *Salvia sagittata* is among her favorite salvias because "the flowers seem to hover above the plant and the intensity of the blue is most appealing." (pers. comm.). She adds that in Sydney, plants sucker very nicely when grown in part shade. She encourages this suckering characteristic to obtain an attractive patch of foliage with brilliant blue flowers.

In my garden, winter temperatures frequently fall to the low 20's F (around -6°C), so I grow *Salvia sagittata* in a container as a precaution. After nighttime temperatures dip to 32°F (0°C), I move it into the greenhouse, where it continues to bloom freely throughout autumn and well into January. In fact,

SALVIA SAGITTATA

as it needs a rest, you should cut it back in March and return it to the outdoors when there is no danger of frost. Its natural habit and dimensions make it eminently suitable for a container because it requires little, if any, pruning or deadheading. You could follow the attractive Mediterranean practice of placing many pots of the same species of plants at the edge of a patio or pool, or along steps or a walkway.

Salvia scabra Linnaeus

From the southeastern strand of South Africa's Cape of Good Hope comes the wiry and assertive *Salvia scabra*. Named by Linnaeus in 1781, this salvia has a habitat that is limited to sandy shores, coastal brush, and hilly slopes. It is found from sea level to a height of 600 ft (180 m). From this habitat information you might deduce that the plant is difficult to establish in gardens, but the opposite is true. With minimal cultural conditions, this tough little plant will adjust to almost any sunny situation and produce flowers, on and off, from spring through autumn. Both the leaves and a water extract from the roots have been used in traditional medicine in its native habitat for well over a hundred years.

Introduced to California gardeners in approximately 1996, *Salvia scabra* has proven to be readily adaptable. It was propagated from seed that had been identified and collected by Rod and Rachel Saunders, who own and operate Silverhill Seeds in South Africa. This plant's small size, perky, pinkish flowers, and tenacity when establishing itself have resulted in its widespread use in many gardens, including those in England, France, and Italy.

Described by botanists as a perennial herb, *Salvia scabra* builds up woody stems that are pale brown, rounded, and lightly covered with short hairs. In its native habitat it reaches 3 ft (1 m) in height, but in the United States and on the Continent it is usually 1.5 ft (45 cm) tall and 1 ft (30 cm) wide. The leaves are shaped like a lyre and are lobed. As the plant matures, the lobing becomes more pronounced. Midgreen in color, the leaves along the stem appear to grow in thick bunches. However, closer examination reveals that because leaves emerge from the petiole and because there is

Salvia scabra

Alive with flowers, *Salvia scabra* is a very neat plant that seeds itself around the garden without being a pest. (Ginny Hunt))

opposite branching, they have little space in which to expand, which makes the leaves appear bunched. The specific name, *scabra*, means "rough-leaved" and aptly describes the leaf's surface. The short inflorescence sometimes has six flowers in each whorl. The long, straight, tubed flowers are 0.5 in (1.3 cm) in length and they can vary in color from pale pink to pale lilac. The calyx is short, hairy, and tinged with purple. It expands as the seed it holds ripens. *Salvia scabra* is a good seed-producing plant, so it is not unusual to find seedlings that have germinated near the mother plant. Although sowing seed is the easiest means of propagation, you can also take cuttings. This salvia will survive and continue to look healthy and handsome when temperatures dip to the low 20°s F (around -6°C) for short periods.

A combination of plants for the front of a sunny border might include three or more plants of both *Salvia scabra* and *Ageratum houstonianum* 'Blue Bouquet', which is less than 2 ft (60 cm) tall. The spreading *Verbena rigida* 'Polaris', which has silver-blue flowers and leaves that are reminiscent of *S. scabra*, could be encouraged to weave among the other plants. All these plants flower from midsummer into autumn, and all have the same requirements: good garden soil, regular water, and lots of sunshine.

Salvia sclarea Linnaeus
clary sage

A striking herbaceous plant that is classified as both biennial and perennial, *Salvia sclarea* has been recognized for its essential oils and used extensively since well before the birth of Christ. Theophrastus, Dioscorides, and Pliny all wrote at length about its useful properties. In the wild, it is found throughout the northern Mediterranean region and in limited parts of North Africa and central Asia. It is commonly known as *toute-bonne* or *sauge sclarée* in France, *sclarea* in Italy, *hierba de los ojos* in Spain, and *clary* in Britain. Requiring little water or attention and being adaptable to temperatures below 0°F (-18°C), this salvia has become naturalized in central Europe.

An early summer-blooming plant, *Salvia sclarea* can develop in a year's time from a seedling to a plant 3–4 ft (1–1.3 m) tall when in flower. Stems are square and covered with hairs and oil globules. Leaves vary in size from 1 ft (30 cm) long at the bottom of the plant to less than half that size at the top. They may be sessile or have a short petiole when growing at the top of the plant. The length of the petiole varies too. The leaf surface is rugose and covered with short hairs and oil globules. Leaves are grassy green on the surface, and on the underside there are pronounced, creamy white veins. The entire edge is saw-toothed. Flowers number between two and six in each verticil and are held in large, colorful floral bracts that are pale mauve to lilac or white to pink with a pink marking at the edge. The lilac or pale blue corolla is about 1 in (2.5 cm) in length, and the lips are held wide open in the shape of a scythe. The colors of the inflorescence I mention are only an indication of the range that may be observed.

Eleanour Sinclair Rohde (1936) refers to an unusually tall and handsome form of clary sage as the "Vatican strain." Jim and Jenny Archibald saw such plants in Turkey in 1984 and collected seed. They subsequently gave reports of large and grand plants from that seed.

Occasionally, a form may be found in the wild with white flowers and white floral bracts tinged with pink. This is the cultivar 'Turkestanica', which comes true from seed. In my garden, 'Turkestanica' has pinkish stems and petioles, and the leaves are

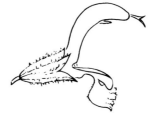

Salvia sclarea

Revered for centuries for its healing powers and beauty, *Salvia sclarea* is a striking plant in the summer border. Companions here are *Convolvulus mauritanicus* in front, S. 'Indigo Spires' to the left, and *S. recognita* to the right. (Betsy Clebsch)

The impressive *Salvia sclarea* 'Turkestanica'. (Robert Kourik)

more yellow-green than the clary sage. It requires weekly water in order to attain 3–4 ft (1–1.3 m).

Clary sage needs full sun, a soil low in nutrients, and fast drainage. Watering on a weekly basis will make plants in a border flourish. Once flowers start to look shabby and tan at the edges, cut flowering stems back to encourage perennial vigor. This procedure precludes seed production and avoids large numbers of seedlings germinating at the base of the plant. Even with this prudent practice, plants may

SALVIA SCLAREA

be short-lived, so it is judicious to have a few young plants developing. Propagation is quite easily accomplished from seed.

Salvia sclarea is not suitable as a cut flower because of the powerful odor of the penetrating oils. These essential oils are widely used in making perfume and in imparting a muscatel flavor to wines, vermouths, and liqueurs. The oils are one source of the plant's healing qualities; seed is another. The plant's seeds have traditionally been placed in the eye as a means of producing a thick mucilage; this practice is said to clean the eye of impurities. The name *sclarea* carries the connotation of clear and bright, and it is said that *clary* is an English corruption of *clear-eye*.

Stately in stature, *Salvia sclarea* is among our most arresting border plants. In a bed filled with old-fashioned, early summer-blooming plants (for example, roses, foxgloves, Canterbury bells, hollyhocks, delphiniums, pinks, dill, fennel, larkspur, and love-in-a-mist), clary sage provides height and color for almost a full month. It will bloom even longer if inflorescences are cut when they begin to discolor. It is not unusual for plants to rebloom in early autumn when days are warm and nights cool.

Salvia scutellarioides Kunth

In its native habitat, *Salvia scutellarioides* is an evergreen and prostrate plant with graceful, trailing stems. Indigenous to Columbia, Ecuador, and Peru, it occurs in the Cordillera de los Andes at elevations from 3300 to 10,000 ft (1000 to 3100 m) where there is year-round moisture, some rain, and a mild climate. First described by Karl Sigismund Kunth in 1817, it is in 2002 still a rare plant in horticulture. I first grew the plant in 1996 and have rarely seen it listed with nurseries or at botanic garden plant sales. The salvia derives its specific epithet, *scutellarioides*, from its resemblance to *Scutellaria*, a genus in the mint family, Lamiaceae.

Described botanically as a herbaceous, procumbent plant, *Salvia scutellarioides* has trailing stems that are about 1.5 ft (45 cm) in length. Stems of leaves build at the center of the plant, and there are also creeping stems that do not root at the nodes. Forest green, deltoid leaves are held on long petioles and generously cover the stems. They vary in size, but the median dimensions are 3.5 in (9 cm) long and wide. The length of the petiole also varies. Both surfaces of the leaves are lightly covered with hairs, and raised veins are

prominent on the back surface. Flowering is always meager, but in spite of their poor quantity, the brilliant blue flowers are of strikingly fine quality. *Salvia scutellarioides* begins flowering in late summer and repeats sporadically until late autumn. Inflorescences are short, about 6–8 in (15–20 cm) long, with opposite flowers that are a luminous blue. The flowers measure 0.5 in (1.3 cm) or a little more in length and are held in a hairy, tiny green calyx. Plants do not make seed in my climate, so propagation is by cuttings taken in late summer and held over in a greenhouse. Temperatures of 30°F (-1°C) will severely damage this

A ground-hugging plant with creeping stems and handsome arrow-shaped leaves, *Salvia scutellarioides* performs best when grown in a warm and humid climate. (Ginny Hunt)

salvia. In areas where winters are warmer than in my garden, the plant is reported to be semideciduous and is used as a ground cover. The plant keeps quite satisfactorily in a container in the greenhouse over winter and continues to flower lightly until very early in January.

Salvia scutellarioides, which is indisputably a plant that demands shade and moisture, is quite easy to grow. Place it where it receives high shade throughout the day. Morning sunlight for several hours would be acceptable, but the plant will probably require additional water. The plant's basic needs include good garden soil that retains moisture and is well draining. Each spring, spread an additional layer of humus at the plant's base as it will act as mulch to enrich the soil and preserve moisture. This salvia needs to be freely and frequently watered, so a monthly application of liquid fertilizer at half strength on a monthly basis helps keep it green and growing. I have one plant in a large pot that has been raised several feet off the ground so that the handsome stems can flow gracefully over the side of the container.

If you have a retaining wall that is shaded, you can make it the focal point of the area rather than viewing it as a problem. Place containers of *Salvia scutel-*

larioides on top of the wall; the handsome trailing stems will be a visual treat throughout the summer and autumn. Little or no deadheading will be required, but you will need to water the plant on a regular basis.

Salvia semiatrata Zuccarini

Salvia semiatrata is limited in its native habitat to the Mexican province of Oaxaca, where it is found in several locations in the mountains of the Sierra Madre del Sur. Usually located at elevations of 6500 ft (2000 m) or higher, *S. semiatrata* grows quite profusely at the edge of pine forests. It is frequently found on limestone cliffs and banks and in cactus scrub areas that are dry and exposed to the elements. These high mountain areas are very cool at night and receive summer rainfall.

In the wild and under ideal garden circumstances, *Salvia semiatrata* will grow to 6 ft (2 m) in height and 3 ft (1 m) in width. In cultivation, however, this shrubby plant is more likely to be half that size. Deltoid leaves under 1 in (2.5 cm) long that are a lively, grassy green-yellow color lightly cover the plant. Even though they are opposite, the leaves grow in small clusters. The surface of the leaf, which looks velvety, is rugose, and the underside is covered with short, pale cream hairs that make each vein pronounced. Inflorescences tend to be short, about 6 in (15 cm) long, with whorls of one to three flowers in each verticil. Individual flowers are usually 1 in (2.5 cm) in length, occasionally 2 in (5 cm), and splendidly bicolored. The upper lip is covered with hairs and a luminous dark violet color; the lower lip is dusky lavender. The calyx is also covered with hairs and is 0.5 in (1.3 cm) in length. It is a rich violet color with a magenta undertone. The specific epithet, *semiatrata*, means "half blackened" or "darkened," referring to the corolla tube and its two colors. Even though they are small, the individual flowers are eye-catching because of the dark violet-blue blotch on the lower lip.

The culture of *Salvia semiatrata* includes fast drainage, loamy garden soil, and good air circulation. Situate the plant so that it receives sun for at least half a day during winter and summer. Deep watering at least once each week is required, and a little lime sprinkled on top of the roots in late spring is helpful. I recommend pinching and light pruning during the growing season because it is a woody plant that tends to be evergreen. Propagation is by cuttings. I have not grown *S. semiatrata* long enough to test its ultimate hardiness, but it has

Salvia semiatrata has a very dark violet blotch on the flower's lower lip. (Robert Kourik)

wintered over in my garden with temperatures falling to 25°F (-4°C). *Salvia semiatrata* is grown extensively as a garden plant on the French and Italian Rivieras. This salvia grows slowly, comes into full bloom for a while, and then temporarily rests. It repeats this pattern from summer through autumn, though a few flowers may bloom during the winter and spring. Short inflorescences last well as cut flowers and look charming in small vases.

A sloping bank of plants with small-scale habit and foliage might feature three or more plants of each of the following: *Lavandula angustifolia* 'Hidcote', *Salvia semiatrata*, and *Teucrium fruticans* 'Compactum'. The gray, linear foliage of the 1 ft (30 cm) tall lavender will contrast well with the green foliage of the sage and the lanceolate green-gray foliage of the 2 ft (60 cm) tall teucrium. These three plants have flowers in the purple-blue color range. All require the same culture, including moderate amounts of water.

Salvia serpyllifolia Fernald

A handsome woody perennial, *Salvia serpyllifolia* has a limited habitat in the province of San Luis Potosí in Mexico. Fernald described it in 1900 and gave it the specific epithet, *serpyllifolia*. The epithet calls attention to the salvia's small and shiny leaves, which recall the tiny leaves of *Thymus serpyllum*. The plant was introduced to horticulture in 1990 from seed that had been collected at 7000 ft (2100 m) in the province of San Luis Potosí by Sally and Tim Walker of Southwestern Native Seeds. At the time of its introduction, this salvia was called a purple form of *S. microphylla*. In 2001, James Compton saw specimens of the plant and determined its specific name. *Salvia serpyllifolia* has been grown in a very limited way in northern California since 1990.

A plant with a handsome habit, *Salvia serpyllifolia* has vivid flowers in spring and autumn.
(Ginny Hunt)

A shapely and small mounding plant, *Salvia serpyllifolia* is 2 ft (60 cm) in height and 3 ft (1 m) in width. In the course of a growing season it makes woody stems. Bright, glossy green leaves lightly cover the stem and are usually less than 0.5 in (1.3 cm) long. Plants are evergreen in a mild climate, and the leaves release a faint, strawlike odor when crushed. The beetroot-purple flowers are small at less than 0.7 in (1.8 cm) long and they appear sporadically in summer and autumn. With whorls of two to six flowers, the plant looks as though it is in light bloom throughout a long growing season. The heaviest bloom occurs in early summer. My plant does not set seed even though many insects and hummingbirds visit the flowers. Cuttings can be taken in late summer, and rooted stems can easily be removed from the base of the plant.

This salvia will take full sun but it grows and flowers well with only a half day of direct sunlight. Given good drainage and a gritty or loamy soil, plants of *Salvia serpyllifolia* require a minimal amount of water. Deadheading after each flowering will promote more flowers. In midsummer, lightly clip the plant so that it keeps its attractive shape through the remainder of the grow-ing season. This salvia is cold tolerant to the low 20°s F (around -6°C) and in my garden has come back from the roots when temperatures dipped into the teens (-10°C). Keep in mind that it must have fast drainage to survive wet and cold winters. After all danger of frost has passed, take out all the heavy, wooded stems and prune the plant to a pleasing, small shape. After warm weather arrives, it will quickly reach attractive proportions.

In a Mediterranean climate, *Salvia serpyllifolia* can be a primary plant in a sunny border that requires low amounts of water. If the border is big, three of these salvias with three of the gray-foliaged *S. dentata* from South Africa would sufficiently fill the area. If there is space in which to tuck other plants, *Thymus serpyllum* has almost 30 cultivars from which to choose. Growing the plant after which the salvia was named is truly appealing. All these plants require the same culture and a lot less water than gardeners have used in the past.

Salvia sessei Bentham

In the wild, *Salvia sessei* may be found in seven or more provinces in central Mexico. Occurring from 600 to 7000 ft (200 to 2100 m), the plant usually grows on the edge of woodlands and pine forests. This salvia was first collected by the Spanish botanist Don Martin de Sessé and his learned fellow botanist Jose Moçiño, who was of pure Spanish descent but born in Mexico. These two were the key participants in the Royal Botanical Expedition of 1777 commissioned by King Charles III of Spain. Plants including *S. sessei* were collected from Guatemala and a large portion of Mexico over a period of approximately 10 years. A very large herbarium was amassed that included excellent drawings by the talented Atanasio Echeverría, for whom the genus *Echeveria* is named, as well as the work of another artist. This material was shipped to Spain for the purpose of preparing a *Flora Mexicana* under the supervision of the distinguished Swiss botanist, Augustin-Pyramus de Candolle. Unfortunately, the project, which involved hardship and heartbreak, was abandoned. The participants in the expedition suffered mental and physical miseries, and large numbers of their pressed plants were ravaged by insects and water. Incidentally, Sessé became among the first professors of botany at the University of Mexico in 1788 and immediately started the establishment of a botanic garden in Mexico City.

A treelike shrub in the wild, *Salvia sessei* will reach 15 ft (4.5 m) in its native habitat, but in cultivation it is half that size. Leaves can be variable in size and shape but generally are 2–5 in (5–13 cm) long and deltoid in shape. They have a fresh green color throughout the growing season and cover the plant well. The color of the flowers is a remarkable blending of soft red and chartreuse that is very beautiful and similar to *S. regla*. Unfortunately, flowering stems hold up as cut flowers for only a few hours. Susceptible to cold air, *S. sessei* can be grown outdoors in mild, frost-free areas, where it tends to bloom for three months or more. The most floriferous display occurs during summer. Propagation is by cuttings taken in late August. The rooted cuttings are then placed in the greenhouse in late October or November to assure plants for the garden the following spring. The production of seed on garden plants is rare.

This salvia needs full sun and a bed prepared with humus for a moist rootrun. Good drainage as well as weekly water are necessities too. Growing requirements are simple in a frost-free climate. A popular plant on the French and Italian Rivieras, *Salvia sessei* is often topped at about 4 ft (1.3 m) and encouraged to form a treelike trunk. I have seen it used in this way as a hedge or background within a border. If you are able to grow the plant year-round in the garden, remember to prune it in spring when active growth begins, as this assures new stems that will flower during the summer and autumn.

Salvia sessei is a spectacular plant for the border because it grows so rapidly. It can be shaped for the back of a perennial or shrub border; if there is space, it can be encouraged to develop into a specimen shrub. Its upright habit is an asset when companions such as the 3 ft (1 m) *Nandina domestica* 'Fire Power' are included in the border. The leaves of the nandina are flushed wine-red, and in autumn they turn a soft orange color. The stoloniferous *S. blepharophylla*, with its red-orange flowers, will cover the ground and tie the composition together.

Salvia shannoni Smith

A tender shrub that is found in Chiapas, Mexico, as well as Guatemala, El Salvador, and Honduras, *Salvia shannoni* usually occurs in or near pine-oak forests. In El Salvador it is called *monte amargo*, which means "bitterwood," and it is used domestically for treating malaria. Its habitat range encompasses altitudes from 3000 ft (900 m) to a little more than 5000 ft (1500 m). These mountainous habitats receive plenty of moisture in the form of fog, rain, and streams. The weather is very mild, the chilliest temperatures coming in January when temperatures may fall to 40°F (5°C). When temperatures drop to 32°F (0°C) in my garden for even a few hours, the plant shows signs of leaf burn. Although a frost cloth would shield the plant from a few hours of cold air, it

Salvia shannoni needs greenhouse protection and low light to flower repeatedly throughout autumn, December, and January.
(Sonja Wilcomer)

would be safest to pot the plant and move it to a greenhouse for the entire winter. Make sure that all chances of frost have passed before you replant it in the garden.

Collected in the wild by William Cummings Shannon, it was named for him by Captain John Donnel-Smith, the botanist who first described the plant in 1893. These men apparently served in the United States Army at the same time. Although *Salvia shannoni* has been known and often grown in Central America for many, many years, it is new to California gardeners. Strybing Arboretum occasionally distributes this salvia through its plant sales.

Salvia shannoni is such a handsome, well-proportioned, and shapely shrub that it is not only worth the extra effort to pot up but it is also worth the space it takes up in the greenhouse. In the greenhouse it rewards the grower by continuing to bloom well into February. *Salvia shannoni* first comes into bloom in summer. It has short, fat inflorescences that are 2.5–3.5 in (6–9 cm) in length, and only a few of the vibrant violet or lilac flowers bloom at the same time. The upper lip is small, narrow, and covered with hairs. The lower lip is wide and showy. Large and conspicuous bracts that subtend the flowers contribute to the stubby but not unattractive appearance of the inflorescence. This lime-green calyx is long in comparison to other salvia calyces. The obovate leaves have a thickish texture and are 2.5–4.5 in (6–11 cm) in length. The upper surface is mid-green, and when the weather turns cold or crisp, a layer of brown covers the surface. The underside is whitish, and the veins are quite pronounced. When taken together, all these characteristics present quite an attractive, though tender, shrub.

Needing protection from the hot sun, *Salvia shannoni* can be placed where there is high shade in the garden. My plant receives noonday sun for a brief time but is protected throughout the rest of the day by high shade from very large roses and trees such as crabapples. Well-draining soil that is enriched with humus and regular water are this plant's additional requirements. If you keep the salvia in a container during the summer, give it liquid fertilizer at half strength once a month, as that will furnish the nutrients needed for growth and flowering. With greenhouse space and protection, *S. shannoni* will continue to bloom throughout the winter. This salvia is propagated by cuttings taken in September and wintered over in the greenhouse. It has seldom been known to set seed in the San Francisco Bay area.

There are several perennial plants that will make admirable companions for *Salvia shannoni*. The autumn-blooming *Aconitum carmichaelii*, which will reach 4 ft (1.3 m), is an attractive partner with dark purple flowers that remain fresh for many days. Another good partner is the graceful, spring-blooming, white-spiked *Francoa ramosa*, which has evergreen leaves. Even though *F. ramosa* does not bloom at the same time as the salvia, its low-growing foliage is a welcome addition to the composition. If there is still space, you could fill it with one of the many ornamental, dark purple-leaved heucheras that you see in most nurseries. Heuchera cultivars such as 'Chocolate Ruffles', 'Pewter Veil', 'Plum Pudding', and 'Purple Petticoats' barely start the lengthy list.

Salvia sinaloensis Fernald
Sinaloa sage

Rarely do gardeners find a truly blue flowering plant, but several salvias from Mexico are almost true blue. *Salvia sinaloensis* possesses that exceptional flower color. It has been found only in the Mexican province of Sinaloa, usually in the foothills of the Sierra Madre Occidental. Introduced to horticulture in California in the 1980s, Sinaloa sage has also been available to gardeners in Britain and France since then. Look for it when you visit the national collections of salvias in both countries. It is also available through nurseries in the United States.

Salvia sinaloensis is a small herbaceous perennial with many graceful stems, about 1 ft (30 cm) long that spread on underground runners into a small 1 ft (30 cm) wide clump. Over the summer it makes rapid growth and produces many upright flowering stems. It is a charming plant because of its growth habit and those deep, intensely blue flowers, which have only the slightest hint

Salvia sinaloensis is a densely compact and clumping plant. (Christine Andrews)

of violet. Flowering begins in summer and continues for three or four weeks with recurrent bloom in autumn.

Small lance-shaped leaves about 1 in (2.5 cm) long and 0.5 in (1.3 cm) wide are closely spaced along the stem. When new leaves first appear they are plum-purple, which adds a subtle shade to the small plant. They age to a mid-green with a gray undertone. Plants grown in full sun retain this color but require more water. The flowers appear in whorls of six and are less than 1 in (2.5 cm) in length. They come into bloom one whorl at a time so there is never a lot of blue-violet showing at any one time. The lower lip of the flower has a spot of white, and each flower is held in a wine-colored 0.5 in (1.3 cm) long calyx that persists after the flowers have dropped. The calyces may be checked for seed, and if seed is forming the entire inflorescence should be left in place until maturity. In my garden, plants produce a small amount of seed. Propagation is by seed, cuttings, or careful division of the rootstock.

Salvia sinaloensis needs good drainage, acidic, peaty soil that is enriched with humus, and a half day of sunlight. Deep watering at least once a week is necessary for the plant to produce large clumps. Remember to give plants in full sun extra water. It is helpful to fertilize at least twice during the active growing season. Plants are hardy to 20°F (-7°C), perhaps even lower if given the pro-

SALVIA SINALOENSIS

tection of other plants. *Salvia sinaloensis* does best with shelter from cold air, so look for a protected nook in the garden for it. Planted with large plants such as roses, it would soon make a ground cover at their base. The pale pink rose 'Souvenir de la Malmaison' or the blush-pink, lilac-striped 'Honorine du Brabant' would give shelter and shade to this delightful little salvia. To enjoy its plum-purple leaves for an extended period, plant *S. sinaloensis* at the front of a border that receives full sun and water on a regular basis. Cool and very dry weather promote purplish leaves.

Salvia somalensis Vatke
Somalia sage

Among the early summer-blooming sages, *Salvia somalensis* usually begins flowering towards the end of May and continues, off and on, until the end of October. An aromatic shrub reaching 4–5 ft (1.3–1.5 m) in height and 3 ft (1 m) across, it is multistemmed and rangy with an irregular outline. Endemic to Somalia, it has a limited geographical and altitudinal range. Occurring at 4000–7000 ft (1200–2100 m), it grows in forest clearings, where it is a very common or dominant undershrub, or at the edge of forests.

Oblong, yellow-green leaves amply cover the plant. The longest and largest measure approximately 4 in (10 cm) in length and 1 in (2.5 cm) in width. The flowers are a rather pale wisteria-blue and are usually in closely spaced, many-flowered whorls. The inflorescences are exceptional in that they do not all occur at the top of the stems. Even though each stem has terminal inflorescences, flowering branchlets occur along each main stem. I can think of no other salvia that flowers in this manner. Fertile seed is freely produced, and propagation is easily achieved with seeds, cuttings, or divisions.

Either light shade or almost full sun is suitable for *Salvia somalensis*, along with good drainage and friable soil amended with humus. It also needs weekly water in summer. In the early 1980s after a hard freeze, I lost this plant to 11°F (-12°C) temperatures. Luckily, and much to my amazement, seeds under the old plant germinated a few months later when warm weather arrived. My original plant came from cuttings of a plant grown by seed collected in 1973 in Somalia by the Huntington Botanical Gardens.

A combination of summer- into autumn-blooming plants that takes advantage of this lightly but persistently blooming salvia includes the 3–5 ft (1–1.5 m) *Lavatera maritima*, which has large, lavender, hollyhock-like flow-

ers and gray-green foliage. A mass of the 3 ft (1 m) *Phlox carolina* 'Miss Lingard', with its large clusters of fragrant white flowers, can be highlighted with the 3 ft (1 m) *Nicotiana alata*, Sensation hybrids, which are classified as perennials but treated as annuals. These tobacco plants come in a wide range of white, pink, and rose, and are especially pleasing when mixed throughout the planting. In the evening, they are sweetly scented. *Salvia somalensis* is also a fine companion for the stout, herbaceous, and heavy blooming *Phygelius* 'Winchester Fanfare'. The softly colored, coral-red flowers of the phygelius do not overpower the pale flowers of the salvia.

The summer-blooming *Salvia somalensis*. (Ginny Hunt)

Salvia sonomensis Greene
creeping sage, Sonoma sage

The indigenous *Salvia sonomensis* can be found in three unconnected areas in California: the foothills of the Sierra Nevada, the Coast Ranges from Siskiyou County to Napa County, and from Monterey County to San Diego County. All the habitats are below 6500 ft (2000 m) and consist of dry slopes and woodland forests. The specific epithet, *sonomensis*, refers to the county of Sonoma, one of the plant's many native habitats.

A low-growing perennial herb that tends to form mats, *Salvia sonomensis* is called creeping sage because of its growth habit. It is a highly variable species: the shape of the leaf can range from long and narrow to short and almost rounded; the color of the leaves ranges from yellow-green to dusky green, even to gray-green. Flower color varies too, from pale lavender to lavender-purple; one selection has sparkling lavender-blue flowers. Plants are usually under 1 ft (30 cm) in height with 6 in (15 cm) tall inflorescences rising above the foliage.

Salvia sonomensis at peak bloom in East Bay Regional Parks Botanic Garden, Oakland, California. (Bart O'Brien)

A dry hillside that affords good drainage with light or high shade is needed for all selections of creeping sage. It has the reputation of being hard to grow because of its susceptibility to various fungal rots. Fortunately, I have had no such problems. I recommend a gritty soil low in humus or organic material as I find this type of soil indispensable in obtaining a healthy, long-lived ground cover. You should water plants only until they become established because this species is exceedingly drought tolerant. Creeping sage will not survive in gardens that are regularly watered or have heavy clay soil. Plants are hardy to 10°F (-12°C) or less and do not seem to attract deer.

Easy to propagate, creeping sage tends to root as it enlarges its mat. These rooted pieces can be potted until a good root system has formed and then planted in the garden. Cuttings are the usual method of propagation and ensure the desired selection.

Many different selections have been made based mainly on shape and leaf color. These selections have been collected and propagated from numerous habitats but have seldom been differentiated. Two selections made by Brett Hall of the Arboretum of the University of California, Santa Cruz, were made for hardiness, appearance, and the tendency to not die back in the center of its mat.

Both selections—'Cone Peak' and 'Serra Peak'—are named for their high altitude collection sites.

An excellent form of *Salvia sonomensis* with white flowers was introduced by California Flora Nursery in 1998 and has the cultivar name 'John Farmar-Bowers'. It is named for the late Farmar-Bowers who owned Skylark Nursery in Sonoma County, California. The form has proven to be a handsome and reliable garden subject that blooms exuberantly in spring. Grown on well-draining clay soil, this salvia needs no summer water after it is established.

A hybrid of *Salvia mellifera* and *S. sonomensis* occurred in the Berkeley, California, garden of Helen Beard as a chance seedling and has been grown at the University of California Botanical Garden, Berkeley, since 1965. This hybrid has been distributed and is known as *Salvia* 'Mrs. Beard'. Growing 2 ft (60 cm) in height and 4–6 ft (1.3–2 m) in width, it needs regular pinching to keep wood from building up in the center of the plant. Dull green leaves have a grayish cast, and its tiny flowers are pale lavender. Not subject to fungal attacks, it is drought tolerant but will accept additional water if given fast drainage. This plant is an excellent choice for edging informal dry beds or paths.

Salvia 'Dara's Choice' is thought to be a hybrid of *S. mellifera* and *S. sonomensis*. Introduced in the 1980s, it was named by Nevin Smith of Wintergreen Nursery in Watsonville, California, for Dara Emery, who made the selection at the Santa Barbara Botanic Garden. Taller and more mounding than creeping sage, this hybrid is aromatic with mid-green leaves that make a fresh background for the 8 in (20 cm) tall flowering spikes. Tiny, 0.5 in (1.3 cm) long, violet flowers are held in tight, interrupted whorls. Many spikes come into bloom at the same time making what Marjorie Schmidt (1980) called a "misty effect." This hybrid is easier to cultivate than the species but is subject to verticillium wilt, a fungal problem. Branches, even whole sections, may suddenly die, but a part of the plant usually withstands the attack.

With appropriate cultural conditions, *Salvia sonomensis* makes either a fine ground cover that clambers among rocks or a noteworthy mat for the front of a dry border. A graceful, 4–5 ft (1.3–1.5 m) companion is the pink-flowering currant, *Ribes sanguineum* var. *glutinosum*. Both plants bloom at the same time and require high shade. *Myrica californica*, the evergreen wax myrtle that responds so well to pruning, eventually reaches 10 ft (3 m) or more in height and makes an admirable backdrop or hedge for the other plants.

Salvia spathacea Greene
crimson sage, pitcher sage, hummingbird sage

Salvia spathacea is endemic to California and can be found in the wild at low elevations in the central and coast ranges from San Bruno Mountain in the north to Orange County in the south. It is a robust herbaceous perennial with creeping rhizomes that form dense and handsome mats. In its native habitat it colonizes in soils rich with humus in the light shade of trees or on protected hillsides.

Though not very well known in horticultural circles, *Salvia spathacea* has been grown in gardens in California since the 1970s. Several nurseries distribute unnamed clones that vary in intensity of flower color. Nevin Smith, a California plantsman, introduced his selection 'Kawatre' through his Wintergreen Nursery in 1979. He found it in the Santa Lucia Mountains near Kawatre, a Girl Scout camp. This particular selection has more deeply colored flowers than are commonly found. Smith (1991) calls crimson sage among the most beautiful California native perennials and notes that its appearance is unlike other native California sages and more like the herbaceous sages of Europe and Asia.

A selection made by Bert Wilson of Las Pilitas Nursery in Santa Margarita, California, is called 'Powerline Pink'. The selection is notable because it stands 3 ft (1 m) tall before it flowers, and its flowering stalks add another 3 ft (1 m) to the height of the plant.

The leaves of *Salvia spathacea* 'Kawatre' are evergreen and hastate. The largest measures 8 in (20 cm) in length and 4 in (10 cm) across at its base. A rich lettuce green on the surface, the leaf has an the underside that is covered with short hairs, is pale pastel green, and has prominent veining. The entire edge is scalloped. Flowering stalks 1–3 ft (30–90 cm) in height form in early spring. Late February through June is the blooming period, though there are occasional flowerings in autumn. Splendid, beetroot-purple flowers that are over 1 in (2.5 cm) in length emerge from a large hair-covered calyx that is a dark ruby-red. Bracts of a similar description subtend the calyces. The flowers, calyces, and bracts are in tight whorls spaced about 2 in (5 cm) apart. The calyces and bracts are predominant on the inflorescence, and their whorls are the size of small lemons. Even

Salvia spathacea

The splendid California native *Salvia spathacea* with California poppies in the foreground. (Robert Kourik)

after the flowers have bloomed and dropped, the calyces and bracts remain intact and are a handsome and interesting feature of the sage. All parts of the inflorescence that are hairy have glands that release a pleasant, fruity fragrance when stroked. Crimson sage makes a good cut flower and lasts well in fresh or dry arrangements.

Salvia spathacea does best with a half to full day of sun in a mild climate where temperatures remain above 20°F (-7°C). Well-draining garden soil enriched with humus will encourage colonies. Categorized as a drought-tolerant plant, this salvia should nonetheless be watered once every two weeks or so if it is in full sun. Propagation is by division of the rootstock, cuttings, or seed.

Colonies of crimson sage planted on north- or east-facing hillsides along with California poppies and annual nemophilas will make a riot of color in late spring. *Nemophila menziesii*, baby blue eyes, has charming blue flowers, and the creamy white petals of *N. maculata*, fivespot, are blotched at the tips with purple or violet markings. All are plants that require the same culture, and their lengthy blooming periods overlap. Another favorable site for crimson sage is under trees in filtered light. Planted in patches, its fragrant foliage looks handsome year-round.

Salvia splendens Roemer & Schultes
scarlet sage

Salvia splendens is found in the wild only in Brazil at altitudes of 6500–9800 ft (2000–3000 m) where it is warm year-round, frequently with high humidity. It is usually 4 ft (1.3 m) tall in its native habitat, the selections of which are seldom seen in our gardens. A popular dwarf strain of *S. splendens* is often planted in public gardens and shopping malls in Europe, the United States, Argentina, and Chile. These dwarf strains, which are 2 ft (60 cm) tall, have a proclivity to flower heavily. Millions of these plants are produced from seed and sold each year. They are treated as annuals, and almost every year a new cultivar is introduced. Several strains—for example 'Salsa' and 'Sizzler'—are commonly planted en masse.

Salvia splendens, meaning shining or brilliant, was described botanically in 1822, and then described in both Latin and English in James Ridgeway's *Botanical Register* and given the common name Lee's scarlet sage. The register includes the explanation that Mr. Lee from Hammersmith Nursery introduced the salvia. A beautiful hand-colored drawing of the plant's inflorescence is also included. Ridgeway's notation may mark the beginning of *S. splendens* in horticulture. At that time plants were easily grown from seed and kept in greenhouses where they flowered freely for a long period. (Because plant breeders made the plant small and took away its marvelous habit, I do not provide a general description of *S. splendens*.) These plants varied greatly in size, anywhere from 2 to 9 ft (0.6 to 3 m) in height. The cultivar 'Van Houttei' was an early Dutch selection that was made before the short compact forms were selected and became popular bedding plants. *Salvia splendens* 'Van Houttei' was named for Louis Benoit Van Houtte, the indefatigable nurseryman and editor known as "the father of Belgian horticulture." Of a gentle nature, Van Houtte had a scientific mind and pursued botany as well as art. A great traveler himself, he maintained contact with missionaries and far-flung botanists through letters when he was at home.

A herbaceous perennial, *Salvia splendens* 'Van Houttei' has numerous, ovate, yellow-green leaves with saw-toothed edges that give the plant a leafy look. Plants reach 3–4 ft (1–1.3 m) in both height and width by the time they start flowering in mid- to late August. Flowering continues until frost. The 2 in (5 cm) long, dark red flowers are in verticils of two to six and are held in a 1 in (2.5 cm) long calyx that is the same hue of red as the lower lip of the flower. The two reds combined produce a maroon, brownish red color. When the plant is in flower in autumn it is a stunning sight, particularly when back lit.

In a mild climate, *Salvia splendens* 'Van Houttei' will develop a woody base after a few years. However, because it makes rapid growth,

Salvia splendens 'Van Houttei'

Salvia splendens 'Van Houttei' adds drama to the autumn garden. (Ginny Hunt)

cuttings taken in August and wintered over in a greenhouse will flower the following August. Propagation is by cuttings. This salvia is tender and is damaged at 30°F (-1°C). In my garden in frost-free winters, 'Van Houttei' does survive, but it fails to grow rapidly in the spring or to develop into a fulsome plant. I advise setting out new plants grown from cuttings and then getting them into the border as soon as the earth has warmed. Occasional applications of half-strength liquid fertilizer will speed the growth of 'Van Houttei'.

Part shade is a necessity for siting *Salvia splendens* 'Van Houttei' in the garden, as is good drainage and friable soil that has been amended with humus. Regular water and a mulch of humus to keep roots cool are also helpful. Flowering stems hold well as cut flowers if conditioned by being cut under water. Cutting the flowering stems has the additional benefit of keeping the plant shapely and in flower over a two-month period.

In an area protected by high shade, *Salvia splendens* 'Van Houttei' interplanted with the 4 ft (1.3 m) evergreen *Viburnum utile* provides the backbone of a restful and refreshing border. *Ajuga reptans* 'Jungle Beauty', the rather flat, dark green ground cover, completes the picture. Other possible ground covers are *Heuchera micrantha* or the marble-leaved hybrid *Heuchera* 'Genevieve'. Planted in groups, both these heucheras make 1 ft (30 cm) companions that repeat bloom off and on over a long period.

SALVIA SPLENDENS

Salvia sprucei Briquet

A tall, woody-based perennial, *Salvia sprucei* is an endemic of Ecuador. It is found at high elevations, sometimes more than 7000 ft (2100 m), in dense scrub on steep and often wet slopes. Described by the botanist John Isaac Briquet in 1898, this salvia was named for Richard Spruce, a plant collector who worked in South America for 15 years for the Royal Botanic Gardens, Kew. In 1857 he spent a year collecting in Ecuador, and it is likely that he discovered *S. sprucei* at that time.

A large aromatic plant with many branches, *Salvia sprucei* will attain 10–12 ft (3–4 m) in height and 6 ft (2 m) in width. Leaves vary in size, are ovate or egg shaped, and measure, on average, about 3.5 in (9 cm) long and 1.5 in (4 cm) wide. The upper surface is green with a yellow undertone, and the back of the leaf has pronounced whitish veining that is covered with hairs. Inflorescences are branched with loosely held whorls of flowers that are a light and clear watermelon pink. The flowers are large and measure 1.5 in (4 cm) in length. The lower lip is wide and has a little flange on either side that is marked with a white line. The upper lip is hooded, straight, and covered with fine hairs. The yellow-green, two-lipped calyces that hold the flowers are unusually long, measuring 0.75 in (2 cm). Calyces are the same bright green as the leaves, and they call attention to themselves because they are positioned in a way that makes their entire length visible after the flowers drop. Coming into bloom in late December or early January, this salvia continues to bloom throughout March. On two occasions I have lost my *S. sprucei* specimens when temperatures dipped into the 30°s F (around 1°C); it is clearly a plant for a frost-free garden.

Salvia sprucei is easy to care for in a moderate and warm climate. Full sun and gritty soil with some humus will mirror its native habitat. It needs good drainage and light irrigation throughout the year. The plant should be pruned to the ground in March after new growth has sprung from its base. Even though flowers must be sacrificed, cutting the plant back hard will give it a rest before flowering begins the next winter. A virtue of *S. sprucei* is that it holds itself erect. Some pinching back of new shoots will help reduce its 10–12 ft (3–4 m) height at the time of flowering. After new stems reach 3 ft (1 m), prune about 1 in (2.5 cm) from the top with sharp clippers. This procedure slows the growth of the stems and can be repeated several times. The plant should be in the range of 6–7 ft (2–2.3 m) when flowering.

A winter-blooming plant, *Salvia sprucei* needs a mild climate to produce watermelon-pink flowers with prominent white beelines. (Ginny Hunt)

Several California native plants that bloom when days are short would make both handsome and substantial companions for *Salvia sprucei*. *Arctostaphylos* 'John Dourley' has evergreen, bluish green leaves and blooms profusely in February. A substantial shrub, it will reach 3 ft (1 m) in height and eventually 7–8 ft (2.3–2.5 m) in width. The salvia planted behind the arctostaphylos with the deciduous, very early spring-blooming *Ribes malvaceum* 'Montara Rose' tucked throughout the bed would all bloom in concert. The long drooping clusters of this California native's rosy pink flowers make it an elegant companion. Unlike *S. sprucei*, which requires a moderate amount of water on a weekly basis, the ribes requires no summer water once well established. If you irrigate your garden you would easily be able to withhold water from both the arctostaphylos and the ribes after they are established.

Salvia staminea Montbret & Aucher ex Bentham

A spring-blooming perennial herb, *Salvia staminea* is found in the wild in Asia Minor. Its large habitat is comprised of eastern Turkey, Georgia, Armenia, and Iran, where it occurs at altitudes between 6000 and 14,000 ft (1800 and 4100 m).

Growing in alpine meadows, screes, and cliffs, it is also found with scrub oak as well as on limestone or igneous rocky slopes. *Salvia staminea* is described as being a highly variable plant because of distinct variants in localized habitats throughout its range. Reported to be closely related to *S. austriaca*, a perennial of eastern Europe, *S. staminea* was described botanically in 1836. It has become known only very slowly in horticultural circles, coming into cultivation in England, France, and the United States in the early 1990s. It is occasionally on a few seed lists but is rarely listed with nurseries.

A small, erect, herbaceous plant, *Salvia staminea* is 1.5–2.5 ft (45–80 m) in height and less in width. The plant is covered with medium to dark green ovate leaves that are held on a petiole. The leaves vary in size, the

Coming into delightful bloom during spring and early summer, *Salvia staminea* has handsome foliage that warrents the plant a permanent space in the perennial border. (Ginny Hunt)

largest being 6 in (15 cm) long and 2 in (5 cm) wide. The inflorescence is branched and about 2 ft (60 cm) long. Clasping leaves subtend the inflorescence, which has two to six flowers in spaced whorls. The creamy to off-white flowers are small, less than 0.5 in (1.3 cm) in length, with a narrow upper lip and a spreading and divided lower lip. Flowers are held in a two-lipped, hairy calyx that is frequently reddish brown on its upper lip. Even though the flowers are small, many come into bloom at the same time, creating a pleasant display for about a month. Cutting material can be found on plants, although the usual method of propagation is by sowing seed; some flowers should therefore be permitted to mature. If you did some deadheading, however, you can both encourage and enjoy a repeat bloom in late summer.

Plant *Salvia staminea* where it will receive full sun throughout the growing season. Plants are dormant in winter. Ordinary garden soil with good drainage and water on a regular basis are this salvia's additional needs. The plant's water requirements are minimal but it is not drought tolerant. It is a plant of high elevations so will withstand temperatures into the low teens (-11°C).

Salvia staminea, being of modest size, can be sown or planted into a border of perennial plants that bloom in late spring and early summer. The large 4–5 ft (1.3–1.5 m), yellow-blooming *Euphorbia characias* subsp. *wulfenii* forms the year-round backbone of a sunny border. Two other euphorbias can be counted on for handsome foliage and spectacular yellow flowers: 'Portuguese Velvet', which is a selection of *E. characias*, is 2 ft (60 cm) tall and wide and has beautiful velvetlike, gunmetal-gray foliage, and 'Cherokee' is a cool and restrained hybrid of *E. characias* subsp. *wulfenii* and *E. ×martinii* that grows to 3 ft (1 m) tall and equally as wide with dark green foliage that becomes grayish with summer heat. All you need to complement this yellow and white combination are touches of blue, which you can get from *Centaurea cyanus*, bachelor's buttons, *Linum perenne*, perennial blue flax, and *Consolida ajacis*, annual larkspur. All these plants enjoy a similar culture.

Salvia stenophylla Burchell ex Bentham

A small perennial, *Salvia stenophylla* has an extensive native habitat in South Africa that includes, but is even larger than, the habitat of *S. repens*. Closely allied to *S. repens* and three other *Salvia* species that occur in that area, *S. stenophylla* grows on grassy or stony slopes, on cultivated land or wasteland, and in open and bushy countryside. Photochemical work was done on this salvia in South Africa in the 1980s, and many promising compounds were found in its essential oil. It is rich in one particular oil, an anti-inflammatory agent known as epi-a-bisabolol. An important additive for skin-care products, epi-a-bisabolol has been isolated from other chemicals in this salvia for further study. There is a persistent woodlike odor from the compounds in *S. stenophylla*. Some South Africans burn the plant as a means of disinfecting huts after sickness. It is also mixed with tobacco and smoked, but I find no reference to it being used traditionally for skin care. George Bentham described the plant botanically and named it in 1833, the specific name, *stenophylla*, calling attention to and denoting its narrow leaves.

A much-branched, erect, and bushy aromatic herb, *Salvia stenophylla* reaches 1 ft (30 cm) tall and wide in my garden. It is reported to occasionally reach 2 ft (60 cm) in height and width in its native habitat. Square stems are lightly covered with hairs and appear almost bare. Leaves are sparsely spaced on the stems, the largest ones measuring 2 in (5 cm) long and 0.5 (1.3 cm) wide. They are pinnatifid, parted almost to the midrib, with up to 10 pairs of narrow segments that are glandular. These glands, when brushed, have a light wood odor. Blooming in summer, this salvia has pale blue flowers that are in whorls of six to eight, which are spaced less than 1 in (2.5 cm) apart. Flowers are tiny and held in a calyx that is covered with hairs and oil glands. When in fruit, the small calyces appear to be pressed against the stem.

Both *Salvia stenophylla* and *S. repens* are little known by gardeners and are rarely seen in cultivation. Full sun, water on a weekly basis, and ordinary garden soil that drains well are this salvia's requirements. No pruning is necessary except to remove stems bearing ripe seed. This procedure will keep the plant tidy and healthy. Plants tend to be evergreen in a mild winter and are hardy to temperatures in the low 20°s F (around -6°C) for short periods. Unlike *S. repens*, which has a great capacity to reproduce rapidly by both seed and underground runners, *S. stenophylla* produces a modest amount of seed from which it can be propagated. A small amount of cutting material can be eased from the plant in late summer.

Being diminutive in size, plants of *Salvia stenophylla* can be used to great advantage as a ground cover. For example, a bed of annuals grown for cut flowers would be enhanced with the salvia's delicate and spidery foliage. Both *Zinnia elegans* 'Parasol Mixed', which is 1 ft (30 cm) tall, and *Z. angustifolia* 'Golden Eye', which has single, snow-white flowers and a deep yellow center, can be used for bouquets all summer. The naturally dwarf *Osteospermum hybrida* 'Passion Mixed', which blooms in shades of purple, rose, and white, is only 1 ft (30 cm) tall but has the added advantage of being drought tolerant. It will make a delightful combination when planted with *S. stenophylla*. An assortment of pansies, *Viola*, which are usually grown for their charming colors and splashy blotches, can also be enhanced when in partnership with this salvia.

Salvia taraxacifolia Hooker
dandelion leaved sage

A charming herbaceous perennial, *Salvia taraxacifolia* is found in the wild only in southwest Morocco. It grows in the Atlas Mountains at both high and low altitudes that range from 2000 ft (600 m) to 8000 ft (2500 m). Occurring on rocky limestone slopes, by stony riversides, or in forest clearings, this plant is

The dainty pink flowers of *Salvia taraxacifolia.*
(Robert Kourik)

truly adaptable to many different habitats. Given this adaptive ability, it is surprising that the plant has not been found elsewhere in the wild. Another peculiarity of the plant, as Hedge (1974) points out, is that it has no close allies and occupies an isolated position in the genus.

The leaves of *Salvia taraxacifolia* are gray-green and remain so year-round. Shaped like a lyre, they are about 3–4 in (8–10 cm) long and grow in thick basal rosettes. The dense hairs covering the back of the leaf give it a white appearance. When lightly rubbed, the glands on the hairs release an aromatic citrus odor that is most pleasing. In mild climates where temperatures remain above 20°F (-7°C), the plant is evergreen. Rosettes of foliage are about 6–8 in (15–20 cm) across and equally as high. The epithet, *taraxacifolia*, is probably of Persian origin and means "with leaves shaped like a dandelion."

Abundant, upright, flowering stalks are 6–8 in (15–20 cm) in height with pinkish cream flowers. The flowers, which will be in bloom by the beginning of June, appear in whorls spaced about 1 in (2.5 cm) apart along the inflorescence. The plant tends to form large mats, which makes the numerous inflorescences and little, pale pink flowers a pretty sight.

Dandelion leaved sage will thrive in all kinds of sites and variable conditions. To encourage matting, plant this salvia in three-quarters to a full day of sun and make sure the soil is enriched with humus and has good drainage. Gritty soil is excellent. An application of lime once a year will help produce more robust plants, and deep watering every 10 or 12 days seems to be adequate. Remove spent flowering stalks to encourage repeat bloom. Propagation is easily accomplished by seed or division.

Whether in bloom or not, *Salvia taraxacifolia* is handsome when massed as a ground cover or planted in the front of a border. It blends well with most shades of green because of its gray-green leaves. A combination chosen specifically for texture and foliage color could include the mat-forming, white-flowering perennial *Arenaria montana*, which has small, rich green leaves, and clumps of the 6–8 in (15–20 cm) grass *Festuca amethystina* 'Superba', which has finely textured, bluish, gray-green blades. *Salvia taraxacifolia* completes this selection of pleasing foliage.

Salvia thymoides Bentham

Indigenous to a small geographical area in Mexico where the provinces of Oaxaca and Puebla adjoin one another, *Salvia thymoides* grows in high, cloud forest habitats. The eastern side of these provinces has mountains that rise 7000–9000 ft (2100–2800 m) and that catch lots of moisture in the form of rain and fog—the entire area is bathed in humidity. Described by the botanist George Bentham in 1833 as a herbaceous perennial, this salvia was introduced to horticulture in a limited way in the 1980s. It is little known and rarely grown even though its unique charms are endearing.

An upright, evergreen perennial, *Salvia thymoides* has tiny gray-green leaves that are barely 0.25 in (0.6 cm) in length and that amply clothe stems that are usually about 1 ft (30 cm) tall and wide. The specific name, *thymoides*, refers to the leaves of the plant, which are like thyme. Flowering can take place any time of the year but in my garden the plant is more reliably in bloom during winter and spring. A tiny dark purple calyx holds small purple-blue flowers that measure about 0.5 in (1.3 cm) in length. The flowers are in whorls on a short 2 in (5 cm) long inflorescence. Few flowers are in bloom at any given time. The lower lip of the flower is expanded and has two teardrops of white, which guides insects to the nectary. This salvia is beautifully proportioned, both as a whole and in all its separate parts, and even though it is a shy bloomer, it is enchanting.

The cultural requirements for growing *Salvia thymoides* are simple and easy. Good drainage is essential, and a soil that drains fast and has some humus in it seems to suit the plant well. A south-facing slope with full sun and the protection offered by several rocks would make a perfect setting. Be sure that rocks or other plants do not cast a shadow on the salvia. *Salvia thymoides* could also be grown in a container that has gritty soil with some humus in it. I have never used fertilizer on this plant but have simply watched and waited for its slow development. Light frosty spells do not cause a problem; the plant tolerates tem-

Salvia thymoides at Strybing Arboretum. (Christine Andrews)

peratures into the 20°s F (around -6°C) for short periods. It produces seed sporadically, but cuttings taken in midsummer are the more usual method of propagation. It is also possible to tease away rooted shoots at the base of the plant.

The petite *Salvia thymoides* is a first-rate candidate for a rock garden. Its upright habit makes a good contrast with the bun and mat shapes of more traditional rock garden plants. You could also grow it in a trough with other plant treasures or in a container by itself. This is a reliable salvia just waiting to be discovered by gardeners.

Salvia tingitana Etlinger

Both an ample and handsome herbaceous perennial, *Salvia tingitana* has long been called a perplexing and enigmatic plant. First described by the botanist Andreas Ernst Etlinger in 1777, the plant had no type specimen, the herbarium specimen to which a name is permanently attached. The salvia's place of origin is equally as mysterious. Two botanists at the Royal Botanic Garden, Edinburgh, F. Sales and Ian Hedge have concluded that *S. tingitana* is indeed a species but a species without a definite and definable native habitat. The distribution of the plant has never been accurately determined. The specific epithet, *tingitana*, refers to Tingi, a town in Mauritania that is now called Tangiers, but the plant has never been collected from that location. An unanticipated twist to this story occurred in 1989 when Sheila Collenette, an English botanist living in Saudi Arabia, reported collecting specimens in the middle of and adjacent to a date palm grove in the western part of that country. Laying aside all the mystery that surrounds this plant, the gardener will soon find this winsome and attractive perennial a valuable addition to the border.

About 2 ft (60 cm) in height and the same in width, *Salvia tingitana* has many square, leafy stems that make an upright mound. The leaves are an unusual, pale lime green—in bright sunlight they are almost the color of lime sherbet. The top surface is very rugose and fractures the light that falls on it. The underside is prominently veined and netted with a few long hairs along the center vein. Both sides have glands that release a pungent and penetrating odor when brushed. Ovate leaves have irregular, wavy edges and are graduated in size, the largest being about 6 in (15 cm) long and 5 in (13 cm) wide. The long petiole is lightly covered with long hairs. Flowering begins in late spring and continues for about a month. The inflorescence is about 1 ft (30 cm) in length and frequently branched. Many inflorescences come into bloom simultaneously making this shapely plant look very dramatic. The small, pale, bicolored flowers are less than 1 in (2.5 cm) long and are in whorls that are subtended with persistent floral leaves. The flower's upper lip is a very pale lavender and falcate, whereas the lower lip is a very pale yellow and shorter than its counterpart. Each flower is held in a hair-covered calyx that is 0.25 in (0.6 cm) in length. Plants produce seed, which is the usual means of propagation, though there is cutting material on the plant that can be used in late August or early September. In my experience, the plant normally takes one year to become established when seed is sown and it blooms in the second year.

I recommend planting this salvia where it receives five or more hours of sunlight each day. It is important for the plant to receive good drainage and soil that is not rich in nutrients. You can place a layer of mulch around the base of the plant after the weather has warmed. It will need regular water throughout the growing season. Care for *Salvia tingitana* is minimal and consists of removing the spent inflo-

Salvia tingitana

Noted for its precisely designed erect habit and unusual pale lime-green leaves, *Salvia tingitana* can be placed to great effect in the garden. (Ginny Hunt)

rescences and pruning only a stem or two to keep the plant shapely. Staking is not necessary. It will survive temperatures in the low 20°s F (around -6°C) for short periods.

Salvia tingitana makes a fine addition to the perennial border not only because of its beautiful lime green leaves but also because of its attractive habit. Whether the border is in bloom or resting, this salvia will continue to look handsome and shapely throughout a long growing season. A combination of foliage plants that will produce a quiet effect to a section of the garden might include the evergreen *Berberis calliantha*, which is 2 ft (60 cm) tall and wide. It is a graceful shrub with young stems that are crimson and dark green leaves that are completely white on the underside. You can use two or three *S. tingitana* plants in the foreground, depending on the amount of space available, interspersed with the sprawling and repeat-blooming *Geranium* 'Patricia', which has a magenta flower with a dark eye. A gray-foliaged plant you could use for the front of the group is *Tanacetum haradjanii*, its silver-white foliage bringing out the salvias' lime-green leaf color. Another ground cover plant that will spread and tie the group together is *Marrubium rotundifolium*. Its foliage is almost the same color as that of the salvia. The edge of its leaf, which is slightly scalloped and almost white, is stunning, especially when wet. All these plants need minimal care and enjoy the same culture.

Salvia transsylvanica Schur

A very hardy herbaceous perennial, *Salvia transsylvanica* has a wide distribution from northern and central Russia through Romania. The specific epithet, *transsylvanica*, refers to the central area of Romania that is bounded on the south by the Transylvanian Alps. It was described botanically in 1853 but its introduction to gardeners through seed catalogs was only in the late 1980s.

When first becoming established, the very leafy *Salvia transsylvanica* forms a clump of leaves from which are produced many lax stems 2 ft (60 cm) or more in length. The leaves at the base of these stems are large and they decrease in size towards the top of the stem. They are dark yellow-green on top with pale undersides and prominent yellow veining. Each petiole varies in length in proportion to the size of the leaf. The beauty of the foliage lies not only in its rich color and texture but also in the pronounced scalloping around the entire edge of the leaf.

Flowering begins in early summer and will continue until frost if spent inflorescences and a large portion of their lax stems are removed. The flowers are arranged in loose whorls and spaced about 0.5 in (1.3 cm) apart. Many flowers come into bloom at the same time and their rich violet color makes a lovely showing. The flowers are at least 0.5 in (1.3 cm) in length, so a lot of color can be seen on each inflorescence. These flowering stems are lax, but even so they make a fine display. As a cut flower, this salvia lasts for many days in a bouquet.

Propagation is easiest by seed, although cuttings can be used. After the mother plant is established, self-sown seedlings may be found at its base. It takes a full year for young plants to develop a large rootstock with a tap root that will subsequently produce abundant flowering stems.

The cultural requirements of *Salvia transsylvanica* include a half to full day of sun, good drainage, and humus incorporated in friable garden soil. Deep watering once a week and a liquid fertilizer applied at half-strength several times during the growing season are recommended. Considering this salvia's native habitat, I would expect these plants to be hardy to 0°F (-18°C) and quite possibly to even lower temperatures. Place conifer boughs over the crown of the plant to prevent heaving in a cold climate.

Salvia transsylvanica needs a space that measures 3 ft (1 m) if it is to develop fully. It reaches almost 2 ft (60 cm) in height but because of its lax, sprawling habit, it makes a fine companion plant and looks lovely with shrub roses. The climbing form of the old tea rose 'Mme Caroline Testout', with its subdued pink flowers, or the white-flowered, upright hybrid tea 'Frau Karl Druschki' would be enhanced by *S. transsylvanica*, which clothes the nearby spaces but does not grow directly underneath the roses. All have the same cultural requirements. The front of a herbaceous border is also a desirable place for this attractive salvia with dark green leaves and blooms that repeat throughout the summer as it almost crawls along the ground.

A mound of foliage supports *Salvia transsylvanica* in the center of this photo. Directly behind it is the tall *Anigozanthos flavidus*, with the yellow-flowered *S. ×jamensis* 'Cienega de Oro' to the left and an unidentified verbascum on the right. (Ginny Hunt)

Salvia tubiflora Smith

A tall and leafy shrub that is classified botanically as a perennial, *Salvia tubiflora* makes woody stems only at its base. It has a limited habitat in western Peru and in northern Chile near the tropic of Capricorn, where it grows at low altitudes between 800 and 1600 ft (250 and 500 m). I have not been able to find any information as to its habitat conditions, but plants growing in the general area of where I live in California have proven to be adaptable and easy to establish in gardens. The specific epithet, *tubiflora*, refers to the plant's long tubular flowers.

Salvia tubiflora begins blooming in my garden as the days grow short. The earliest flowers appear in late September or early October, and with a spell of warm days and nights, flowering will continue into early December. The shortened hours of sunlight do not stop the flowering and in fact may trigger it. At the latitude where *S. tubiflora* is native, the hours of daylight and darkness are more evenly divided the year-round. Reaching 9 ft (3 m) in height and about 4 ft (1.3 m) in width in a long growing season, plants achieve approximately these same dimensions in Peru and Chile. Leaves are yellow-green and held on a long petiole. The largest are heart shaped and about 3–4 in (8–10 cm) long and 2 in (5 cm) or more wide. The veins are prominent on the back of each leaf with tiny hairs that are arranged in a row like eyelashes. The petioles and stems also have these tiny hairs. Inflorescences vary little in length and usually reach 8–12 in (20–30 cm). They are held in a stiff, upright position at the top of the shrub. Flowers are an attractive, almost dark and dull cranberry-red color and are not abundant; there are usually only two or three in a whorl. The two-lipped flower is a long, straight, and slender tube that is about 1 in (2.5 cm) in length. It is held in a distinctive reddish green calyx that is 0.75 in (2 cm) long and covered with tiny hairs and glands. Some gardeners regard this salvia as coarse, but when it is in flower and at its prime it is an impressive addition to the autumn border. At its best—when the cranberry-red flowers are silhouetted against a heavenly blue sky—*S. tubiflora* can easily be called remarkable. Tolerant of cold weather to about 25°F (-4°C), this salvia in my garden has come back from its roots in the spring after a winter low of 20°F

Salvia tubiflora

An autumn-blooming plant, *Salvia tubiflora* has cranberry-red flowers that are at the very top of its shrublike growth. (Sonja Wilcomer)

(-7°C). *Salvia tubiflora* is easy to root from cuttings taken in late August before it blooms. In spring, when its base shows signs of life and growth, rooted stems may be removed and potted for extra plants. After all danger of frost has passed, cut all the stems back to two active nodes at the plant's base. This procedure is usually the only pruning you will need to do.

Plant *Salvia tubiflora* in good garden soil that drains well and place it where it will receive over a half day of sunlight. It requires water on a weekly basis, more during hot spells. Although fertilizer is not needed, a mulch of several inches of humus at the base of the plant in late spring will furnish food for the growing season.

Useful as a tall screening plant, *Salvia tubiflora* can be paired with an evergreen shrub such as *Osmanthus fragrans* or *Berberis julianae*, both of which are about 6 ft (2 m) tall, to make a handsome and impenetrable barrier. The upright, deciduous *B. sherriffi*, which reaches 6 ft (2 m), has leaves that turn lovely shades of apricot and red in autumn. It would also make a companion that is well timed for seasonal color.

Salvia uliginosa Bentham
bog sage

In the early part of the 19th century, *Salvia uliginosa* was found in specific localities in southern Brazil, Uruguay, and Argentina, and was described and named by the distinguished English botanist George Bentham. In its native habitat it is found growing in bogs and wet places. In fact, the specific epithet, *uliginosa*, means "of swamps and marshes." Introduced to horticulture in 1912, *Salvia uliginosa* has steadily been gaining recognition among gardeners. There are good reasons for this increased popularity: it has beautiful sky-blue flowers, it flourishes in a multitude of growing conditions, and the rootstock is easily divided.

A herbaceous perennial that will reach 3–6 ft (1–2 m) in height in a season, bog sage spreads fairly rapidly on underground runners. It has very thin stems that are deeply grooved, and its leaves are yellow-green and shaped like a lance. They are of varying sizes, serrated on the edge, and tend to grow in clusters—all these features give the thin, multiple stems a fairylike, graceful appearance, particularly when they move in a breeze. The bright azure-blue flowers are about 0.5 in (1.3 cm) in length and have a white beeline in the throat to guide insects to pollen and nectar. The flowers appear in whorls and many usually come into bloom at the same time. Flowering begins in summer and continues until daylight hours shorten. Hardy to 15°F (-9°C) and probably lower, *Salvia uliginosa* is a favorite of Beth Chatto (1982), who tells of it surviving nine out of ten winters in her cold Essex garden with a cover of mulch.

As bog sage is far from particular about growing conditions, I recommend good drainage, garden soil enriched with humus, and infrequent watering. With little water the plant stays within the 4 ft (1.3 m) range and does not spread as rapidly. It tolerates full sun but looks prettiest with some shade. It is not evergreen, and all stems should be cut to the ground in late winter or early spring. Propagation is by seed, cuttings, or division, although division is by far the easiest method. Bog sage makes a very nice cut flower throughout its long summer- into autumn-blooming period.

In a high-shade border, *Salvia uliginosa*, white or pink Japanese

Salvia uliginosa

The light and airy *Salvia uliginosa* interplanted with *S. dumetorum*. (Christine Andrews)

anemones, and the spring- and autumn-flowering *Geranium* 'Russell Prichard' with its reddish rose flowers make an attractive late summer combination. In my garden I have planted bog sage with the late spring-blooming rose 'Félicité Perpétue' to give life to the green foliage of the rose during the summer after it has flowered.

Salvia urica Epling

An attractive salvia that comes from a warm and moist habitat, *Salvia urica* is a herbaceous perennial well suited for gardens with mild climates. Indigenous to the mountainous regions of Guatemala, Belize, Honduras, and Chiapas, Mexico, it is reported to be more plentiful in Guatemala. It grows in Guatemala at elevations from 1000 to 8500 ft (400 to 2600 m) in many different habitats that include thickets, open fields, slopes, dense and mixed forests as well as open pine-oak woodlands. Temperatures in this large but contained area vary little from summer to winter, but there is more precipitation, including rain, fog, and drizzle, during the winter months. Carl Epling described this salvia in 1939 and gave it the specific epithet, *urica*, which means "caterpillar" or "canker-worm." I assume the epithet refers to the whorls of flowers, calyces, and bracts that are held tightly together before expanding and blooming.

Coming into bloom in late summer, *Salvia urica* is a well-proportioned plant that reaches about 4 ft (1.3 m) or less in both height and width. Stems, leaves, and calyces are covered with long white hairs. The leaves are soft to touch because of these hairs, and as the leaves are glandular they release a light and pleasant scent when brushed. Deltoid in shape, they are also thin and measure 2–6 in (5–15 cm) long with a margin that is barely saw-toothed. Whorls of small but rich blue-violet flowers numbering three to six are held in green calyces and are just under 0.5 in (1.3 cm) long. The upper lip of the flower is narrow and covered with short hairs, and the lower lip is wider and has distinct white markings. The flower is just a little longer than the calyx that holds it. The flowers produce some seed but propagation is usually by cuttings that are taken in late summer or early autumn. Cuttings held in the greenhouse can be planted out when there is no danger of a late frost. They will

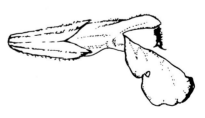

Salvia urica

develop rapidly with regular water and the addition of liquid fertilizer at half strength applied every two weeks.

Salvia urica is a plant for the mildest climates as it is a tender salvia that cannot tolerate temperatures in the 20°s F (around -6°C); even 30°F (-1°C) will cause it serious difficulties. Plant this salvia where it receives at least a half day of sunlight in good garden soil that drains well and is enriched with humus. Several inches of humus added each spring as a mulch will insure a cool root run that encourages steady and uniform growth. In a warm climate, this salvia tends to keep producing flowers even when the days grow short. When there is no danger of frost, you can cut it back into a pleasing shape for the upcoming growing season.

A late summer- through autumn-blooming border containing *Salvia urica* will become substantial with several of the old-fashioned shrub roses in the background. For example, 'La Marne', which reaches 5 ft (1.5 m) in height and width, has small but prolific pink flowers that repeat bloom unfailingly and provide a most agreeable contrast to the salvia's blue-violet flowers. You could plant *S. urica* on either side of the roses and in front of both add some 3 ft (1 m) tall, late-blooming asters. There is a long list of asters from which to choose, but the three I recommend are *Aster divaricatus*, which has large white flowers; *A. pringlei* 'Ochtendgloren'; which has starry pink flowers; and *A. petiolatus* 'Photograph', which has darkish purple-lavender flowers and stems. *Salvia lycioides*, a very low-growing salvia that repeats bloom lavishly in autumn, could fill the front of the border. Usually under 1.5 ft (45 cm) tall and spreading 2 ft (60 cm), this salvia has gray-green leaves and twinkling cornflower-blue flowers. All these plants require the same culture of friable soil, good drainage, regular water, and lots of sunlight.

Salvia verticillata Linnaeus

Widely distributed in the wild, *Salvia verticillata* is found across central Europe and into western Asia. Naturalized in northern Europe and North America, this sage apparently adapts easily to different climates and soils. It was described by Linnaeus in 1753, but I find no mention of it in early gardening literature or herbals and must assume that it lacks medicinal and culinary properties.

A herbaceous perennial, *Salvia verticillata* has a leafy base of mid-green leaves that are covered with short hairs, giving them a soft green appearance and making them velvety to the touch. Stems covered in leaves carry branched inflorescences that frequently reach 3 ft (1 m) in height and 2.5 ft (0.8 m) in width. Whorls of tiny, densely packed, lavender flowers are held in equally tiny calyces that are lime green tinged with purple. The specific epithet, *verticillata*, refers to these tightly packed whorls of flowers in verticils. Graham Stuart Thomas (1990a) calls the plant stately but not showy and I would have to agree with him. However, in the early 1990s the long-blooming cultivar 'Purple Rain' was introduced, and this cultivar is indeed showy. This selection was made by Piet Oudolf of the Netherlands and is distributed from his nursery. Not as large or lax as the species, 'Purple Rain' is usually about

Salvia verticillata 'Purple Rain' blooms without interruption in the summer and autumn. (Robert Kourik)

2 ft (60 cm) tall, and its upright position supports whorls of small but plentiful purple flowers held in tiny violet calyces. When conditioned by being cut under water, the stems of *S. verticillata* and its cultivar 'Purple Rain' both make fine cut flowers.

Friable garden soil improved with humus along with good drainage and water at least once a week are required for these salvias. I recommend full sun because the inflorescences tend to become leggy and lax with shade. *Salvia verticillata* and 'Purple Rain' are both cold tolerant to 0°F (-18°C). In a cold climate, place pine boughs over the crown of plants to prevent heaving.

Salvia verticillata and 'Purple Rain' are good candidates for a spot in a sunny border that requires flowers of a dusky hue. One end of a summer-flowering border might include clumps of *Origanum laevigatum* 'Hopleys', with its vibrant pink flowers and bracts, and *Origanum* 'Santa Cruz', with its heavily flowering lilac-pink spikes. Both are about 2 ft (60 cm) in height. *Thymus vulgaris* 'Argentea', silver thyme, is less than 1 ft (30 cm), and can be interplanted to weave the composition together. The lovely, summer-blooming *Buddleja alternifolia* 'Argentea', with its silver, willowlike leaves and lilac-purple flowers, makes a fine background for drifts of *S. verticillata* or 'Purple Rain'. The spreading and lax *B. davidii* 'Nanho Purple', which has dark red-purple flowers with an orange eye, serves the same purpose equally well. Crocus or narcissus bulbs could be included for a touch of color in early spring. The bulbs' foliage will have matured and been removed before the salvia comes into bloom.

Salvia villosa Fernald

A tender and rather dainty perennial herb, *Salvia villosa* has been collected in two Mexican provinces, Coahuila and San Luis Potosí. Collection sites have been at 4000 ft (1200 m) in areas that are mainly dry and have little or no frost. It is a handsome plant, and though it is not hardy, it should be known to gardeners because of its pretty, delicate appearance.

Eventually reaching 1–1.5 ft (30–45 cm) in both height and width, *Salvia villosa* is a low, mounding plant. Small blue-green leaves, the largest about 1 in (2.5 cm) in length, hold themselves upright along the stems and amply cover the plant. The leaves are thin and covered with short hairs, and the margins are outlined with tiny hairs too. The specific epithet, *villosa*, means "hairy" and refers to these soft hairs. Slender and wiry inflorescences rise above the foliage about 8 in (20 cm). Irregularly spaced verticils hold two to six flowers. The flowers are tiny, often less than 0.5 in (1.3 cm) long, but their bright violet-blue color attracts attention, particularly in the sunlight. The lower lip has a white beeline that extends into the throat. *Salvia villosa* never comes into what would be referred to as full bloom, but it has a few flowers continuously from spring through autumn.

Full sun and a fast-draining, gravelly soil are important conditions for this salvia. It needs regular weekly water throughout the summer. In my garden, it grows and fills out more rapidly if there are low-growing companion plants around it. It will survive temperatures into the high 20°s (around -2°C) for short periods. Propagation is by seed or cuttings. To be on the safe side, take cuttings in late August to be wintered over in the greenhouse.

A sun-filled rock garden is an ideal setting for *Salvia villosa*. A vast number of low-growing plants can be considered as companions, and I have listed a few of varying heights. All thrive in the same culture as *S. villosa*.

The small, blue-flowered *Salvia villosa* blooms in spring and autumn. It makes a fine partner for the unidentified red salvias. (Betsy Clebsch)

Achillea ageratifolia, filigree-like, silvery-gray foliage and white flowers, 6 in (15 cm).

Achillea umbellata, divided gray foliage and white flowers, 6 in (15 cm).

Artemisia pycnocephala, finely cut, silvered foliage, 2 ft (60 cm).

Ballota acetabulosa, handsome, rounded, gray-green foliage, 2 ft (60 cm).

Eriogonum latifolium, flat, pearl gray foliage and pink flowers, 8 in (20 cm).

Frankenia thymifolia, gray-blue foliage and tiny pink flowers, 2 in (5 cm).

Helichrysum italicum, bright silver, linear foliage and small straw-yellow flowers, 1.5 ft (45 cm).

Santolina pinnata 'Edward Bowles', narrow, divided, gray-green leaves, 1.5 ft (45 cm). Particularly attractive pale lemon flowers.

Tanacetum haradjanii, finely cut, feathery, silver-white foliage, 4 in (10 cm).

Salvia viridis Linnaeus

Salvia viridis is an erect herbaceous annual occurring in the wild in a region extending from the Mediterranean into Crimea and Iran. *Salvia viridis* was known as *S. horminum* for many years, but some botanists have determined that the earlier specific name *viridis* is the correct one. In 1753, Linnaeus described *Salvia viridis* and *Salvia horminum* as separate species, and some botanists today agree they are separate. *Viridis* is from the Greek and means "green," covering every shade of the color. Youth and vigor are also implied. *Horminum* is the Greek for sage. Since the late 1500s, when *S. viridis* was brought into cultivation, many selections have been made and are named for the colorful sterile bracts that adorn each inflorescence and give the plant its unique charm.

This is a delightful plant for the front of a summer border, growing 1–2 ft (30–60 cm) tall and 1 ft (30 cm) wide. It is an annual that develops rapidly and has a long period of bloom that lasts over a month. The colorful bracts do well as cut flowers. Nearly hidden beneath the bracts are the tiny two-lipped flowers. These almost secret flowers are cream-colored with a tinge of either purple or rose on the top lip, reflecting the colorful bract on top. In addition to being useful in fresh arrangements, the inflorescences may be cut and dried for winter bouquets.

Three-quarters to a full day of sun, good drainage, friable soil, and moderate water are the plant's cultural requirements. Applications of liquid fertilizer are helpful to push the plants along to full bloom. Plants growing in an area that has a lengthy and warm autumn will bloom twice if inflorescences are cut back after they reach peak bloom. This pruning should be done before seed production begins and probably no later than at the end of July. I recommend regular feeding and watering to encourage a second bloom.

Salvia viridis

Sow seed indoors in late March to get a jump on the season or sow them in place in the border when the soil has warmed and the danger of frost has passed. Germination takes more or less 15 days if soil temperature has reached 70°F (21°C). Seedlings are stout and transplant readily. When winters are very mild, self-sown seedlings may appear, but they should

Salvia viridis shown with *S. albimaculata* in the foreground and the outstanding gray-foliaged *Brachyglottis* 'Sunshine' in the background. (Christine Andrews)

not be counted on. *Salvia viridis* used to be known as "red-topped sage," implying that the bracts were deep pink or rose. This common name was probably used to distinguish *S. viridis* from *S. officinalis* 'Purpurascens', commonly called red sage. For several centuries, both sages have been widely grown and used in Britain and on the continent. Breeders have been busy and are able to offer many color selections; the cultivar name usually describes the color of the showy bracts. I have tried and enjoyed each of the following cultivars: 'Alba', 'Bluebeard', 'Oxford Blue', 'Pink Sunday', and 'Rose Bouquet'. One British seed list offers 'Claryssa Blue', 'Claryssa Pink', and 'Claryssa White'. I have also grown these cultivars and find them just as enjoyable.

Elizabeth Lawrence (1942) warns gardeners in the hot and humid southern United States that this showy annual must be grown for a late spring display. In those conditions it seldom repeats bloom in the way it does in more favorable climates.

In their extraordinary work *A Modern Herbal*, M. Grieve and C. F. Leyel (1931) provide a wide range of information on herbs and their uses. In discussing *Salvia viridis*, they state that the seeds and leaves used to be added to fermenting vats in order to "greatly increase the inebriating quality of the liquor." An infusion of the leaves was a treatment for sore gums, and powdered leaves were used for snuff. This sage was also noted as a honey-yielding plant. We no longer grow these pretty plants for their versatile, life-enhancing properties; instead we grow and enjoy them for their lively beauty in the garden.

If you have leggy roses, such as 'First Love' or 'Silver Jubilee', a group of *Salvia viridis* would skirt the shrubs and give additional color. Plant this salvia in drifts in the border so that the colorful bracts can be enhanced by the silver-gray foliage of *Artemisia arborescens* or the almost silver-white foliage of the attractive California native *A. pycnocephala*.

Salvia viscosa Jacquin

An erect herbaceous perennial, *Salvia viscosa* was described in 1781 by Nicolaus Joseph von Jacquin, a distinguished botanist at the University of Leiden in the Netherlands. This salvia has been known botanically since the 1780s, but I have not been able to find it mentioned in any gardening literature. In the 1990s, however, there are reliable reports of it being sold in nurseries in England, France, and the United States. It is ironic that it has taken 200 years for a well-described plant that is easily grown to be discovered by gardeners. *Salvia viscosa* has a very limited native habitat that is comprised of the mountainous regions of both Lebanon and Israel.

Salvia viscosa forms a small attractive clump of soft, misty green leaves that are ovate-oblong in shape and 3–4 in (8–10 cm) long and 1.5–2 in (4–5 cm) wide. Both the upper and lower surfaces of the leaves are covered with soft hairs, the lower being prominently marked with whitish green veining. In midsummer the 3 ft (1 m) tall inflorescence rises above the cluster of leaves. Although the salvia is tall, it is difficult to see the inflorescence because the plant has thin stems and widely spaced whorls of flowers that are remarkably small. Flowers are a beautiful burgundy-red and measure about 0.75 in (2 cm) in length. They are held in a tiny hair-covered calyx that is wine colored. These darkish red colors simply make the flowers disappear in the border. The salvia makes copious amounts of seed, and young plants are invariably found around and near the mother plant. In late summer cutting material may be teased away from the cluster of leaves at the base of the plant. Deciduous in a cold winter, *S. viscosa* completely disappears in 20°F (-7°C) weather but reappears with moderate spring temperatures. It tends to come into bloom in midsummer, and if you remove inflorescences before seeds are formed, the plant will repeat bloom for a full month or so.

This salvia is not at all fussy about its cultural conditions. It can be sited in a half to full day of sunlight and grown in clay or ordinary garden soil. Drainage is not as critical to its well-being as it is for other salvias, and it requires only a moderate amount of water. Pruning is not necessary except to remove the flowering stalk before seed is produced in order for the plant to repeat bloom. Its overall care is both simple and straightforward.

I must admit that I have never found a way of showing *Salvia viscosa* to its best advantage. It is a self-sufficient salvia, so I let it seed by chance among other shrubs and herbaceous plants. Although this salvia fills any nook or cranny between plants, it is also almost impossible to see either the outline of the plant or its flowers

An adaptable plant that seeds itself into vacant niches in the garden, *Salvia viscosa* has flowers of rich burgundy-red that attract hummingbirds and insects. (Ginny Hunt)

when it is growing in a casual or mixed border. I saw it planted in the south of France in a narrow border with walkways on either side where it was combined with shorter-growing and heavy-flowering *S. greggii* cultivars. This combination complemented both salvias very well. This salvia's inflorescence is held in an upright position so it could be planted to good advantage behind a collection of origanums. Having a similar blooming period, the shorter-growing origanums, when in flower with soft and dusky pinks, mauves, and purples, would blend with the rich burgundy-red flowers of the salvia. These plants all require the same culture, including little water.

Salvia wagneriana Polakowsky

Even though *Salvia wagneriana* is found at elevations of 4000–6500 ft (1200–2000 m), suggesting it is cold tolerant, the climate in the mountainous areas where it is found is warm and moist. In fact, this salvia frequently grows in thickets that are both wet and warm. It is a beautiful species and very popular with gardeners in the parts of the world where it occurs naturally. Frequently found at moderate elevations in Guatemala, El Salvador, Nicaragua, Costa Rica, and the province of Chiapas in Mexico, it is among the few salvias taken from the wild and grown in gardens in these localities. Its ease of adaptability has resulted in it becoming established outside the parameters of many of its native habitats.

Described by botanists sometimes as a herb and sometimes as a shrub, *Salvia wagneriana* is shrublike in stature, attaining 3–9 ft (1–3 m) in height and 4 ft (1.3 m) or more in width. Leaves are yellowish green, sometimes with purple veins, and smooth on top. On the underside of the leaf the veins are distinctly raised. Flower color can vary from bright red to rose to pinkish cream. The bracts that cover the emerging flowers are highly colored, as are the calyces. When you observe them closely, you will see that the flowers, calyces, and bracts are all slightly different colors. Flowers are at least 1 in (2.5 cm) in length, frequently as long as 3 in (8 cm). They are held in a calyx that is 0.75 in (2 cm) long and showy. The bracts are usually slightly darker in color than the flower and fall away as the plump flowers emerge in whorls. Seeds of *Salvia wagneriana* germinate readily and cuttings root quickly.

Blooming begins in late autumn and continues through January. Short days probably trigger flowering but the plant certainly needs warm air and soil to promote blooming. I have been able on only one occasion to bring this plant into bloom. The winter preceding bloom was without frost, allowing the plant to grow to about 3 ft (1 m) in height. The following autumn the plant reached 6 ft (2 m) and began flowering on the first day of November. It was in full gorgeous bloom by Thanksgiving. Soon after that we had a killing frost and the plant melted away. In the spring there was no sign of life at its base.

Site *Salvia wagneriana* under high shade with protection from hot sun and wind. A very warm, mild climate is a prerequisite for this salvia, as is well-draining garden soil amended with humus. Annual mulching and regular deep watering are also necessary.

In a frost-free garden, *Salvia wagneriana* is a handsome partner for flowering maple, *Abutilon*, and there are many free-flowering selections from which to choose. 'Nabob', for example, is covered with dark leaves and has large maroon flowers. 'Pink Parasol' is charming, with satinlike leaves and almost mauve flowers. The hybrid *Abutilon suntense*, so popular in Britain, has open, lavender-violet flowers 3 in (8 cm) wide. All these plants like partial shade, water, and warmth.

Salvia 'Waverly'

In approximately 1994, a splendid new salvia came to the attention of nurserymen and plant people in California. Quickly, the plant acquired an excellent reputation and became well known. It was both rapidly and widely distributed up and down the coast because it is quite easy to propagate. The names of people who first distributed it and the nurseries or gardens where it was grown were not recorded making it difficult, if not impossible, to determine its origin. Because of 'Waverly's' phenomenal vigor, it is thought to be of hybrid origin.

A substantial plant in both shape and performance, Salvia 'Waverly' thrives in a mild climate where temperatures do not go below 32°F (0°C).

Flowering heavily for many months, *Salvia* 'Waverly' grows in gardens all over the world that have Mediterranean climates. (Sonja Wilcomer)

It has proven to take temperatures in the low 20°s F (around -6°C) for short periods, however. This salvia is evergreen with very little wood at its base, its stems are herbaceous and square in shape. With regular garden water throughout the year it attains about 5 ft (1.5 m) in both height and width. It is a very heavy bloomer with inflorescences frequently 2 ft (60 cm) in length. Blooming begins in late spring and continues until cold weather and short days stop all growth. The leaves are lanceolate in shape and glabrous. The upper surface is dark green, rugose, with indented veining. The underside is light green with prominent veining. The petiole varies in length according to the size of the leaf. Medium-sized leaves measure 2.5 in (6 cm) in length and have petioles 0.5 in (1.3 cm) in length. Flowers, numbering on the average

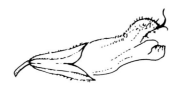

Salvia 'Waverly'

about ten, are in whorls and as the inflorescence elongates the space between each whorl also lengthens. The largest flowers are 1 in (2.5 cm) in length and are held in a two-lipped green calyx with purplish tips that is 0.4 in (1.2 cm) in length. The flowers emerge pale lavender and frequently mature white. However, some flowers are completely lavender. The lower lip is wide and spreading, the upper lip is hooded and lightly covered with hairs. The overall plant conveys a picture of agreeable abundance.

A sunny border with well-draining garden soil are the cultural needs for growing *Salvia* 'Waverly'. Regular water and a 3 in (8 cm) or more layer of mulch each spring will assure good growth. This plant wants to produce leaves and flowers and will do so vigorously. Some summer pruning will assure a shapely plant and regular deadheading will promote more flowering. Fertilizer is not advised. Propagation is by cuttings that will root easily and may be taken at any time during the growing season. 'Waverly' is not known to have produced any seed, leading once again to the conjecture that it may be a hybrid.

Many large, herbaceous, shrubby plants are desirable companions for 'Waverly'. Dahlias, agastaches, and nicotianas are all late summer- into autumn-blooming herbaceous plants. Buddlejas, lavateras, and abutilons too are sizable and late-blooming shrubs. In a wide and generous sunny border, I can picture two shrub roses in the background, the pale pink and fragrant 'Souvenir de la Malmaison' with three plants of 'Waverly' between the roses. In the foreground, drifts of the lavender-blue flowered *Aster* ×*frikartii* 'Monch', the white-flowered with dark leaves *A. lateriflorus* 'Lady in Black', and the *Sedum* 'Vera Jameson' with rosy flowers and purple tinged leaves fill all the spaces. These are all noteworthy companions for a salvia without a known or documented past but with a bright and promising future as a garden subject.

SALVIA 'WAVERLY'

Where to See Salvias

The following are a few of the public gardens with particularly fine collections of salvias.

UNITED STATES

Cabrillo College Salvia Garden
6500 Soquel Drive
Aptos, California 95003
Tel 831-479-6439

Denver Botanic Gardens
909 York Street
Denver, Colorado 80206
Tel 303-331-4000

East Bay Regional Parks
Botanic Garden
Tilden Regional Park
11500 Skyline Boulevard
Oakland, California 94619
Tel 510-562-7275

Elizabeth F. Gamble Garden Center
1431 Waverley Street
Palo Alto, California 94301
Tel 650-329-1356

Huntington Botanical Gardens
1151 Oxford Road
San Marino, California 91108
Tel 818-792-6141

Quarryhill Botanical Garden
12825 Sonoma Highway
Glen Ellen, California 95442
Tel 707-996-3166

Rancho Santa Ana Botanic Garden
1500 North College Avenue
Claremont, California 91711
Tel 909-625-8767

Santa Barbara Botanic Garden
1212 Mission Canyon Road
Santa Barbara, California 93105
Tel 805-682-4726

Strybing Arboretum Society
Ninth Avenue at Lincoln Way
San Francisco, California 94122
Tel 415-661-1316

University of California Botanic
Garden, Berkeley
Centennial Drive
Berkeley, California 94720
Tel 510-642-3343

University of California, Santa Cruz,
Arboretum
1156 High Street
Santa Cruz, California 95064
Tel 831-427-2998

Wave Hill Gardens
675 W 252nd Street
Bronx, New York 10471
Tel 718-549-3200

FRANCE

Pépinière Filippi
R.N. 113
34140 Mèze
Tel 04 67 43 88 69

AUSTRALIA

Unlimited Perennials
369 Boomerang Drive
Lavington, NSW 2641
Tel 02 6025 458

BRITISH ISLES

British National Collections
Dyffryn Botanical Gardens
St Nicholas
Cardiff, CF5 6SU
Tel (01222) 593328

Kingston Maurward Gardens
Kingston Maurward
Dorchester
Dorset, DT28PY
Tel (01305) 264738

Pleasant View Nursery
Two Mile Oak
Near Denbury
Newton Abbot
Devon, TQ12 6DG
Tel (01803) 813388

Where to Buy Salvias

The following list contains suggestions for sources of salvias. An asterisk (*) denotes a source for seed rather than plants. A dagger (†) denotes a mail-order nursery.

UNITED STATES

Alplains*
P.O. Box 489
Kiowa, Colorado 80117
Tel 303-621-2590

California Flora Nursery
Somers & D Street
P.O. Box 3
Fulton, California 95439
Tel 707-528-8813

Berkeley Horticultural Nursery
1310 McGee Avenue
Berkeley, California 94703
Tel 510-526-4704

Canyon Creek Nursery†
3527 Dry Creek Road
Orville, California 95965
Tel 530-533-2166

Heronswood Nursery†
7530 NE 288th Street
Kingston, Washington 98346
Tel 360-297-4172

J. L. Hudson, Seedsman*
Rt. 2 Box 337
La Honda, California 94020

Joy Creek Nursery†
20300 NW Watson Road
Scappoose, Oregon 97056
Tel 503-543-7474

Logee's Greenhouses†
55 North Street
Danielson, Connecticut 06239
Tel 860-774-8038

The Sandy Mush Herb Nursery†
316 Surrett Cove Road
Leicester, North Carolina 28748
Tel 826-683-2014

Seedhunt*
P.O. Box 96
Freedom, California 95019

Sierra Azul Nursery and Garden
2660 East Lake Avenue
Watsonville, California 95076
Tel 831-763-0939

Southwestern Native Seeds*
Box 50503
Tucson, Arizona 85703

Western Hills Nursery
16250 Coleman Valley Road
Occidental, California 95465
Tel 707-874-3731

Yucca Do Nursery†
P.O. Box 907
Hempstead, Texas 77445
Tel 979-826-4580

AUSTRALIA

The Digger's Club
Heronswood
105 La Trobe Parade
Dromana, Victoria 3936
Tel 03 5987 1877

Unlimited Perennials
369 Boomerang Drive
Lavington, NSW 2641
Tel 02 6025 4585

BRITISH ISLES

Jim and Jenny Archibald*
'Bryn Collen'
Ffostrasol
Llandysul
Dyfed, SA44 5SB
Wales

Brian Hiley
25 Little Woodcote Estate
Wallington
Surrey, SM5 4AU
Tel (0181) 647 9679

The Beth Chatto Gardens
Elmstead Market
Colchester
Essex, CO7 7DB
Tel (01206) 822007

Chiltern Seeds*
Bortree Stile
Ulverston
Cumbria, LA12 7PB

Four Seasons
Forncett St Mary
Norwich, NR16 1JT
Tel (01508) 488344

Green Farm Plants
Bentley
Farnham
Surrey, GU10 5JX
Tel (01420) 23202

Hollington Nurseries
Woolton Hill
Newbury
Berkshire, RG15 9XT
Tel (01635) 253908

Hopleys Plants
High Street
Much Hadham
Hertfordshire, SG10 6BU
Tel (01279) 842509

Pleasant View Nursery
Two Mile Oak
Near Denbury
Newton Abbott
Devon, TQ12 6DG
Tel (01803) 813388

FRANCE

Alain Daubas
Avenue du Bérange
34160 Saint Drezery
Tel 67 86 92 36

Pépinière Filippi
R.N. 113
34140 Mèze
Tel 67 43 88 69

SOUTH AFRICA

Silverhill Seeds
P.O. Box 53108
Kenilworth 7745
Cape Town
Tel 021 762 4245

Further information on plant sources may be found in the current editions of
the following books:

BRITISH ISLES
The Plant Finder. London:
Royal Horticultural Society.

EUROPE
PPP Index: European Plantfinder, by
Anne Erhardt and Walter Erhardt.
Ashbourne, Derbyshire: Moorland

NORTH AMERICA
*The Andersen Horticultural Library's
Source List of Plants and Seeds.*
Chanhassen: Minnesota Landscape
Arboretum.

Flowering Guide by Season

Species marked * repeat bloom in autumn

SPRING FLOWERING SALVIAS

africana-lutea*
algeriensis
apiana
brandegei
caespitosa
candidissima
carduacea
chionophylla*
columbariae
dentata

disermas*
dominica
eigii
frigida
fruticosa
hierosolymitana
indica
jurisicii
leucophylla
lycioides*

mellifera
merjamie
palaestina
pratensis
recognita
serpyllifolia*
sonomensis
spathacea
staminea
tingitana

SUMMER FLOWERING SALVIAS

aethiopis
africana-caerulea
albimaculata
argentea
arizonica*
austriaca*
barrelieri
blepharophylla*

broussonetii
buchananii
cacaliifolia*
canariensis
canescens
    var. daghestanica*
castanea
cedrosensis

chamaedryoides*
chamelaeagnea*
chiapensis*
clevelandii
coahuilensis*
coccinea*
corrugata
coulteri*

cyanescens*
darcyi*
desoleana
digitaloides
discolor*
dolomitica
farinacea*
flava
forsskaolii*
gilliesii*
glechomifolia*
glutinosa
greggii*
guaranitica*
hians
hirtella*
'Indigo Spires'*
interrupta*
×jamensis*
koyamae*
lanceolata
lanigera
lavandulifolia

leucantha*
longispicata*
melissodora*
mexicana*
microphylla*
miltiorrhiza
moorcroftiana
muirii
namaensis
napifolia
nemorosa
nilotica
nubicola
officinalis
oppositiflora
patens
prunelloides
przewalskii
'Purple Majesty'
repens
reptans*
ringens

roborowskii
roemeriana*
rubescens*
rypara
sagittata*
scabra
sclarea
scutellarioides
semiatrata*
serpyllifolia*
sessei*
sinaloensis*
somalensis*
stenophylla
taraxacifolia
transsylvanica
uliginosa*
urica*
verticillata
viridis*
viscosa
'Waverly'*

AUTUMN FLOWERING SALVIAS

africana-lutea
arizonica
austriaca
axillaris
azurea var. grandiflora
blepharophylla
cacaliifolia
canescens var.
  daghestanica
chamaedryoides
chamelaeagnea
chiapensis
chionophylla

coahuilensis
coccinea
confertiflora
coulteri
cyanescens
darcyi
discolor
disermas
disjuncta
dombeyi
elegans
farinacea
forsskaolii

'Frieda Dixon'
fulgens
glechomifolia
greggii
guaranitica
hirtella
'Indigo Spires'
interrupta
involucrata
×jamensis
koyamae
leucantha
littae

longispicata
lycioides
madrensis
melissodora
mexicana
microphylla
miniata
polystachya
puberula
'Purple Majesty'
recurva

regla
reptans
roemeriana
rubescens
rypara
sagittata
semiatrata
serpyllifolia
sessei
shannoni

sinaloensis
somalensis
splendens
  'Van Houttei'
thymoides
tubiflora
uliginosa
villosa
viridis
wagneriana
'Waverly'

WINTER FLOWERING SALVIAS

africana-lutea
disjuncta
dombeyi
dorisiana

gesneriiflora
holwayi
iodantha
karwinskii
littae

purpurea
sprucei
thymoides
wagneriana

Cold Tolerance Guide

The following species are cold tolerant to 10°F (-12°C) or below:

aethiopis
albimaculata
argentea
arizonica
austriaca
azurea var. *grandiflora*
caespitosa
candidissima
canescens
   var. *daghestanica*

castanea
cyanescens
digitaloides
eigii
flava
forsskaolii
frigida
glutinosa
hians
jurisicii
moorcroftiana

nemorosa
nubicola
officinalis
pratensis
recognita
ringens
sclarea
staminea
transsylvanica
verticillata

Shade Tolerance Guide

The following species are shade tolerant:

arizonica	*dorisiana*	*prunelloides*
blepharophylla	'Frieda Dixon'	*recurva*
broussonetii	*glutinosa*	*roemeriana*
buchananii	*hirtella*	*rypara*
cacaliifolia	*holwayi*	*sagittata*
castanea	*involucrata*	*scutellarioides*
chamelaeagnea	*koyamae*	*shannoni*
chiapensis	*littae*	*sinaloensis*
corrugata	*miltiorrhiza*	*splendens*
digitaloides	*miniata*	'Van Houttei'
discolor	*polystachya*	*sprucei*
divinorum		*wagneriana*

Salvias for a Hot and Humid Climate

The following species are well suited for a hot and humid climate:

azurea var. *grandiflora*
blepharophylla
buchananii
chamaedryoides
chiapensis
coccinea
confertiflora
darcyi
elegans
farinacea
greggii
guaranitica

'Indigo Spires'
involucrata
iodantha
koyamae
leucantha
littae
madrensis
melissodora
mexicana
microphylla
miniata

patens
puberula
'Purple Majesty'
regla
reptans
splendens
 'Van Houttei'
urica
uliginosa
villosa
viridis
'Waverly'

Water-wise Salvias

The following salvias do well receiving little water throughout the summer:

africana-lutea
apiana
brandegei
canariensis
carduacea
cedrosensis
chamaedryoides
clevelandii
coahuilensis
coulteri
desoleana
disermas

dolomitica
dominica
fruticosa
greggii
×jamensis
lanceolata
lanigera
lavandulifolia
leucantha
leucophylla
lycioides

mellifera
muirii
nilotica
officinalis
palaestina
recognita
repens
sclarea
sonomensis
taraxacifolia
thymoides
villosa

Salvias with Especially Handsome Foliage

The following species have especially handsome foliage:

aethiopis

algeriensis

apiana

argentea

broussonetii

buchananii

cacaliifolia

canescens
 var. *daghestanica*

chiapensis

chionophylla

corrugata

desoleana

discolor

disermas

frigida

fruticosa

indica

interrupta

lanigera

madrensis

namaensis

officinalis
 and all its cultivars

ringens

sagittata

semiatrata

sinaloensis

somalensis

spathacea

thymoides

tingitana

Salvias for Containers

The following salvias are well suited to container growing:

albimaculata
algeriensis
argentea
blepharophylla
buchananii
canescens
  var. *daghestanica*
cedrosensis
chiapensis
chionophylla
dentata
discolor
divinorum
dorisiana
elegans
farinacea cultivars
frigida

fruticosa
greggii
indica
×*jamensis*
jurisicii
lanigera
leucantha
lycioides
microphylla
  'Graham's Sage'
muirii
namaensis
officinalis
  and all its cultivars
oppositiflora
patens

reptans
roemeriana
sagittata
scabra
scutellarioides
semiatrata
shannoni
sinaloensis
splendens
  'Van Houttei'
taraxacifolia
thymoides
tingitana
verticillata
  'Purple Rain'
villosa
viridis

Color Designations of Unusual Flower or Foliage Color

The following is a list of salvias with unusual flower or foliage color. The exact or nearest possible color of flower or foliage is given using the Royal Horticulture Society Colour Chart, which is available from the R.H.S. Garden at Wisley in the United Kingdom.

africana-lutea, emerging corolla Yellow-Green Group 151B, calyx Yellow-Green Group 152A. Mature corolla Greyed-Orange Group 164A, calyx Greyed-Orange Group 176A.

albimaculata, corolla Violet Group 88A, spotted with white.

apiana, leaf surface Greyed-Green Group 190A.

argentea, leaf surface Greyed-Green Group 191A.

arizonica, corolla Violet-Blue Group 93B.

austriaca, corolla Yellow Group 10D.

azurea var. *grandiflora,* corolla Violet-Blue Group 94A.

blepharophylla, corolla Red Group 43A.

brandegei, corolla Purple Group 76B, calyx Violet Group 83B, leaf surface Green Group 137B, underside Greyed-Green Group 191C.

buchananii, corolla Red-Purple Group 74A.

cacaliifolia, corolla Violet-Blue Group 94A.

canariensis, corolla Purple-Violet Group 80B, calyx Red-Purple Group 71B.

carduacea, corolla Purple Group 75A.

cedrosensis, corolla Violet-Blue Group 93B, leaf surface Greyed-Green Group 194A.

chamaedryoides, corolla Violet-Blue Group 94A, leaf surface Greyed-Green Group 194A.

chamaedryoides 'Desert Green', corolla Violet-Blue Group 94A, leaf surface Greyed-Green Group 191A.

chamelaeagnea, corolla Violet-Blue Group 92A.

chiapensis, corolla Red-Purple Group 74A.

clevelandii 'Allen Chickering', corolla Violet-Green Group 88C.

clevelandii 'Santa Cruz Dark', corolla Violet Group 86B.

clevelandii 'Winnifred Gilman', corolla Violet Group 88B, stem Red-Purple Group 59A.

coahuilensis, corolla Purple Group 78A.

columbariae, corolla Violet-Blue Group 89B.

confertiflora, corolla Orange-Red Group, calyx Greyed-Red Group 178A.

coulteri, corolla Violet-Blue Group 93B.

cyanescens, corolla Purple-Violet Group 82C.

'Dara's Choice', corolla Violet Group 88B.

darcyi, corolla Red Group 45C.

discolor, corolla Violet-Blue Group 89A, calyx Green Group 139D, leaf surface Green Group 139B, underside Greyed-Green 192B.

disjuncta, corolla Red Group 42A.

dolomitica, corolla Purple Group 76A with cream center.

dominica, corolla White Group 155C.

dorisiana, corolla Red-Purple Group 71B, calyx Yellow-Green Group 144B, leaf surface Yellow-Green Group 144A.

eigii, upper lip of corolla Red-Purple Group 74C, lower lip Red-Purple Group 62D, calyx Red-Purple Group 59A.

elegans, corolla Red Group 42A.

elegans 'Honey Melon', corolla Red Group 45B.

elegans 'Pineapple Sage', corolla Red Group 45A.

flava, corolla Yellow Group 13B with a blotch of Violet Group 83A on the lower lip.

forsskaolii, corolla Violet Group 87A.

'Frieda Dixon', corolla Red Group 50B.

fruticosa, corolla Purple Group 75A, calyx Greyed-Purple Group 183B, underside of leaf Greyed-Green Group 138B.

fulgens, corolla Red Group 45B, calyx Greyed-Red Group 178B.

gesneriiflora, corolla Red Group 44B, calyx Yellow-Green Group 146A.

gesneriiflora 'Tequila', corolla Red Group 44B, calyx Greyed-Purple Group 187A.

glechomifolia, corolla Violet-Blue Group 94B, calyx Violet-Blue Group 95C.

glutinosa, lips of corollas Yellow Group 9C, upper lip flecked with dots of Red-Purple Group 59B.

greggii 'Purple Haze', sparkling color of corolla is not found on Chart. The nearest is Purple-Violet Group 81A.

greggii 'Purple Pastel', corolla Purple-Violet Group 82B, calyx Violet Group 83A with green.

guaranitica, corolla Violet-Blue Group 89C.

guaranitica 'Costa Rica Blue', corolla Violet-Blue Group 93B, calyx base Yellow-Green Group 145A with purple tips.

hians, corolla Violet Group 87A.

hirtella, corolla Red Group 44B, calyx Greyed-Purple Group 183A.

holwayi, corolla Red Group 53B.

'Indigo Spires', corolla Violet-Blue Group 89B, calyx Purple Group 79B.

interrupta, corolla Violet Group 87A with 83B in center.

involucrata, corolla, calyx, and bracts Red-Purple Group 71B.

involucrata 'El Cielo', corolla Red-Purple Group 61A, calyx Greyed-Purple Group 183A.

iodantha, corolla Red-Purple Group 74A.

×*jamensis* 'Cienega de Oro', corolla Yellow Group 10C.

×*jamensis* 'Sierra San Antonio', corolla Yellow-Orange Group 16C.

jurisicii, corolla Violet Group 83D. White-flowered form Yellow-White Group 158D.

karwinskii, corolla Red Group 51A, calyx Greyed-Purple Group 183A.

koyamae, corolla Yellow Group 12C.

lavandulifolia subsp. *blancoana*, corolla Violet Group 87A, leaf surface Yellow-Green Group 147B.

leucantha, corolla White Group 155D, calyx Purple-Violet Group 81A.

leucantha 'Midnight', corolla Purple-Violet Group 80A, calyx Purple Group 77A.

leucophylla, corolla Purple Group 78C, leaf surface Greyed-Green 189A.

littae, corolla Red-Purple Group 61A.

longispicata, corolla Violet Group 33A.

lycioides 'Guadalupe Mountain', corolla Violet-Blue 89B, leaf surface Green Group 138B.

madrensis, corolla Yellow-Orange Group 16B, calyx Yellow-Orange Group 14C.

melissodora, corolla Violet-Blue Group 89C, lower lip Violet Group 84C.

mellifera 'Terra Seca', corolla White Group 155D with purple stamens.

mexicana 'Limelight', corolla Violet-Blue Group 89B, calyx Yellow-Green Group 144B.

mexicana 'Lollie Jackson', corolla Violet-Blue Group 89B, calyx green splashed with violet-blue.

microphylla, corolla Red-Purple Group 57C.

microphylla 'Graham's Sage', corolla Red Group 52A.

microphylla 'Forever Red' corolla Red Group 43A.

microphylla 'Rosita', corolla Red-Purple Group 57C.

microphylla 'San Carlos Festival', corolla Red Purple Group 61B.

microphylla var. *wislizeni*, corolla Red-Purple Group 67A.

miniata, corolla Red Group 43A.

'Mrs. Beard', corolla Violet Group 85B.

nubicola, corolla Yellow Group 10A with markings of Greyed-Purple Group 184B.

patens, upper lip of corolla Violet-Blue Group 96B, lower lip Violet-Blue Group 95B.

penstemonoides, corolla Red-Purple Group 72A.

polystachya, corolla Violet-Blue Group 89C, graduating to white at lip edge.

pratensis, corolla Violet Group 88A, calyx Brown Group 200A.

przewalskii, corolla Violet Group 88B, calyx Purple Group 79A.

puberula, corolla Red-Purple Group 67A, calyx Red-Purple Group 70A, bracts Red-Purple Group 67B.

'Purple Majesty', corolla Violet Group 83A, calyx Purple Group 79A.

purpurea, corolla Purple-Violet Group 80B.

recognita, upper lip of corolla Red-Purple Group 73C, lower lip Red-Purple Group 72D.

regla, corolla Red Group 44B, upper side of calyx Greyed-Orange Group 171A, lower side Greyed-Yellow Group 160A.

reptans, corolla Violet-Blue Group 96B, stems facing sun Brown Group 200B.

roborowskii, corolla Yellow Group 4C.

roemeriana, corolla Red Group 45B.

sclarea, corollas vary in color from Violet Group 85A to Violet Group 87C. Bracts Red-Purple Group 69A fading to White Group 155B.

sclarea 'Turkestanica', bracts White Group 155B edged pink, petioles Red-Purple Group 74C.

semiatrata, upper lip of corolla Violet Group 84A, lower lip Violet Group 83B, calyx Purple Group 79C.

sinaloensis, corolla Violet-Blue Group 95A. Mature leaf Greyed-Green Group 189A. New leaf Purple Group 79.

somalensis, corolla Violet-Blue Group 92A.

spathacea 'Kawatre', corolla Red-Purple Group 71A, calyx Red-Purple Group 59A.

splendens 'Van Houttei', lower lip of corolla Red Group 45A, upper lip, tube, and calyx Red-Purple Group 59B.

taraxacifolia, corolla Purple Group 75C, leaf Greyed-Green Group 189A.

thymoides, corolla Violet-Blue Group 89C, leaf Greyed-Green 191B.

transsylvanica, corolla Violet Group 88A.

uliginosa, corolla Violet-Blue Group 96B.

verticillata, corolla Purple-Violet Group 82C, calyx Yellow-Green Group 145A, green tinged with purple.

verticillata 'Purple Rain', corolla Violet-Blue Group 89C, calyx Violet Group 86B.

villosa, corolla Violet-Blue Group 95A.

wagneriana, corolla and bracts Red-Purple Group 59C, calyx Red-Purple Group 57A. Pinkish form, corolla Red-Purple Group 62A, calyx Red-Purple Group 63C, bracts Orange-White Group 159.

Geographical Origin of *Salvia* Species

This list is included to show the reader quickly the geographical origins of a number of salvias now in cultivation. The list is not exhaustive and more detail of specific locations can be found in individual species entries.

AFRICA

africana-caerulea
africana-lutea
algeriensis
chamelaeagnea
dentata
disermas

dolomitica
interrupta
lanceolata
merjamie
muirii
namaensis

nilotica
repens
scabra
somalensis
stenophylla
taraxacifolia

ASIA

aethiopis
albimaculata
austriaca
caespitosa
candidissima
castanea
cyanescens
digitaloides
eigii
flava

forsskaolii
frigida
glutinosa
hians
indica
koyamae
miltiorrhiza
moorcroftiana
nemorosa

nubicola
palaestina
pratensis
przewalskii
recognita
roborowskii
sclarea
staminea
sylvestris
verticillata

CALIFORNIA

apiana	*clevelandii*	*mellifera*
brandegei	*columbariae*	*sonomensis*
carduacea	*leucophylla*	*spathacea*

EUROPE

aethiopis	*glutinosa*	*ringens*
austriaca	*jurisicii*	*sclarea*
canescens	*nemorosa*	*transsylvanica*
var. *daghestanica*	*pratensis*	*verticillata*

MEDITERRANEAN

aethiopis	*dominica*	*officinalis*
argentea	*fruticosa*	*tingitana*
broussonetii	*hierosolymitana*	*verticillata*
canariensis	*lanigera*	*viridis*
desoleana	*lavandulifolia*	*viscosa*
	napifolia	

MEXICO

apiana	*darcyi*	*leucantha*
arizonica	*disjuncta*	*littae*
axillaris	*divinorum*	*longispicata*
blepharophylla	*elegans*	*lycioides*
brandegei	*farinacea*	*madrensis*
cacaliifolia	*fulgens*	*melissodora*
cedrosensis	*gesneriiflora*	*mellifera*
chamaedryoides	*glechomifolia*	*mexicana*
chiapensis	*greggii*	*microphylla*
chionophylla	*holwayi*	*miniata*
clevelandii	*involucrata*	*patens*
coahuilensis	*iodantha*	*polystachya*
columbariae	×*jamensis*	*prunelloides*
coulteri	*karwinskii*	*puberula*

purpurea
recurva
regla
reptans
roemeriana

semiatrata
serpyllifolia
sessei
shannoni
sinaloensis

thymoides
urica
villosa
wagneriana

SOUTH AND CENTRAL AMERICA

cacaliifolia
chiapensis
coccinea
confertiflora
corrugata
discolor
disjuncta
dombeyi
dorisiana

gilliesii
guaranitica
hirtella
holwayi
karwinskii
miniata
oppositiflora
patens
polystachya
purpurea

rubescens
rypara
sagittata
scutellarioides
splendens
sprucei
tubiflora
uliginosa
wagneriana

UNITED STATES (excluding California)

arizonica
azurea var. grandiflora
columbariae

farinacea
greggii
lycioides
microphylla

regla
reptans
roemeriana

Bibliography

Alziar, Gabriel. 1988. Catalogue synonymique des *Salvia* du monde. *Biocosme Mesogéen, Revue d'Histoire Naturelle* 5 (3–4).

Barbour, M., B. Pavlik, F. Drysdale, and S. Lindstrom. 1993. *California's Changing Landscapes*. Sacramento: California Native Plant Society.

Bawden, Harold, and Joan Bawden. 1970. *Woodland Plants and Sun Lovers*. London: Faber & Faber.

Chatto, Beth. 1978. *The Dry Garden*. Portland, Oregon: Sagapress.

———. 1982. *The Damp Garden*. Portland, Oregon: Sagapress.

———. 1988. *Beth Chatto's Notebook*. Portland, Oregon: Sagapress.

Compton, James, ed. 2000. *Salvia*. In *The European Garden Flora*, vol. 6. Cambridge: Cambridge University Press.

———. 1992. *Salvia*. In *The New Royal Horticultural Society's Dictionary of Gardening*. New York: Stockton Press.

———. Feb. 1994a. Mexican salvias in cultivation. *The Plantsman* 15 (4): (180–192).

———. May 1994b. *Salvia darcyi*. *Kew Magazine* 2 (2): (52–55).

Epling, C. 1938. The California salvias; a review of *Salvia* section *Audibertia*. *Annals of the Missouri Botanical Garden* 25: 95–152.

———. 1939. A revision of *Salvia*, subgenus *Calosphace*. *Repertorium Specierum Novarum Regni Vegetabilis, Beihefte*, vol. 110.

Grieve, M., and C. F. Leyel 1931. *A Modern Herbal*. New York: Dover.

Hareuveni, Nogah. 1980. *Nature in Our Biblical Heritage*. Kiryat Ono, Israel: Neot Kedumin.

Harper, Pamela J. 1991. *Designing with Perennials*. New York: Macmillan Publishing.

Hedge, Ian C. 1974. A revision of *Salvia* in Africa, including Madagascar and the Canary Islands. *Notes from the Royal Botanic Garden Edinburgh* 33:1.

———. 1982a. *Flora of Turkey*, vol. 7. Edinburgh: Edinburgh University Press.

———. 1982b. *Flora Iranica*. Ed. K. H. Rechinger. Graz, Austria: Akademische Druck.

Hobhouse, Penelope. 1985. *Color in Your Garden*. Boston: Little, Brown.

Illingworth, John, and Jane Routh, eds. 1991. *Reginald Farrer*. Occasional paper no. 19. Lancaster: Lancaster University.

Jekyll, Gertrude. 1908. *Colour in The Flower Garden*. London: Country Life.

Jelitto, L., and W. Schacht. 1990. *Hardy Herbaceous Perennials*. Rev. ed. Portland, Oregon: Timber Press.

Lawrence, Elizabeth. 1942. *A Southern Garden*. Chapel Hill: University of North Carolina Press.

———. 1990. *Through The Garden Gate*. Ed. Bill Neal. Chapel Hill: University of North Carolina Press.

Li, Hsi-wen, and Ian C. Hedge. 1994. Lamiaceae. In *Flora of China*, Wu Zheng-yi and Peter Raven. St. Louis: Missouri Botanical Garden.

Lovejoy, Ann. 1993. *The American Mixed Border*. New York: Macmillan Publishing.

Lloyd, Christopher. 1973. *Foliage Plants*. London: Collins.

Mattern, A., and M. Moskowitz. 1994. The life and works of Ernst Pagels. *Journal of the Hardy Plant Society* 16 (1).

Mitchell, Sydney. 1932. *From a Sunset Garden*. New York: Doubleday, Doran.

Nottle, Trevor. 1984. *Growing Perennials*. Kenthurst, New South Wales: Kangaroo Press.

O'Brien, Bart. 1997. Horticulture and classification of the section *Audibertia* of the genus *Salvia*. Occasional publication no. 2. Claremont, California: Rancho Santa Ana Botanic Garden.

Parsons, Mary Elizabeth. 1921. *The Wild Flowers of California*. Rev. ed. San Francisco: H. S. Crocker.

Quest-Ritson, Charles. 1992. *The English Garden Abroad*. London: Viking.

Ridgeway, James. 1822. *Botanical Register*. Vol. 8. London.

Robinson, William. 1933. *The English Flower Garden*. Rev. ed. Sagaponack, New York: Sagapress.

Roemer, Ferdinand. 1935. *Roemer's Texas*. Trans. Oswald Mueller. San Antonio, Texas: Standard Printing Company.

Rohde, Eleanour Sinclair. 1936. *Herbs and Herb Gardening*. London: The Medici Society.

Schmidt, Marjorie. 1980. *Growing California Native Plants*. Berkeley: University of California Press.

Schmidt, Marjorie, Stephen P. Edwards, Ron Lutsko Jr., Wayne Roderick, and Nevin Smith. 1990. *Native Plants for Your Garden*. Sacramento: California Native Plant Society.

Smith, Nevin. 1991. Growing natives: The shrubby salvias. *Fremontia* 19 (1): 25–28.

———. 1991. Growing natives: The other salvias. *Fremontia* 19 (2): 23–25.

Starr, Greg. 1985. New world salvias for cultivation in southern Arizona. *Desert Plants* 7 (4): 167–207.

Steele, Arthur Robert. 1964. *Flowers for the King, The Expedition of Ruiz and Pavón and the Flora of Peru*. Durham, North Carolina: Duke University Press.

Sutton, John. 1999. *The Gardener's Guide to Growing Salvias*. Portland, Oregon: Timber Press.

Thomas, Graham Stuart. 1990a. *Perennial Garden Plants*. Rev. ed. Portland, Oregon: Sagapress/Timber Press.

———. 1990b. *Plants for Ground-Cover*. Rev. ed. Portland, Oregon: Sagapress/Timber Press.

Yeo, Christine. 1995. *Salvias*. Pleasant View Nursery, Devon.

———. 1997. *Salvias II*. Pleasant View Nursery, Devon.

Index of Plant Names

Page numbers in italic indicate illustrations.

Abutilon, 306
Abutilon 'Nabob', 306
Abutilon 'Pink Parasol', 306
Abutilon ×*suntense*, 306
Acacia boormanii, 168
Achillea ageratifolia, 155, 169, 301
Achillea ageratum 'W. G. Childs', 155
Achillea clavenae, 162, 169
Achillea 'Fire King', 45
Achillea 'Hoffnung', 45
Achillea 'King Edward', 40, 215
Achillea 'Moonshine', 45
Achillea 'Paprika', 45
Achillea 'Taygetea', 144
Achillea tomentosa, 170
Achillea umbellata, 301
Aconitum carmichaelii, 271
Aesculus parryi, 48
Agapanthus inapertus, 206
Agastache, 215
Agastache 'Apricot Sunrise', 94
Agastache barberi, 215
Ageratum houstonianum 'Blue Bouquet', 260

Agrimonia, 213
Agrostemma githago, 45
Ajuga reptans 'Jungle Beauty', 106, 280
Allium oreophilum, 125
Aloysia triphylla, 185
Amarylis belladonna, 60
Anigozanthos flavidus, 292
Anthemis cretica, 134
Anthoxanthum odoratum, 228
Arbutus unedo, 244
Arbutus unedo 'Compacta', 53
Arctostaphylos 'John Dourley', 282
Arctostaphylos pajaroensis, 30
Arctostaphylos stanfordiana subsp. *bakeri* 'Louis Edmunds', 30, 159
Arctostaphylos 'Winterglow', 30
Arenaria montana, 287
Artemisia absinthium 'Lambrook Silver', 152
Artemisia arborescens, 127, 304
Artemisia californica, 35, 48
Artemisia caucasica, 34, 56
Artemisia 'Powis Castle', 211
Artemisia pycnocephala, 301, 304

Artemisia pycnocephala 'David's Choice', 204, 211

Artemisia schmidtiana 'Nana', 162

Artemisia schmidtiana 'Silver Mound', 72

Asarum magnificum, 41

Aster cordifolius, 254

Aster divaricatus, 298

Aster ×*frikartii*, 40

Aster ×*frikartii* 'Monch', 40, 140, 308

Aster ×*frikartii* 'Wonder of Staffa', 40

Aster lateriflorus, 140

Aster lateriflorus 'Lady in Black', 308

Aster novae-angliae, 235

Aster novi-belgii, 235

Aster petiolatus 'Photograph', 298

Aster pringli 'Ochtendgloren', 298

Aster ×*versicolor*, 129

Ballota acetabulosa, 91, 301

Ballota pseudodictamnus, 168

Ballota undulata, 111

Berberis calliantha, 290

Berberis darwinii, 249

Berberis hookeri, 133, 249

Berberis julianae, 294

Berberis sherriffii, 294

Berberis stenophylla 'Irwinii', 208

Berberis thunbergii 'Red Chief', 240

Beschorneria yuccoides, 66

Boltonia asteroides 'Snowbank', 235

Brachyglottis 'Sunshine', 144, *303*

Bracteantha bracteata 'Dargan Hill Monarch', 244

Briza media, 94

Buddleja alternifolia 'Argentea', 300

Buddleja davidii 'Nanho Purple', 215, 300

Bulbinella robusta, 28

Calamagrostis ×*acutiflora* 'Stricta', 254

Calylophus hartwegii, 82

Campanula rotundifolia, 76

Carex buchananii, 161

Ceanothus, 187

Ceanothus 'Dark Star', 187

Ceanothus gloriosus var. *porrectus*, 91, 187

Ceanothus maritimus 'Roger's Dark', 159

Centaurea cyanus, 284

Centranthus ruber, 35, 217

Ceratostigma griffithii, 105

Ceratostigma willmottianum, 255

Cercidium microphyllum, 68

Cercis canadensis 'Forest Pansy', 140

Cercis occidentalis, 176

Chaenomeles, 150

Chaenomeles 'Enchantress', 151

Chaenomeles 'Nivalis', 151

Chasmanthium latifolium, 199

Chimonanthus praecox, 164

Chrysanthemum paludosum, 247

Cistus ladanifer, 98

Cistus libanotis, 146

Cistus palhinhae, 30

Cistus 'Peggy Sammons', 204

Cistus salviifolius 'Prostratus', 222

Cistus ×*skanbergii*, 204, 221

Citronella, 66

Consolida ajacis, 284

Consolida ambigua, 45

Convolvulus mauritanicus, 262

Coreopsis bigelovii, 64

Coreopsis 'Early Sunrise', 142–143

Coreopsis verticillata, 255

Cotoneaster horizontalis, 224

Cotoneaster horizontalis 'Variegatus', 250

Cynara cardunculus, 168

Cyrtomium falcatum, 224

Datura meteloides. See *D. wrightii*

Datura wrightii, 232

Daucus carota, 141

Dianthus 'Danielle Pink', 185
Dianthus deltoides, 32
Dianthus 'Devon Dove', 204
Dianthus gratianopolitanus, 32
Dianthus 'Jealousy', 185
Diascia barberae, 32
Diascia 'Ruby Field', 206
Dudleya caespitosa, 189

Echeveria, 268
Echeveria elegans, 134
Echinops bannaticus 'Blue Globe', 257
Echinops ritro, 120
Elymus magellanicus, 189
Encelia californica, 48, 68
Epilobium canum subsp. canum, 40
Epimedium ×rubrum, 123
Erigeron glaucus, 134
Erigeron karvinskianus, 213
Erodium corsicum 'Album', 34, 98
Erodium corsicum 'Rubrum', 34, 98
Eriogonum arborescens, 92
Eriogonum fasciculatum, 37
Eriogonum giganteum, 30
Eriogonum grande var. rubescens, 202
Eriogonum latifolium, 37, 301
Eriogonum umbellatum 'Shasta Sulfur', 57
Erysimum 'Jubilee Gold', 28
Erysimum pulchellum, 104
Eschscholzia californica, 93, 146
Euphorbia characias 'Portuguese Velvet', 68, 284
Euphorbia characias subsp. wulfenii, 217, 284
Euphorbia 'Cherokee', 284
Euphorbia ×martinii, 80, 284
Euphorbia myrsinites, 127
Euphorbia rigida, 127
Euphorbia seguieriana subsp. niciciana, 100

Festuca amethystina 'Aprilgrün', 94
Festuca amethysina 'Superba', 287
Festuca cinerea 'Blausilber', 82
Folia salviae, 126
Francoa ramosa, 271
Frankenia thymifolia, 301
Fremontodendron californicum subsp. crassifolium, 187

Gaura lindheimeri, 152, 174
Genista cinerea, 170
Geranium dalmaticum, 75, 142
Geranium incanum, 213
Geranium macrorrhizum 'Album', 122
Geranium 'Patricia', 290
Geranium 'Russell Prichard', 297
Geranium sanguineum, 218
Geranium sanguineum 'Minutum', 162
Gesneria, 129
Glechoma, 133
Glechoma hederacea 'Variegata', 135

Hedera helix 'Helena', 113
Helenium autumnale, 255
Helenium 'Moerheim Beauty', 255
Helianthus ×laetiflorus 'Morning Sun', 122
Helichrysum bracteatum, 244
Helichrysum italicum, 301
Helichrysum petiolare, 144
Helichrysum splendidum, 52, 53
Helictotrichon sempervirens, 202
Helleborus argutifolius, 230
Heuchera 'Chocolate Ruffles', 271
Heuchera 'Genevieve', 280
Heuchera micrantha, 280
Heuchera 'Pewter Veil', 271
Heuchera 'Plum Pudding', 271
Heuchera 'Purple Petticoats', 271
Hibiscus syriacus 'Diana', 205
Hydrangea quercifolia, 252

Hydrangea quercifolia 'Snow Queen', 41
Hyptis emoryi, 68

Iberis sempervirens 'Purity', 164
Ilex, 117

Juniperus conferta, 182

Kerria, 151
Kerria japonica, 151
Koeleria cristata, 228

Lathyrus latifolius, 45
Lathyrus latifolius 'Pink Pearl', 45
Lathyrus latifolius 'White Pearl', 45
Lavandula angustifolia 'Blue Cushion', 63
Lavandula angustifolia 'Compacta', 63
Lavandula angustifolia 'Hidcote', 266
Lavandula angustifolia 'Loddon Blue', 82
Lavandula angustifolia 'Melissa', 63
Lavandula angustifolia 'Nana', 63
Lavandula 'Goodwin Creek Grey', 60
Lavandula lanata, 170
Lavatera maritima, 273
Lavatera thuringiaca 'Barnsley', 204
Leonotis leonurus, 255
Lespedeza thunbergii 'Alba', 257
Leucanthemum vulgare, 228
Limonium latifolium, 202
Linum narbonense, 174
Linum perenne, 284
Lobelia 'Crystal Palace', 143
Lonicera nitida 'Baggesen's Gold', 54
Lychnis flos-jovis, 115
Lycium, 182

Magnolia dawsoniana, 192
Marrubium rotundifolium, 290
Miscanthus sinensis, 131
Miscanthus sinensis 'Condensatus', 157

Miscanthus sinensis 'Morning Light', 166
Myrica californica, 276

Nandina domestica 'Fire Power', 269
Narcissus jonquilla, 165
Nemophila maculata, 278
Nemophila menziesii, 278
Nepeta 'Blue Wonder', 104
Nepeta ×*faassenii*, 112, 240
Nicotiana alata Sensation hybrids, 274
Nicotiana langsdorffii, 133

Oenothera speciosa, 52
Origanum dictamnus, 201, 213
Origanum 'Kent Beauty', 96
Origanum laevigatum 'Hopleys', 299
Origanum rotundifolium, 92
Origanum 'Santa Cruz', 299
Origanum vulgare 'Aureum', 218
Osmanthus, 117
Osmanthus fragrans, 88, 294
Osmanthus fragrans 'San Jose', 88
Osmanthus heterophyllus, 234, 237
Osmanthus heterophyllus 'Goshiki', 230
Osteospermum hybrida 'Passion Mixed',
    285

Panicum virgatum, 88, 123
Pelargonium crispum, 206
Pelargonium peltatum, 118
Penstemon 'Apple Blossom', 53
Penstemon barbatus, 35
Penstemon 'Garden Star', 257
Penstemon 'Garnet', 179
Penstemon heterophyllus, 35
Penstemon heterophyllus 'Blue Bedder',
    96
Penstemon 'Hidcote Pink', 53
Penstemon 'Huntington Pink', 209
Penstemon 'Midnight', 53, 179

Penstemon 'Sour Grapes', 179, 257
Penstemon spectabilis, 35
Perilla frutescens, 232
Perovskia 'Blue Spire', 255
Philadelphus 'Avalanche', 230
Philadelphus 'Bouquet Blanc', 230
Phlomis fruticosa, 30, 120
Phlox carolina 'Miss Lingard', 274
Phormium tenax 'Atropurpureum', 213
Phygelius 'Salmon Leap', 94
Phygelius 'Winchester Fanfare', 274
Picea religiosa, 127
Pimpinella major 'Rosea', 198
Pinus oaxacana, 236
Platanus mexicana, 93
Polygonum, 213
Prunella vulgaris, 228
Prunus 'Mt. Fuji'. See P. 'Shirotae'
Prunus 'Shirotae', 115
Pteris cretica, 224

Quercus coccifera, 206

Rhamnus alaternus, 234
Rhamnus californicus, 234
Rhus integrifolia, 48
Rhus ovata, 186
Ribes malvaceum 'Montara Rose', 282
Ribes sanguineum var. glutinosum, 276
Rosa 'Ballerina', 158, 198, 249
Rosa 'Baltimore Belle', 200
Rosa 'Blanc Double de Coubert', 180
Rosa 'Buff Beauty', 43
Rosa 'Charles Austin', 48
Rosa 'Crepuscule', 48
Rosa 'Duchesse de Brabant', 158, 226
Rosa 'Felicia', 249
Rosa 'Félicité Perpétue', 297
Rosa 'First Love', 304
Rosa 'Francesca', 48

Rosa 'Frau Karl Druschki', 291
Rosa 'Honorine du Brabant', 273
Rosa 'Kathleen', 200
Rosa 'La Marne', 141, 298
Rosa 'Little White Pet', 240
Rosa 'Lyda Rose', 179
Rosa 'Mary Rose', 226
Rosa 'Mevrouw Nathalie Nypels', 198
Rosa 'Mme Caroline Testout', 291
Rosa 'Mons. Tillier', 59
Rosa 'Mrs. Joseph Schwartz', 158
Rosa 'Mrs. Oakley Fisher', 226
Rosa 'Nathalie Nypels', 142
Rosa 'Roseraie de l'Hay', 180
Rosa rugosa 'Rubra', 223
Rosa 'Silver Jubilee', 304
Rosa 'Souvenir de la Malmaison', 273, 308
Rosa 'Sparrieshoop', 59
Rosa 'The Fairy', 240
Rosa 'Tuscany', 223
Rosa 'Tuscany Superb', 223
Rosa 'Wise Portia', 185
Rosmarinus 'Ken Taylor', 91
Rosmarinus officinalis 'Collingwood
  Ingram', 28, 112, 127
Rosmarinus officinalis 'Miss Jessop's
  Upright', 28, 221
Rosmarinus officinalis 'Spice Islands', 221
Rosmarinus officinalis 'Tuscan Blue', 35,
  221
Rudbeckia hirta, 122

Salvia aethiopis, 25–26, 26, 109
Salvia africana-caerulea, 27, 27–28, 28
Salvia africana-lutea, 28–30, 29, 30
Salvia albimaculata, 30–32, 31, 56, 303
Salvia algeriensis, 32–34, 33, 51, 222
Salvia angustifolia. See S. reptans
Salvia 'Anthony Parker', 173, 174
Salvia apiana, 34, 34–36, 35, 49, 175, 186

Salvia argentea, 36–37, *37*, 118

Salvia arizonica, 37–39, *38*

Salvia aurea. See *S. africana-lutea*

Salvia austriaca, 39–40, *40*, 283

Salvia axillaris, 40–42

Salvia azurea var. *grandiflora*, 42–43

Salvia barrelieri, 43–46, *44*, *45*

Salvia blepharophylla, 46, *46–48*, *47*, 147, 269

Salvia blepharophylla 'Sweet Numbers', *47*

Salvia brandegei, 48, *48–49*, *49*, 109

Salvia broussonetii, 49–51, *50*

Salvia buchananii, 52, *52–53*, *53*

Salvia bulleyana, 119

Salvia cacaliifolia, 53, *53–54*, *54*, 147

Salvia caespitosa, 55, *55–57*, *56*, 125

Salvia canariensis, 57, *57–59*, *58*

Salvia canariensis var. *candidissima*, 57, *58*, *59*

Salvia candelabrum, 153–155

Salvia candidissima, 59–61, *60*, *61*, 92

Salvia canescens var. *daghestanica*, 61–63, *62*, *63*

Salvia cardinalis. See *S. fulgens*

Salvia carduacea, 22, 63, *63–66*, *64*, *65*, 186

Salvia castanea, 66–68, *67*

Salvia cedrosensis, 21, 68–70, *69*

Salvia chamaedryoides, 70–72, *71*, *72*, 77, *193*

Salvia chamaedryoides 'Desert Green', 71

Salvia chamelaeagnea, 27, 68, 72–74, *73*, 100, 109, 206

Salvia chiapensis, 74–76, *75*

Salvia chionophylla, *76*, *76–78*, *77*

Salvia clevelandii, 35, *78*, 78–81, 177, 186

Salvia clevelandii 'Allen Chickering', 80

Salvia clevelandii 'Aromas', 80

Salvia clevelandii 'Betsy Clebsch', 80

Salvia clevelandii 'Pozo Blue', *80*

Salvia clevelandii 'Santa Cruz Dark', 80

Salvia clevelandii 'Whirly Blue', 80

Salvia clevelandii 'Winnifred Gilman', *79*

Salvia coahuilensis, 81–82, *82*

Salvia coccinea, 82–84, *83*, *84*, 129

Salvia coccinea 'Brenthurst', *83*, 84

Salvia coccinea 'Lactea', 84

Salvia columbariae, 85, 85–86, 93, 186

Salvia confertiflora, 86, 86–88, *87*, 129, *174*

Salvia corrugata, 88, 88–90, *89*

Salvia coulteri, 90–92, *91*

Salvia cuneifolia. See *S. axillaris*

Salvia cyanescens, 92–93

Salvia 'Dara's Choice', 276

Salvia darcyi, 93, 93–94, *94*

Salvia dentata, 95, 95–96, *96*, 268

Salvia desoleana, 96–98, *97*, *98*

Salvia digitaloides, 98–100, *99*

Salvia discolor, 100, 100–102, *101*

Salvia disermas, 102–104, *103*, *104*

Salvia disjuncta, 104–106, *105*

Salvia divinorum, 106–108, *107*

Salvia dolomitica, 108–109, *109*

Salvia dombeyi, 109–110, *110*

Salvia dominica, *111*, *111–112*

Salvia dorisiana, 112–113, *113*

Salvia dumetorum, 296

Salvia eigii, 113–115, *114*

Salvia elegans, 115–117, *116*, 122, *173*

Salvia elegans 'Honey Melon', *116*, 129, 184, 250

Salvia elegans 'Scarlet Pineapple', 115

Salvia farinacea, 117–118, 151, 180

Salvia farinacea 'Alba', 118

Salvia farinacea 'Blue Bedder', 118

Salvia farinacea 'Mina', 118

Salvia farinacea 'Victoria', 118, 144

Salvia farinacea 'White Porcelain', 118

Salvia flava, 118–120, *119*

Salvia forreri, 39

Salvia forsskaolii, *120*, 120–122, *121*

INDEX OF PLANT NAMES

Salvia 'Frieda Dixon', 122–123, *123*

Salvia frigida, *124*, 124–125

Salvia fruticosa, 125–127, *126*

Salvia fulgens, 127–129, *128*, *183*

Salvia gesneriiflora, *129*, 129–131

Salvia gesneriiflora 'Mole Poblano', 130

Salvia gesneriiflora 'Tequila', *130*, 131, 234

Salvia gilliesii, *131*, 131–133, *132*

Salvia glabrescens, 165

Salvia glechomifolia, 133–135, *134*

Salvia glutinosa, 135, 215

Salvia grahami. See *S. microphylla*
   'Graham's sage'

Salvia graveolens. See *S. dominica*

Salvia greatae, 66

Salvia greggii, 51, *136*, 136–140, 160, 193,
   222, 305

Salvia greggii 'Alba', *140*

Salvia greggii 'Big Pink', *136*, 140

Salvia greggii 'Cherry Chief', *137*, 138

Salvia greggii 'Cherry Queen', 140

Salvia greggii 'Dark Dancer', 182

Salvia greggii 'Desert Pastel', *138*, *139*, *140*

Salvia greggii 'Dwarf Pink', 140

Salvia greggii 'Furman's Red', *136*, 222

Salvia greggii 'Keter's Red', 140

Salvia greggii 'La Encantada', 140

Salvia greggii 'Plum Wine', 140

Salvia greggii 'Purple Haze', 138

Salvia greggii 'Raspberry Royale', 140

Salvia greggii 'Rosea', 140

Salvia guaranitica, 140–143, *141*, *142*, 234,
   238

Salvia guaranitica 'Argentina Skies', *141*,
   142

Salvia guaranitica 'Black and Blue', 142

Salvia guaranitica 'Blue Enigma', 142

Salvia guaranitica 'Blue Ensign', 142

Salvia guaranitica 'Costa Rica Blue', 142

Salvia guaranitica 'Purple Splendour', 142

Salvia hians, *143*, 143–144, *144*

Salvia hierosolymitana, *145*, 145–146

Salvia hirtella, 146–147, *147*

Salvia hispanica, 85

Salvia holwayi, 22, *148*, 148–149

Salvia horminum. See *S. viridis*

Salvia indica, 97, 149–151, *150*

Salvia 'Indigo Spires', 151–152, *152*, 180, 262

Salvia interrupta, *153*, 153–155, *154*

Salvia involucrata, 155–158, 232

Salvia involucrata 'Bethellii', 156

Salvia involucrata 'Deschampsiana', 156

Salvia involucrata 'El Butano', 156

Salvia involucrata 'El Cielo', *156*

Salvia involucrata 'Hidalgo', 156

Salvia involucrata 'Mulberry Jam', *157*

Salvia iodantha, 158–159, *159*

Salvia ×jamensis, *136*, 159–161, *160*, 193

Salvia ×jamensis 'Cienega de Oro', *160*,
   161, 292

Salvia ×jamensis 'El Duranzo', 161

Salvia ×jamensis 'La Luna', 161

Salvia ×jamensis 'San Isidro Moon', 161

Salvia ×jamensis 'Sierra San Antonio',
   160, 161

Salvia jurisicii, *161*, 161–162, *162*

Salvia jurisicii 'Alba', 161

Salvia karwinskii, 162–165, *163*

Salvia koyamae, *165*, 165–166

Salvia lanceolata, 166–168, *167*, *168*

Salvia lanigera, 168–170, *169*, 188

Salvia lavandulifolia, 77, 170–171

Salvia lemmonii. See *S. microphylla*

Salvia leptophylla. See *S. reptans*

Salvia leucantha, *171*, 171–174

Salvia leucantha 'Midnight', *172*, 173

Salvia leucantha 'Santa Barbara', *172*, *173*

Salvia leucophylla, 35, 174–177, *175*, 186

Salvia leucophylla 'Bee's Bliss', *177*, 177

Salvia leucophylla 'Figueroa', 177

Salvia leucophylla 'Point Sal', 177
Salvia littae, *178*, 178–179, *179*
Salvia longispicata, 151, 179–180
Salvia lycioides, 180–182, *181*, 298
Salvia lycioides 'Guadalupe Mountain
    Form', 182
Salvia madrensis, 88, 117, 128, 182–184, *183*,
    215, 235
Salvia 'Mainacht', 211
Salvia 'Marine Blue', *72*
Salvia 'May Night'. See *S.* 'Mainacht'
Salvia melissodora, 184–185, *185*
Salvia mellifera, 48, 66, 85, 109, 175,
    186–187, *187*, 276
Salvia mellifera 'Little Sur', 187
Salvia mellifera 'Prostrata'. See *S. mellifera*
    'Terra Seca'
Salvia mellifera 'Terra Seca', 187
Salvia merjamie, 51, 188–189, *189*
Salvia mexicana, 117, 129, 189–192, *191*
Salvia mexicana 'Limelight', *190*, 192
Salvia mexicana 'Lollie Jackson', *191*
Salvia mexicana 'Ocampo', 192
Salvia microphylla, 136, 160, 192–196, 266
Salvia microphylla 'Cerro Potosi', 195
Salvia microphylla 'Desert Blaze', 196
Salvia microphylla 'Forever Red', *194*, 196,
    226
Salvia microphylla 'Graham's Sage', 71,
    193, 195, 196
Salvia microphylla 'Hoja Grande', 195
Salvia microphylla 'Kew Red', 195, 196
Salvia microphylla 'La Foux', 196
Salvia microphylla 'La Trinidad Pink', 195
Salvia microphylla 'Newby Hall', 196
Salvia microphylla 'Pink Blush', 196
Salvia microphylla 'Red Velvet', *194*, 196
Salvia microphylla 'Rosita', *196*, 232
Salvia microphylla 'San Carlos Festival',
    196

Salvia microphylla 'Wild Watermelon', 196
Salvia microphylla var. *wislizenii*, 195
Salvia miltiorrhiza, 196–198, *197*
Salvia miniata, *198*, 198–199
Salvia moorcroftiana, 199–200, *200*
Salvia mouretii, 32
Salvia 'Mrs. Beard', 187, 276
Salvia muelleri, *201*, 201–202
Salvia muirii, 202, 202–205, *203*
Salvia munzii, 48
Salvia namaensis, 205–206, *206*
Salvia napifolia, 206–208, *207*
Salvia nemorosa, 208, 208–211
Salvia nemorosa 'Amethyst', 210
Salvia nemorosa 'Blauhügel', 210
Salvia nemorosa 'Blaukönigin', 210
Salvia nemorosa 'Lubecca', 210
Salvia nemorosa 'Lye End', 210
Salvia nemorosa 'Mainacht', 210, 211
Salvia nemorosa 'Ostfriesland', *209*, 210,
    211
Salvia nemorosa 'Plumosa', 210
Salvia nemorosa 'Rose Queen', 210
Salvia nemorosa 'Rubin', 210
Salvia nemorosa 'Schneehügel', 210
Salvia nemorosa 'Superba', 210
Salvia nemorosa 'Tänzerin', 210
Salvia neurepia. See *S. microphylla*
Salvia nilotica, 188, 211–213, *212*
Salvia nipponica, 165
Salvia nivea. See *S. lanceolata*
Salvia nubicola, 135, *213*, 213–215, *214*, 215
Salvia officinalis, 17, 126, 216–219, *217*
Salvia officinalis 'Albiflora', 217
Salvia officinalis 'Aurea', 216
Salvia officinalis 'Berggarten', 109, 216, 218
Salvia officinalis 'Compacta', 216, 219
Salvia officinalis 'Crispa', 217
Salvia officinalis 'Grete Stolze', 217
Salvia officinalis 'Holt's Mammoth', 216

Salvia officinalis 'Icterina', *116*, 216, *218*
Salvia officinalis 'Milleri', 217
Salvia officinalis 'Purpurascens', 60, 96, 216, 217, *218*, 303
Salvia officinalis 'Salicifolia', 217
Salvia officinalis 'Sturnina', 217
Salvia officinalis 'Tricolor', 216
Salvia oppositiflora, 219, *219*–220, *220*
Salvia palaestina, 220–222, *221*
Salvia patens, 222–223, *223*
Salvia patens 'Alba', 222
Salvia patens 'Cambridge Blue', 222
Salvia patens 'Chilcombe', 222
Salvia patens 'Guanajuato', 222
Salvia patens 'Oxford Blue', 222
Salvia penstemonoides, 223–224
Salvia polystachya, 86, *225*, 225–226
Salvia pratensis, 210, 226–228, *227*
Salvia pratensis subsp. *haematodes*, 227
Salvia pratensis 'Tenorii', 227
Salvia prunelloides, 228–230, *229*
Salvia przewalskii, 230–232, *231*, *232*
Salvia puberula, 232–234, *233*
Salvia 'Purple Majesty', 215, 234–235, *235*
Salvia 'Purple Pastel', 51, 138, 222
Salvia purpurea, 235–237, *236*
Salvia recognita, 237–240, *238*, *239*, 262
Salvia recurva, 240–241, *241*
Salvia regla, 184, *242*, 242–244, *243*, *244*
Salvia regla 'Mount Emory', 242, 244
Salvia regla 'Royal', 242, 269
Salvia regla 'Warnocks Choice', 244
Salvia repens, 245, *245*–246, 284, 285
Salvia reptans, 246, *246*–247
Salvia reptans var. *glabra*, 246
Salvia ringens, 155, 247–249, *248*, *249*
Salvia roborowskii, 250–251
Salvia roemeriana, 251–252, *252*
Salvia rubescens, 252–255, *253*
Salvia rugosa. See *S. disermas*

Salvia rutilans. See *S. elegans*
Salvia rypara, 255–257, *256*
Salvia sagittata, 257, *257*–259, *258*
Salvia scabra, 259, *259*–260, *260*
Salvia sclarea, 97, 238, 261, *261*–263, *262*
Salvia sclarea 'Turkestanica', 261, *262*
Salvia scutellarioides, 263–265, *264*
Salvia semiatrata, 265–266, *266*
Salvia serpyllifolia, 266–268, *267*
Salvia sessei, 268–269
Salvia shannoni, 269–271, *270*
Salvia sinaloensis, 76, 271–273, *272*
Salvia somalensis, 273–274, *274*
Salvia sonomensis, 177, 187, 274–276, *275*
Salvia sonomensis 'Cone Peak', 276
Salvia sonomensis 'John Farmar-Bowers', 276
Salvia sonomensis 'Serra Peak', 276
Salvia spathacea, 49, 277, *277*–278, *278*
Salvia spathacea 'Kawatre', 277
Salvia spathacea 'Powerline Pink', 277
Salvia splendens, 278–280
Salvia splendens 'Salsa', 279
Salvia splendens 'Sizzler', 279
Salvia splendens 'Van Houttei', *279*, *280*
Salvia sprucei, 281–282, *282*
Salvia staminea, 282–284, *283*
Salvia stenophylla, 245, 284–285
Salvia ×*sylvestris*, 208–210
Salvia ×*superba*, 208, 210
Salvia taraxacifolia, 285–287, *286*
Salvia thymoides, 77, 287–288, *288*
Salvia tingitana, 288–290, *289*, *290*
Salvia transsylvanica, 290–291, *292*
Salvia triloba. See *S. fruticosa*
Salvia tubiflora, 293, *293*–294, *294*
Salvia uliginosa, 22, 295, *295*–297, *296*
Salvia urica, 297, *297*–298
Salvia verticillata, 298–300
Salvia verticillata 'Purple Rain', *299*

Salvia 'Vicki Romo', 35
Salvia villosa, 300–301, *301*
Salvia virgata, 210, 227
Salvia viridis, 152, 302, 302–304
Salvia viridis 'Alba', 303
Salvia viridis 'Bluebeard', 303
Salvia viridis 'Claryssa Blue', 303
Salvia viridis 'Claryssa Pink', 303
Salvia viridis 'Claryssa White', 303
Salvia viridis 'Oxford Blue', 303
Salvia viridis 'Pink Sunday', 303
Salvia viridis 'Rose Bouquet', 303
Salvia viscosa, 304–305, *305*
Salvia wagneriana, 305–306
Salvia 'Waverly', *307*, 307–308
Santolina pinnata 'Edward Bowles', 301
Santolina virens, 93
Saponaria 'Max Frei', 32
Saponaria ocymoides 'Splendens', 152
Saponaria vaccaria 'Pink Beauty', 46
Scabiosa farinosa, 189
Scutellaria, 263
Scutellaria resinosa, 63
Sedum cauticola, 208
Sedum spathulifolium, 125
Sedum 'Vera Jameson', 308
Sesleria autumnalis, 78
Sidalcea malviflora 'Elsie Heugh', 35
Silene maritima, 72
Sisyrinchium striatum, 217
Solanum hindsianum, 68
Stipa cernua, 66
Stipa pulchra, 66, 228
Stipa ramosissima, 152
Stipa speciosa, 66

Tagetes patula 'Legion of Honour', 144
Tanacetum haradjanii, 223, 290, 301
Tanacetum parthenium, 215
Teucrium chamaedrys, 70, 93
Teucrium cossonii, 56

Teucrium fruticans, 255
Teucrium fruticans 'Compactum', 266
Teucrium lucidum, 182
Teucrium polium 'Aureum', 56, 62
Teucrium pyrenaicum, 56, 62
Thalictrum delavayi, 241
Thymus ×citriodorus, 96
Thymus serpyllum, 266, 268
Thymus vulgaris 'Argentea', 299
Tithonia rotundifolia 'Aztec Sun', 133

Verbascum chaixii 'Album', 120
Verbascum olympicum, 174
Verbascum phoenicium 'Flush of White',
    104
Verbena ×hybrida, 257
Verbena rigida 'Polaris', 260
Viburnum 'Anne Russell', 166
Viburnum cinnamonifolium, 147
Viburnum davidii, 147
Viburnum japonicum, 147
Viburnum opulus 'Aureum', 54
Viburnum opulus 'Roseum', 184
Viburnum tinus 'Spring Bouquet', 179
Viburnum utile, 280
Viola corsica, 98
Viola tricolor 'Johnny Jump Up', 140

Westringia 'Wynyabbie Gem', 237
Woodwardia fimbriata, 121, 241

Yucca rostrata, 81
Yucca whipplei, 35, 66, 81

Zauschneria. See Epilobium canum subsp.
    canum
Zauschneria californica subsp. cana. See
    Epilobium canum subsp. canum
Zinnia angustifolia 'Golden Eye', 285
Zinnia elegans 'Parasol Mixed', 285